FOOD PROVISIONING IN COMPLEX SOCIETIES

FOOD PROVISIONING IN COMPLEX SOCIETIES

Zooarchaeological Perspectives

EDITED BY
Levent Atici AND Benjamin S. Arbuckle

UNIVERSITY PRESS OF COLORADO
Denver

Published by University Press of Colorado
1624 Market Street, Suite 226
PMB 39883
Denver, Colorado 80202

Printed in the United States of America

The University Press of Colorado is a proud member of the Association of University Presses.

The University Press of Colorado is a cooperative publishing enterprise supported, in part, by Adams State University, Colorado State University, Fort Lewis College, Metropolitan State University of Denver, University of Alaska Fairbanks, University of Colorado, University of Denver, University of Northern Colorado, University of Wyoming, Utah State University, and Western Colorado University.

∞ This paper meets the requirements of the ANSI/NISO Z39.48-1992 (Permanence of Paper).

ISBN: 978-1-64642-098-8 (hardcover)
ISBN: 978-1-64642-256-2 (ebook)
https://doi.org/10.5876/9781646422562

Library of Congress Cataloging-in-Publication Data

Names: Atici, Levent, editor. | Arbuckle, Benjamin S., editor.
Title: Food provisioning in complex societies : zooarchaeological perspectives / edited by Levent Atici, Benjamin S. Arbuckle.
Description: Louisville : University Press of Colorado, [2022] | Includes bibliographical references and index.
Identifiers: LCCN 2021061678 (print) | LCCN 2021061679 (ebook) | ISBN 9781646420988 (hardcover) | ISBN 9781646422562 (ebook)
Subjects: LCSH: Food supply—History. | Animal remains (Archaeology) | Animal industry. | Human-animal relationships. | Nutritional anthropology. | Social archaeology.
Classification: LCC HD9000.5 .F596423 2022 (print) | LCC HD9000.5 (ebook) | DDC 338.1/9—dc23/eng/20220111
LC record available at https://lccn.loc.gov/2021061678
LC ebook record available at https://lccn.loc.gov/2021061679

Cover illustrations from "Pork packing in Cincinnati," 1873. Library of Congress Prints and Photographs Division, Reproduction #LC-USZ62-1056.

CONTENTS

FIGURES AND TABLES

FIGURES

TABLES

ACKNOWLEDGMENTS

The editors would like to thank University Press of Colorado, for the press's interest in this project and patiently moving it through the publication process. The editors would also like to thank all of the participants in the session at the 2014 meeting of the International Council for Archaeozoology (ICAZ) in San Rafael, Argentina, from which this volume developed. Two anonymous reviewers kindly read and provided valuable comments on the volume. Thanks also to the University of Nevada Las Vegas, the University of North Carolina at Chapel Hill, and the Research Labs in Archaeology for support during the production of this volume.

FOOD PROVISIONING IN COMPLEX SOCIETIES

1

Introduction

Global Perspectives on Provisioning Complex Societies

LEVENT ATICI AND BENJAMIN S. ARBUCKLE

This volume, which derives from a productive session at the meeting of the International Council for Archaeozoology in San Rafael, Argentina, addresses a major branch of zooarchaeological inquiry focused on the role of animals in complex societies. Examination of animals in the economies, rituals, and politics of complex societies has been one of the most productive foci of modern zooarchaeological research. From B. Maltby's (1979) *Faunal Studies on Urban Sites: Animal Bones from Exeter*, J. Boessneck and U. von den Driesch and colleagues' (1971) *Die Tierknochenfunde aus dem Oppidum von Manching*, to M. Zeder's (1991) *Feeding Cities*, and Elizabeth Reitz and Elizabeth Wing's (2010) *Mission and Pueblo Santa Catalina de Guale, St. Catherines Island, Georgia (USA)*, faunal specialists have been actively engaged in innovative research exploring the roles of animals in societies characterized by social hierarchies and specialization from the first urban states to European colonial settlements. Influential syntheses of faunal perspectives on complex societies by P. J. Crabtree (1990) and S. deFrance (2009) have defined the avenues that can be explored through faunal remains targeting

https://doi.org/10.5876/9781646422562.c001

themes including political economy, specialization, ritual practices, ideology, identity, and dietary differences within and between communities.

In this volume, authors continue to explore these productive themes within a wide variety of complex societies ranging from Mississippian communities of the American Southeast, to the Great Settlement of Anyang in Bronze Age China, to the Aksumite kingdom of Northeast Africa. Taking a global perspective and including both prehistoric and historic case studies, the chapters in the volume reflect some of the current best practices in zooarchaeology, integrating faunal evidence with archaeological contexts, historical texts, iconography, and ethnohistorical sources to discern ways that animals are key contributors to, and cocreators of, complex societies in all periods and all places.

COMPLEX SOCIETIES

In this volume, we focus on the use of animals in complex societies, which begs the question "what is a complex society?" The line separating what is "complex" and what is not is not always clear and distinct. Thus, answering this question is not as straightforward as it may seem at face value. This ambiguity stems largely from the fact that human societies vary infinitely in their patterning of social, political, and economic organization. The frequent conflation and use without a clear definition of terms such as *city*, *urban center*, *urban society*, *urbanization*, and *state* exacerbate the problem. An inherent false assumption that states didn't exist without cities and/or cities didn't exist without states adds insult to injury. These assumptions make the co-occurrence of city and state superfluous (Cowgill 2004:526). As such, although archaeologists widely disagree on how to define complexity and to identify it in the ground, they may agree on baseline criteria to probe the issue.

From the outset, we acknowledge marked differences among complex societies and their patterns of sociopolitical and economic organization and institutions, as well as among their technologies, natural resources, and settlements. From a Childean vantage point, the study of complex societies requires a set of criteria to aid archaeologists identify and recognize complex forms of social, political, and economic organization. In his seminal work, *The Urban Revolution*, V. Gordon Childe's first sentence reads: "The concept of 'city' is notoriously hard to define" (1950:3). He then goes on to introduce his renowned ten abstract criteria, the archaeologist's *Decalogue*, to distinguish early cities (1950). More than six decades later, Norman Yoffee and Nicola N. Terrenato (2015:2) offer an updated and extended version of the *Decalogue* and postulate that cities

1. have permanent settlements that are large in area;
2. have quite a few people who live closely together;
3. have bureaucracies who keep track of people and things leaving and entering;

4. have a center with impressive architecture that affords and/or restricts political, social, and/or ideological activity;
5. feed people with foodstuffs produced in the related countryside or with imported produce;
6. acquire, through long-distance trade, luxury and utilitarian goods;
7. provide a sense of civic identity;
8. provide arenas in which the rulers demonstrate their special connections to the high gods and the cosmos;
9. contain potential social drama and discontent among various competing/cooperating social groups and their leaders;
10. create and incubate significant environmental and health problems.

Obviously, employing a laundry list approach would not necessarily generate the much-desired theoretical and methodological panacea that can be universally applied to any given ancient society across the globe, due to the plethora of human experience in time and space and to the lack of a uniform socioeconomic system. Hence, it is impossible to agree on a cross-culturally applicable definition of *the* city and *the* state (Cowgill 2004:526). Still, these criteria form a good starting point and offer us a useful explanatory framework to identify some regularity in patterning. Archaeologists, thus, tacitly agree to use criteria that can be summarized under more generic and broader categories as locational, artifactual, administrative, and mortuary with varying sets of tangible material correlates though those, too, are difficult to discern archaeologically. We would like to emphasize that we do not consider social change or a larger scale transformation as a linear evolutionary upgrade from one stage to the next. Following the complex systems approach set forth by J. B. Auban and colleagues (2012), complex societies can be thought to have *many interacting components organized into nested groups that can be represented as organizational hierarchies or hierarchically structured networks* that are governed by a multivalent, dynamic evolutionary process (Auban et al., 2012:23).

WHAT IS FOOD PROVISIONING?

It is no coincidence that food provisioning is on both the original and updated lists of criteria for identifying urbanism, owing to the fact that food is and has always been one of the primary biological needs regardless of the basic and dominant mode of livelihood. Beyond diet and nutrition, food preparation and consumption intersect with many other processes of social life and food systems have effects on public health, social justice, energy, water, land, transport, and economic development (Itulua-Abumere 2013; Morgan 2009). Variations seen in the ways people eat reflect differences of political power, social prestige, economic wealth, and overall health (Gumerman 1997:106).

Cultural anthropologists study food to probe a wide scope of research themes, including classic food ethnographies, single food commodities and substances, food and social change, food insecurity, eating and ritual, eating and identities, food supplies and seasonal rituals of conflict, food resource periodicity and cooperativeness, food avoidances, biological aspects of eating, infant feeding and weaning, and cannibalism, to name but a few (Mintz and DuBois 2002). Food systems have also been directly related to broad societal processes such as political-economic value-creation, symbolic value-creation, and the social construction of memory in anthropological theory building within the framework of cultural materialism versus structuralist or symbolic explanations for human behavior (Mintz and Du Bois 2002:100).

As far as archaeological approaches to food are concerned, one can trace a developmentary trajectory from more subsistence and diet-oriented paradigms to ones that place food within a broader and socially oriented framework, mirroring the transition from scientific to interpretive archaeological theory building (Twiss 2012). This trajectory is evident in the field of zooarchaeology with the emergence of a distinctive "social zooarchaeology," with its explicit emphasis on the social context of engagements with animals and animal products (Ewonus 2011; Orton 2012; Russell 2012). In the context of zooarchaeological research on complex societies, this study incorporates increased interest in exploring the intersection of animals and features of the urban "decalogue" not strictly limited to nutrition and subsistence. These features include recognition of the local and long-distance trade in animals and animal products (Orton et al. 2014; Sharpe et al. 2018); the use of food choice and preparation techniques in the construction of social identity (Crabtree and Campana 2016; Ervynck et al. 2003); engagement with cosmology through food offerings and food symbolism (deFrance 2009; Yuan and Flad 2005); social competition via feasting and gift giving (Knudson et al. 2012; Rowley-Conwy 2018); and the impact on urban health of zoonotic disease, parasites, and animal waste and waste disposal (Bartosiewicz and Gal 2013; Fournié et al. 2017).

As a result of this turn towards the "social life of food," it can be recognized that the study of food provisioning must be embedded within the broader context of political and ritual economies. Economic organization refers to the dynamic relationships among production, distribution or exchange, and consumption (figure 1.1). However, rather than taking place only within a limited range of centralized state institutions—the traditional focus on economic archaeology in complex societies—food and animal economies spill over into a myriad of political and ritual, public and private contexts. Other important attributes of complex economic systems include the management of production; organization of labor; power relationships among different socioeconomic segments; and access to and control of land, infrastructure (e.g., roads, irrigation

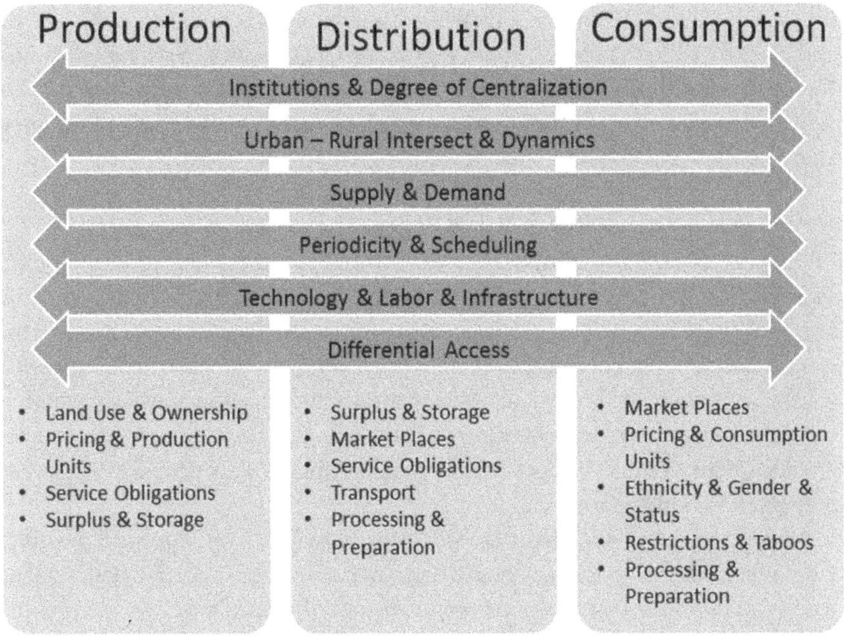

Figure 1.1. *Schematic view of the dynamic variables associated with the production, distribution and exchange, and consumption of animals and animal products in complex societies.*

canals), key raw materials, resources (e.g., beasts of burden), and technology (e.g., carts, wagons, plows, metal tools) (Evans and Webster 2001; Feinman and Nicholas 2004).

According to Melinda Zeder (2003), premodern urban economies are characterized by complex and varying scales of specialized and segregated interactions between centralized/regulated and diffused/unregulated activities during the production, movement, and consumption of goods. She also asserts that some properties of food resources—such as whether the production levels can be predicted and controlled, and whether the resources can be moved and stored to manipulate supply and demand—play significant roles, shaping the nature of urban food provisioning (Zeder 2003:160). J. C. Scott (2017) has further argued that it is the predictable and storable nature of some food resources that form the very basis of state power, social hierarchies, and the features of urbanism listed above.

In regards to animal resources specifically, Zeder (1991:1994) argues that urban settlements are often provisioned via specialized and indirect animal economies characterized by specialized distribution and processing systems reflecting the separation between rural producers and urban consumers. Systems of production may be variably under state control or "farmed out" to independent producers, particularly when involving ruminants such as sheep, goats, cattle, and camels, which require extensive grazing areas. In the Mediterranean and Near Eastern regions, however, pigs and chickens tend to fall outside of the purview of centralized provisioning systems reflecting the presence of multilayered animal economies (Price et al. 2017; Redding 2015; Zeder 1998).

SCOPE AND VISION OF THE BOOK

In the present book, we aim to map out a research agenda for anthropological archaeologists in general and zooarchaeologists specifically, by defining some analytical parameters, perspectives, and concerns associated with food provisioning in complex societies. However, such an exercise will not be received without controversy. We are acutely aware of the fact that our spatiotemporal coverage is not comprehensive. Yet, the breadth shouldn't render what is included here as more important and primary and what is not included as secondary and unimportant.

Studies exploring various socioeconomic aspects of ancient societies have often relied on archaeological, textual, zooarchaeological, and archaeobotanical studies from an isolated perspective and within a disarticulated and fragmented explanatory framework. This volume seeks to develop a picture of food provisioning in complex societies in the Old and New Worlds by bringing together scholars working in Southwest Asia, East Asia, Africa, Europe, North America, and Mesoamerica. We seek to identify how food provisioning in early and more recent complex societies is manifested in the archaeological, historical, and zooarchaeological records.

Theoretically, we focus on centralization and bureaucratic control, asymmetrical access and inequalities, and production-distribution-consumption dynamics. As such, the individual chapters in this book relate to these concepts as a common thread throughout the book. Methodologically, we aim to bring together as many independent lines of evidence as possible, with special emphasis on the combined use of zooarchaeological and historical data to develop comprehensive and fine-resolution pictures of provisioning systems in early complex societies.

Since a book that probes food provisioning in state-level complex societies and/or urban centers across time and space currently doesn't exist, this book represents a first step toward compiling the scattered, disarticulated, and fragmented data on food provisioning. A primary goal of the book is to integrate the work of scholars engaged in archaeology and zooarchaeology with the historians and linguists as a first step toward developing a new synthetic research paradigm that can address issues of urban food provisioning in the ancient world. This book, therefore, represents a unique contribution to our understanding of how food provisioning systems developed in early complex societies. We also fill a gap by shedding new light on a poorly understood, largely neglected, and underinvestigated research topic: urban food provisioning and animal management.

CASE STUDIES

The chapters in this volume are arranged geographically, with chapters 2–6 focusing on case studies from Eurasia and Africa and chapters 7–9 describing examples from the Americas. However, despite this rather predictable geographic bifurcation, themes including specialization, use of wild game, elite ritual, and animals as a reflection of political economy clearly extend beyond regional boundaries.

The first case study, chapter 2, focuses on wild animals in urban economies and evidence for specialized provisioning systems specifically targeting wild resources. Using the Bronze Age urban site of Acemhöyük in central Turkey as a case study and incorporating ancient iconographic and textual records with zooarchaeological analysis, Arbuckle develops a picture of the diverse roles wild animals played in sociopolitical and economic realms during the Bronze Age. Exploring multiple modes of independent and parallel urban-provisioning systems, the chapter documents sophisticated systems aimed at procuring wild animals and their remains at Acemhöyük. These systems include the hunting of aurochs and boar, hunting and perhaps keeping of bears and wolves, the capture of wild equids and breeding and training of equid hybrids, the importation of elephant and hippopotamus ivory for the production of luxury items, and the use of antler and horn in other palace industries. These animals played roles in visual displays, feasting events, ornamentation, and industrial purposes and were used in ways with broad parallels across courtly cultures in Syro-Mesopotamia. This chapter highlights the presence of diverse and specialized provisioning systems in Bronze Age cities designed to provide urban elites with highly valued wild animals and animal products as a means to establish, maintain, and reify economic, political, and social status and to reflect wealth, power, and prestige.

In chapter 3, Meier and colleagues integrate texts, zooarchaeology, and stable isotopes to discuss the roles of animals in wider redistributive economic systems during the Late Bronze Age in the Aegean. They investigate whether centralized palatial bureaucracies imposed on independent herders to support the specialized economy and its attached craftspeople. More specifically, the authors examine evidence for the provisioning at one nonpalatial household, Petsas House, in the Helladic period at the Mycenaean center Mycenae. Here, unique deposits from a well located within the structure are used to identify a combination of indirect and direct access (following Zeder 1991) of this household to animal resources. The analyses reveal the presence of household-level procurement of pigs, a sector of the animal economy thought to reside outside of institutional taxation schemes. Sheep and goat, on the other hand, likely intersected more with the palatial economies, with the Petsas household receiving from and perhaps producing for state herds. This chapter documents how animal procurement varied by taxa and how residents practiced both direct and indirect provisioning in decentralized/domestic and centralized/palatial forms.

Chapter 4 moves to the western margin of Europe, where Beglane targets the dietary contributions of various livestock and animal products at four sites in Ireland, specifically challenging notions of historically constructed Irish diet through a combination of texts, faunal data, and model building. Through the application of textually informed dietary models, Beglane argues for an important role for dairy in the medieval Irish diet, though marked differences in the production and consumption of animal products are identified at three different types of sites: farm, abbey, and castle. This multisited approach reveals the complexity and spatial heterogeneity of animal provisioning systems reflecting differences in social status, religious laws, and economic activities with producer, consumer, and self-sufficient sites each noted archaeologically.

This approach emphasizes the use of livestock, especially cattle, for dairy products, labor, and also as a tangible symbol of wealth—features often difficult to "see" archaeologically—in addition to meat. This case study also emphasizes the benefits of reconstructing a historically informed socioeconomy using faunal remains that provide a higher-resolution understanding of this multisited medieval economy than texts alone. Similar to the previous chapter by Meier, Beglane emphasizes the presence of multiple, contingent provisioning systems structured primarily by social, political, and religious forces and with each individual settlement situated within a uniquely structured economy, the limitations, opportunities, and obligations of which were based on status, function, and wealth.

In chapter 5, Campbell continues to emphasize the importance of status, belief systems, politics, and cosmologies in structuring how food economies are organized. Addressing Shang period animal provisioning in the Yellow River valley in China, Campbell probes provisioning at one of the largest ancient urban centers in the world. This chapter places a special emphasis on the enormous scale of the provisioning system needed to fulfill the subsistence and sacrificial needs (the ritual economy) of the world's largest Bronze Age urban center. More importantly, Campbell deliberately departs from the conventional discussions of subsistence with a singular focus on the roles food played in terms of simply feeding people. The chapter reminds us that both the dead and the living needed feeding; that food was employed as a medium, with differentiated value, to help negotiate sociopolitical status; and that direct and clear entanglement between cosmological and political domains created a ritual economy involving the daily sacrifice of huge numbers of livestock at the Shang capital, Anyang.

Campbell argues that although large numbers of livestock, especially cattle, were consumed in the "Great settlement" of Anyang, there is no evidence from ancient texts for a large-scale centralized provisioning system designed to provide for the caloric, ritual, and political needs of the Shang capital. Instead, Campbell posits, the Shang animal economy was the result of a "myriad self-organized networks" (chapter 5), involving a combination of hierarchical lineage groups, specialist producers, and markets for acquiring needed animal resources. This framework presents a new model of an "acephalous," diverse, and flexible urban provisioning economy, emphasizing the presence of many self-organized and segmented provisioning systems meeting the combined ritual, subsistence, and labor requirements of Anyang's high- and low-status occupants as well as its industrial, commercial, and palatial needs. Here again we see an emphasis on a myriad contemporary provisioning systems operating in unison though not perhaps in direct coordination to meet the needs of a heterogeneous, hierarchical society.

In chapter 6, Woldekiros points out that scholarship on feeding African cities has focused on modern food insecurity and that systems for provisioning ancient cities have received little attention. Turning her attention to the kingdom of Aksum, modern Ethiopia, Woldekiros places a special emphasis on the importance of external trade routes in acquiring high-value resources, especially for elites and on the use of administrative technologies and "police" forces for monitoring, controlling, and maintaining long-distance trade corridors. Using a combination of texts, archaeology, and faunal analysis, Woldekiros argues that the Aksumite state developed a specialized agropastoral system primarily relying on cattle and involving both direct and indirect market-based provisioning of urban populations, thus providing a valuable African model complementing the widely cited model of urban provisioning presented by Zeder (1991) based on Near Eastern examples. Moreover, she also identifies the presence of local and direct access to animals at some sites, arguing that the participation of a wide range of state and nonstate actors in provisioning activities created a resilient and flexible system that was able to meet the diverse needs of both high- and low-status Aksumites. Thus, provisioning systems at Aksum have clear structural parallels with those described in Bronze Age Turkey and Greece, and Shang China.

Moving into the chapters on provisioning complex societies in the Americas, chapter 7 presents the first evidence for animal provisioning at the urban center of Monte Albán in Mexico. In this seminal contribution, Martínez-Lira and colleagues define an urban animal economy focused on a combination of wild (deer, peccary, and rabbit/hare) and domestic (turkey and dog) resources and identify spatial and temporal variations in access to animal products.

In terms of spatial variability, the authors identify differences in the abundance of taxa linked to different functional and status areas of the site, with public spaces exhibiting higher frequencies of deer remains than residential areas, indicating their role in the performance of feasting events. High-status areas are also found to be associated with rabbits—results with parallels at the earlier urban economy at Teotihuacan (Somerville et al. 2017). In terms of change through time, the authors find no evidence for a decline in access to high-status wild game, including deer or peccary, as might be predicted by game depression models, though the frequencies of domestic taxa do increase through time, tracking the increase in population at the site. This increase in domestic taxa suggests that access to large game may have been restricted or controlled by state institutions in order to ensure consistent supplies to meet elite ritual and feasting requirements. Moreover, the authors identify concentrations of high-utility cuts of venison within the city, reflecting a complex and likely specialized system of indirect provisioning, perhaps via multiple mechanisms, including markets or state institutions or based on lineage or occupation. This finding has interesting parallels with Zeder's (1991) model of specialized animal economies in the complex societies of ancient Southwest Asia and suggests that control over the processing and distribution of animal products, whether they derive from wild or domestic taxa, is a central concern of state institutions and urban economies.

In richly illustrated chapter 8, Newman reviews ethnohistorical, iconographical, and zooarchaeological evidence for the role of deer in pre-Columbian Maya subsistence, politics, and cosmology. She shows the complex and multifaceted role of deer hunting as sources of animal products, prestige, and reflections of political and religious power. Deer were also exchanged as property as part of bride price and used as sexual metaphors—important features of complex animal economies rarely addressed in zooarchaeological work in the Americas. Further drawing comparisons with Old World big game hunting, Newman describes evidence that Maya elites engaged in group hunting events for political as well as economic reasons. Moreover, at least by the terminal Postclassic, it is also clear that Maya peoples raised deer within villages, though it remains unclear how deer populations were managed during the height of the Classic Maya period.

Newman follows this review of ethnohistorical sources with a detailed examination of hunting and animal husbandry at the site of El Zotz, Guatemala. She argues that with increasing hierarchy in the Classic period, deer hunting became increasingly intertwined with elite political and religious structures, resulting in an increased emphasis on the most prestigious big game in the region. In fact, white-tailed deer percentages map the rise and fall of the El Zotz ruling dynasty, and, like the case at Monte Albán, state institutions likely deployed wild cervid management strategies in order to maintain access to deer populations. Newman suggests that "garden hunting" was the foundation of wild animal procurement systems in the Maya region with an increase in specialized deer procurement during the Classic Maya. As an outgrowth of garden hunting, Newman recognizes landscape management practices, such as extensive land clearing, as an important mechanism that created increased carrying capacity for deer and other wild taxa and that provided a human-engineered foundation for supplying the wild animals and animal products required to support Maya polities such as El Zotz.

In chapter 9, the final chapter, Peres examines the animal economies from two Mississippian period sites in the American Southeast. She explores how changes in regional settlement patterns from dispersed farmsteads toward population aggregation and more intensive agriculture led to changes in hunting and collecting animal resources. Similar to the previous chapter on Maya hunting economies, Peres places special emphasis on "garden hunting," focusing on themes of risk reduction and resilience. Peres argues that "disturbance taxa" were targeted by garden-hunting strategies as part of a provisioning strategy closely integrated with the agricultural system. Comparing faunal remains from a small farmstead and a larger village, she identifies the development of a more complex provisioning system for the village site, where animals were provided for feasts and other social events as well as subsistence. According to Peres, overrepresentation of deer hind and forequarters suggests a complex and perhaps specialized deer procurement and distribution system, which has parallels at the larger Mississippian center of Moundville (Jackson and Scott 1995) and also in Martínez-Lira and colleagues' chapter on the Zapotec center of Monte Albán.

CONCLUDING REMARKS

The eight individual chapters in this volume encapsulate a wide array of theoretical and conceptual approaches to food provisioning in complex societies, in addition to encompassing a wide spatiotemporal spectrum. Although the specific historical and environmental contexts of each case study are different, each chapter touches on a related series of themes relevant for understanding the nature of animal provisioning in complex societies.

First, in contrast to previous work, which has tended to focus on the role of centralized state institutions in feeding complex societies, based largely on Old World texts addressing palace herds and control over agricultural surplus, the chapters in this volume emphasize the presence of multiple, contingent provisioning systems, organized by a range of institutions, corporate groups, and individual actors. In this emergent model of provisioning complex societies, individual settlements and even households and individuals sit at the center of distinct provisioning systems, each with a unique albeit predictable and structured set of obligations, opportunities, and limitations, reflecting their place in the larger social system. A productive emphasis for future work is therefore on the heterogenous and contingent nature of provisioning systems (with an emphasis on the plural) within early complex societies.

In particular, chapters by Campbell, Woldekiros, and Meier highlight the presence of multiple, flexible, and perhaps acephalous networks utilized to produce, acquire, and distribute animal resources to fill a range of subsistence, industrial, political, and religious obligations and needs at a range of scales from the household to the urban settlement. These systems may involve formal state bureaucracies, but they may also be largely self-organizing and based on social and kin relations rather than market and centralized forces. The diverse and flexible nature of these contingent networks may in fact be a key feature explaining the resilience of animal provisioning systems often evident in archaeological case studies.

A second, related theme is that the production, distribution, display, and consumption of animals and animal products are clearly embedded within social, political, and ritual relationships rather than residing primarily in subsistence-oriented markets. As almost all of the chapters in this volume highlight cleavages along status lines, religious order, sodality, kin group, and so on, they highlight predictable and repeated differences in who has access to what animal resources. In Beglane's chapter on medieval Ireland, access to animals, particularly cattle, is affected by one's position within society, with grange workers, monks, and high-status nobles situated within different provisioning webs, each governed by different sets of rules. Each chapter emphasizes linkages between status and access to specific animal resources, while Campbell, Perez, and Newman show that ritual obligations to feed ancestors and provide offerings for the living and the dead at feasting events are central rather than peripheral features of the economies of ancient complex societies.

In the chapters by Arbuckle, Martínez-Lira, and Newman, wild animals, including aurochs and boar in Anatolia and deer and peccary in the Americas, were accessible in high-status contexts, with suggestions that game reserves and restrictions on nonelite hunting may have been in place in both ancient Mesoamerica and Southwest Asia. In the Mediterranean region, although large sheep and goat herds may have been under the control of palatial authorities, Meier argues, pigs were outside of the obligations and requirements of this redistributive economy; instead, swine provisioning systems were likely organized in a more heterarchical way through personal contacts or kin relationships to local swineherds. This theme emphasizes that faunal assemblages are the aggregated products of social relationships reflecting the social systems in which they were produced. This is particularly the case in ancient complex societies not transformed by the alienating tendencies of later capitalist economic systems.

A third feature is that each case study reveals that elites in complex societies regularly and predictably go to great lengths to create distinctive and specialized provisioning systems designed to highlight their unique ritual and political roles. In many cases, high-status institutions focus on controlling the distribution (i.e., access to) and processing of animals and animal resources for specific events—such as feasts, celebrations, and public rituals—whereas production and acquisition regimes tend to be more distributed and heterogeneous, providing general support for Zeder's (1991) model of urban provisioning.

Because the display, distribution, and consumption of animal products and animals themselves are central parts of the performance and reification of status within hierarchical complex societies, animal remains represent a particularly effective proxy for assessing the nature of hierarchies and status in the archaeological record, particularly when intersite or intrasite contextual analyses are employed. This is the case in both Old and New World contexts, where elite-sponsored feasts are evident in the Mississippian period in the American Southeast, the Oaxaca Valley of Mexico, Bronze Age Anatolia, and Shang China. In addition, big game hunting was an obligation of Maya and Near Eastern kings alike, and lower-status populations accessed animal products through mechanisms such as garden hunting and household swine production as well as through other contingent and resilient strategies outside of centralized provisioning systems.

As a result of the importance of context and relationality in structuring the needs for and resulting uses of animals, the chapters in this volume emphasize the importance of integrating textual and/or ethnohistorical sources in the interpretation of animal provisioning in complex societies. Although the symbolic roles of some animals—particularly those characterized by large size or impressive physical features such as deer, horned cattle, large carnivores, and birds of prey—may fall into predictable cross-cultural patterns in many cases, it is difficult to adequately understand the uses and symbolic importance of many taxa or intrasite variation in foodways and diet in cases where direct historical parallels are not available. In addition, detailed cultural knowledge derived from texts allows zooarchaeologists in historical contexts to further explore the roles of hunting and herding practices in the performance of specific social roles (see examples in chapters by Arbuckle, Beglane, and Woldekiros), cosmologically significant practices, including the recapitulation of mythological events (Newman), or feeding ancestors and other supernatural beings (Campbell).

Finally, although each chapter explores the uses of multiple species in complex societies, the overwhelming importance of large mammals, whether as prey species or livestock, is evident in each case study. In Africa and Eurasia, cattle, and in specific cases camels and horses, are important points of intersection of the realms of wealth, power, production, vitality, alimentation, divinity, and bodily virtue. These large, impressive animals are disproportionately targeted by elites to project and reify positions of power and inequality. In the Americas prior to European colonialism, deer played a very similar role and were controlled, eaten, distributed, and displayed; their roles as nonhuman persons and as supernatural beings were emphasized in political and ritual contexts particularly by elites.

Overall, the chapters in this book provide an optimistic roadmap for ways to further explore the complex, diverse, resilient, and contingent mechanisms involved in provisioning complex societies on a global scale through creative combinations of ethnohistorical evidence, iconography, and contextual analysis of faunal remains. Gone are the days when singular models of top-down, centralized economies can be used to reconstruct premodern urban economies. Instead, in order to address pertinent questions about how cities and complex societies were provisioned, archaeologists must delve deeply into the social lives of the foods that provisioning systems represent. This represents a productive way forward for understanding the unique, yet predictably structured, provisioning systems that emerged in the context of complex societies in all parts of the world.

WORKS CITED

Auban, J. B., A. M. Martín, and C. M. Barton. 2012. "Complex Systems, Social Networks and the Evolution of Social Complexity." In *The Prehistory of Iberia: Debating Early Social Stratification and the State*, edited by M. Berrocal, L. García Sanjuán, and A. Gilman, 23–37. New York: Routledge.

Bartosiewicz, L., and E. Gal. 2013. *Shuffling Nags, Lame Ducks: The Archaeology of Animal Disease*. Oxford: Oxbow Books.

Boessneck, J., A. von den Driesch, U. Meyer-Lemppenau, and E. Wechsler von Ohlen. 1971. *Die Tierknochenfunde aus dem Oppidum von Manching: Ausgrabungen in Manching*. Wiesbaden, Germany: F. Steiner.

Childe, V. G. 1950. "The Urban Revolution." *The Town Planning Review* 21 (1): 3–17.

Cowgill, G. L. 2004. "Origins and Development of Urbanism: Archaeological Perspectives." *Annual Review of Anthropology* 33: 525–549.

Crabtree, P. J. 1990. "Zooarchaeology and Complex Societies: Some Uses of Faunal Analysis for the Study of Trade, Social Status, and Ethnicity." *Archaeological Method and Theory* 2: 155–205.

Crabtree, P., and D. Campana. 2016. "Class and 'Romanization' in Late Roman Egypt: Issues of Identity and the Faunal Remains from the Site of Amheida in the Dakleh Oasis, Western Egypt." In *Bones and Identity: Zooarchaeological Approaches to Reconstructing Social and Cultural Landscapes in Southwest Asia*, edited by N. Marom, R. Yeshuran, L. Weissbrod, and G. Bar-Oz, 293–302. Oxford: Oxbow Books.

deFrance, S. 2009. "Zooarchaeology in Complex Societies: Political Economy, Status, and Ideology." *Journal of Archaeological Research* 17 (2): 105–168.

Ervynck, A., W. Van Neer, H. Huster-Plogmann, and J. Schibler. 2003. "Beyond Affluence: The Zooarchaeology of Luxury." *World Archaeology* 34 (3): 428–441.

Evans, S. T., and D. L. Webster, eds. 2001. *Archaeology of Ancient Mexico and Central America: An Encyclopedia*. New York: Garland Publishing.

Ewonus, P. A. 2011. "Social Zooarchaeology of a Northwest Coast House." *Journal of Island and Coastal Archaeology* 6 (1): 72–97.

Feinman, G. M., and L. M. Nicholas, eds. 2004. *Archaeological Perspectives on Political Economies*. Salt Lake City: University of Utah Press.

Fournié, G., D. U. Pfeiffer, and R. Bendrey. 2017. "Early Animal Farming and Zoonotic Disease Dynamics: Modelling Brucellosis Transmission in Neolithic Goat Populations." *Royal Society Open Science* 4: 160943. https://doi.org/10.1098/rsos.160943.

Gumerman IV, G. 1997. "Food and Complex Societies." *Journal of Archaeological Method and Theory* 4: 105–139.

Itulua-Abumere, F. 2013. "Concepts and Practices of Food Consumptions in Modern Society." *Open Journal of Social Science Research* 1 (4): 78–85.

Jackson, H. E., and S. L. Scott. 1995. "The Faunal Record of the Southeastern Elite: The Implications of Economy, Social Relations, and Ideology." *Southeastern Archaeology* 14 (2): 103–119.

Knudson, K. J., K. R. Gardella, and J. Yaeger. 2012. "Provisioning Inka Feasts at Tiwanaku, Bolivia: The Geographic Origins of Camelids in the Pumapunku Complex." *Journal of Archaeological Science* 39 (2): 479–491.

Maltby, M. 1979. *Faunal Studies on Urban Sites: The Animal Bones from Exeter, 1971–5*, Sheffield: Exeter Archaeological Report 2.

Mintz, S. W., and C. M. Du Bois. 2002. "The Anthropology of Food and Eating." *Annual Review Anthropology* 31: 99–119.

Morgan, K. 2009. "Feeding the City: The Challenge of Urban Food Planning." *International Planning Studies* 14 (4): 341–348.

Orton, D. C. 2012. "Taphonomy and Interpretation: An Analytical Framework for Social Zooarchaeology." *International Journal of Osteoarchaeology* 22 (3): 320–337.

Orton, D. C., J. Morris, A. Locker, and J. H. Barrett. 2014. "Fish for the City: Meta-analysis of Archaeological Cod Remains and the Growth of London's Northern Trade." *Antiquity* 88 (340): 516–530.

Price, M., K. Grossman, and T. Paulette. 2017. "Pigs and the Pastoral Bias: The Other Animal Economy in Northern Mesopotamia (3000–2000 BCE)." *Journal of Anthropological Archaeology* 48 (December): 46–62.

Redding, R. W. 2015. "The Pig and the Chicken in the Middle East: Modeling Human Subsistence Behavior in the Archaeological Record Using Historical and Animal Husbandry Data." *Journal of Archaeological Research* 23 (December): 325–368.

Reitz, E. J., B. Pavao-Zuckerman, D. Weinand, G. Duncan, and D. Thomas. 2010. *Mission and Pueblo Santa Catalina de Guale, St. Catherines Island, Georgia (USA): A Comparative Zooarchaeological Analysis*, Washington, DC: Anthropological papers of the American Museum of Natural History, no. 91.

Rowley-Conwy, P. 2018. "Zooarchaeology and the Elusive Feast: From Performance to Aftermath." *World Archaeology* 50 (2): 221–241.

Russell, N. 2012. *Social Zooarchaeology: Humans and Animals in Prehistory*. Cambridge: Cambridge University Press.

Scott, J. C. 2017. *Against the Grain: A Deep History of the Earliest States*, New Haven, CT: Yale University Press.

Sharpe, A. E., K. Emery, T. Inomata, D. Triadan, G. D. Kamenov, and J. Krigbaum. 2018. "Earliest Isotopic Evidence in the Maya Region for Animal Management and Long-Distance Trade at the Site of Ceibal, Guatemala." *Proceedings of the National Academy of Sciences* 115 (14): 3605–3610.

Somerville, A. D., N. Sugiyama, L. R. Manzanilla, and M. Schoeninger. 2017. "Leporid Management and Specialized Food Production at Teotihuacan: Stable Isotope Data from Cottontail and Jackrabbit Bone Collagen." *Archaeological and Anthropological Sciences* 9 (February): 83–97.

Twiss, K. 2012. "The Archaeology of Food and Social Diversity." *Journal of Archaeological Research* 20 (4): 357–395.

Yoffee, N., and N. Terrenato. 2015. "Introduction: A History of the Study of Early Cities." In *The Cambridge World History*. Vol. 3, *Early Cities in Comparative Perspective 4000 BCE–1200 CE*, edited by N. Yoffee. 1–24. Cambridge: Cambridge University Press. https://doi.org/10.1017/CHO9781139035606.002.

Yuan, J., and R. Flad. 2005. "New Zooarchaeological Evidence for Changes in Shang Dynasty Animal Sacrifice." *Journal of Anthropological Archaeology* 24 (3): 252–270.

Zeder, M. 1991. *Feeding Cities: Specialized Animal Economy in the Ancient Near East*. Washington, DC: Smithsonian Institute Press.

Zeder, M. 1998. "Pigs and Emergent Complexity in the Ancient Near East." In *Ancestors for the Pigs: Pigs in Prehistory*, edited by S. M. Nelson. 109–122. Philadelphia: MASCA Research Papers in Science and Archaeology, vol. 15.

Zeder, M. 2003. "Food Provisioning in Urban Societies: A View from Northern Mesopotamia." In *The Social Construction of Ancient Cities*, edited by M. L. Smith, 156–183. Washington, DC: Smithsonian Books.

2

Provisioning Bronze Age Cities with Wild Animals

Evidence from Acemhöyük, Turkey

BENJAMIN S. ARBUCKLE

Studying how early cities were provisioned has been a central contribution of zooarchaeological research to understanding complex societies in the past (Crabtree 1990; Landon 1997; Maltby 1979; Zeder 1991). This body of work has provided valuable evidence of, and generated theoretical frameworks for, reconstructing the systems that emerged in order to provide urban residents and institutions with the animal products necessary to meet a wide range of needs. These products include postmortem (primary) products such as meat, fat, bone, horn, and skins, as well as antemortem (or secondary) products such as traction, dairy, dung, and animal fiber (Sherratt 1983; Vigne and Helmer 2007). These resources functioned within a wide range of subsistence, industrial, political, and ritual practices, representing diverse and necessary components of specialized urban economies (Campbell 2015; Defrance 2009; Sapir-Hen et al. 2016). In this way, faunal studies have come to play a central role in reconstructing the functioning of ancient urban socioeconomic systems.

In many Bronze Age urban sites in Southwest Asia, which represent some of the earliest complex specialized animal economies, faunal assemblages are

https://doi.org/10.5876/9781646422562.c002

dominated by the remains of livestock that have served as the focus of studies of animal provisioning systems. However, a small yet persistent percentage of urban faunal remains represent wild taxa. Because these wild taxa are represented in low frequencies in urban assemblages, they generally receive little attention (though see Berthon 2014). However, wild animals' ubiquity in the faunal record suggests that they played important and diverse roles in the functioning of Bronze Age urban economic and political systems. These functions are supported by lines of evidence including ancient texts and iconography, which frequently reference wild animals and indicate that the archaeofaunal record systematically underestimates the roles of these taxa in the symbolic, political, ritual, and perhaps even economic practices of early cities (Collins 2002; Van Buren 1939).

Despite abundant evidence for wild animals in urban environments, there have been few systematic attempts to assess how and why Bronze Age urban centers were provisioned with wild animals and wild animal products, nor has there been much effort to clarify the mechanics of these provisioning systems. In this chapter, I focus on evidence for the use of wild animal resources at the Bronze Age site of Acemhöyük, central Turkey, and argue that they were regular and necessary, if small, components of Bronze Age urban systems used in a wide range of social, economic, and political contexts. Wild animal provisioning involved a range of actors but was largely organized by and for elites and was likely characterized by a high degree of specialization emphasizing the importance of regular and uninterrupted access to a range of wild animal resources.

BACKGROUND

Previous faunal work on provisioning systems has focused on addressing the organization of systems of production and distribution of animal products, particularly the primary and secondary products of livestock. For example, in her seminal work on the topic, M. Zeder (1991) assessed evidence for economic specialization in the animal economies of the Bronze Age urban settlement Tal-e Malyan, in western Iran. Working with faunal remains from Tal-e Malyan representing the rise of the settlement into a powerful urban capital, she concluded that all stages of the animal economy—including production, distribution, and processing (butchery)—were highly specialized. However, sheep and goat production in ancient urban settlements was often "farmed out" to local specialized pastoralists: "As long as provisioning needs were met, herders were left to direct their own activities without having to submit to the directives of higher-order specialized administration" (Zeder 1991:254; see also Arbuckle 2012; Wapnish and Hesse 1988).

However, not all animals were subject to the same degree of specialized treatment and institutional control, and recent research has focused on the presence of multiple modes of animal provisioning both within and outside of state institutions. Cattle may have been subject to more centralized economic controls related to their vital roles in intensive agricultural systems as traction animals (Miller et al. 2009), whereas pigs were often utilized as a household-level resource in the Bronze Age with their absence in administrative texts suggesting that urban swine husbandry represents an independent and parallel provisioning system to that of domestic ruminants (sheep, goat, cattle), whose products were more tightly controlled by urban institutions (Price et al. 2017).

Levent Atici (2014) has explored evidence for urban provisioning at the Bronze Age urban site of Kültepe in central Turkey. Here a combination of texts and faunal remains from Middle Bronze Age deposits dating to the early second millennium BC suggests that urban residents had access to whole animals and cuts of meat, as well as cooked meats through various channels. Texts in particular suggest that the specialized processing and distribution of animal products at Kültepe involved both state and nonstate actors, providing important evidence for the presence of parallel public and private provisioning systems. This recent work emphasizes that Bronze Age urban livestock provisioning systems were complex and multivalent, with multiple production, distribution, and processing pathways for different species.

Although faunal studies overwhelmingly focus on the livestock components of urban animal economies, iconography and ancient texts often provide a different perspective on animal provisioning systems that emphasize the regular use of and reference to wild animals in early urban societies in Southwest Asia, particularly among elites (Collins 2002; Heimpel 1968; Van Buren 1939). These complementary sources indicate that big game hunting and the display of symbolically potent game animals were important components of courtly life in the ancient Near East. In particular, it is clear that some wild taxa had central political and ritual significance, that live wild animals were regularly incorporated into urban economies, and that specialized procurement systems were created to ensure elites maintained regular access to these important resources.

Texts and iconography indicate that hunting and displaying large game were frequent features of elite courtly practices in the Bronze Age (Collins 2002; Lewis and Llewelyn-Jones 2018). Hunting functioned within political, ritual, and economic spheres, with T. Allsen (2006) suggesting the near universal role of elite hunting in complex societies. N. Sugiyama (Sugiyama et al. 2014) has emphasized the metaphorical component of capturing and controlling symbolically potent animals and its role in naturalizing the hierarchy of elites as a common strategy relevant to complex societies in both the New and Old Worlds (see also Watanabe 2002).

In Southwest Asia and Egypt, the hunting of bulls was considered a princely activity par excellence and in some cases a religious obligation with elites memorializing successful big game hunts in texts and visual media (Watanabe 2002).

For example, Assyrian king Shalmaneser III (ninth century BC) recorded a hunt in the seventeenth year of his reign marked by the slaughter of sixty-three bull aurochs and the capture of four live animals (Safar 1951; Watanabe 2002:73), while an inscription on a royal scarab of the Egyptian pharaoh Amenhotep III (late second millennium BC) describes in detail a wild bull hunt that took place in his second regnal year. In the latter case, a large herd of aurochs was captured and enclosed within a ditch, allowing the king to kill ninety-six bulls over several days (van Delden 1970). Moreover, scenes depicting royal bull hunts decorated the walls of Ashurnasirpal's (ninth century BC) palace at Nimrud as well as the temple of pharaoh Ramses III (late second millennium BC) at Medinet Habu near Thebes (Albenda 2008; Grayson 1976; Watanabe 2002:69).

Although royal references to aurochs hunting are most common in the late second and first millennium BC, this practice likely has a much deeper history. For example, an Ur III text describes King Shulgi (late third millennium BC) slaughtering aurochs, wild ass, and boar, and a cylinder seal from the Uruk period (fourth millennium BC) shows a high-status male, accompanied by an attendant, and a symbol of the goddess Inanna, shooting arrows at a group of bulls, suggesting that aurochs hunting as an elite activity may have extended back into the earliest urban societies in Southwest Asia (Watanabe 2002:72).

In some cases, written sources indicate a reoccurring interest in procuring specific high-value species and keeping them captive for hunts or other forms of public display (Lion 1992). For example, images from Ashurbanipal's (in seventh century BC) palace at Nineveh show lions being released from cages for royal hunts, clearly indicating these animals had been held in captivity until needed for a ritualized spectacle (Watanabe 2002). King Ashurnasirpal II recorded capturing fifteen lions and fifty cubs and raising them (along with a wide range of other wild animals) for display in the city of Nimrud, while Tiglath-Pileser claimed to have hunted, killed, and captured bull elephants in the land of Harran and to have brought live animals back to Assur in a truly elephantine spectacle (Foster 2002:285).

These inscriptions are among many suggesting that royal menageries may have been common parts of Near Eastern urban settlements (Oates and Oates 2001:34; Watanabe 2002:77). In Anatolia, the well-known Anitta text (ca. 1700 BC) describes King Anitta hunting and capturing a menagerie of wild animals—including lions, boar, and deer—and bringing them back (perhaps alive) to his city Nesa (Kanesh) (Beckman et al. 2007:218). In later Hittite imagery, deer and boar hunting rituals are depicted with some regularity, and texts indicate that these animals were paraded during certain festivals (Baltacıoğlu 1993; Collins 2002; Emre and Çınaroğlu 1993).

In many cases, the scale of wild animal procurement may have involved a handful of wild animals, but in some cases large numbers of animals were involved, suggesting a more organized and "professional" system for capturing, caring for, and transporting wild species. For example, Ashurnasirpal II claimed to have provided 500 stags for a banquet, which indicates a robust provisioning system and perhaps active management of some game animals (Lambert 1960:42). Moreover, a "hunter/trapper" character appears in tablet I of the "Epic of Gilgamesh" (George 2002), implying that wild game were the specific target of specialists in contrast to the commonly held view that game were hunted mostly on an opportunistic basis by pastoralists.

The presence of a specialized system designed to provision urban and elite markets with wild animals is further reflected in third-millennium texts from the sites of Ebla in Syria and Drehem, ancient Puzrish-Dagan, in Iraq. A text from the site of Ebla describes the dowry of Princess Kesh-dut, on the occasion of her marriage to a king of Kish. This dowry includes a large number of livestock (972 bulls, 935 cows, 768 oxen, 277 calves, 1680 sheep) but also 159 equid hybrids (known as *kunga*), 1 horse(?), 5 pigs, 19 bison, and 14 bears (Archi 1987). This list is informative in terms of documenting the scale of royal herds but also indicates the presence of a lively trade in wild animals, including carnivores, which must have been a regular sight in urban palaces and markets in the Bronze Age.

Although Drehem is best known for its role as an imperial livestock distribution center in the Ur III kingdom, texts indicate that wild animals were also transported and inventoried here for redistribution (Steinkeller 1987). In a summary of a single five-year accounting cycle of Nasa, a receiving official at Puzrish-Dagan under King Shulgi, Y. Wu (2010) describes records of the movement of large numbers of live wild animals. This record includes 3,880 gazelle, 458 bears, 404 red deer, 236 fallow deer, 360 wild asses, 727 "large kunga asses," 13 antelope, and possibly one dolphin! An individual named Lu-digir-ra, referred to as a "wild animal keeper," is frequently associated with these animals, an indication of the formalized nature of this profession by the late third millennium BC, when specialists were employed to capture, raise, and facilitate the movement of these valuable wild resources.

Exactly what these animals were needed for is less clear. Some may have been destined for display in game parks and in ritual parades or for gifting to elites in neighboring kingdoms. Others may have been used for sacrifices and/or consumption in temples and in royal and institutional kitchens (i.e., of workers and soldiers), while their skins would have been sent to workshops for manufacturing. In the case of bears, these animals may have also been trained as pets and/or for entertainment, practices that continued well into the twentieth century (e.g., Mattick 2015).

The wild asses (*Equus hemionus*) and "large kunga asses" (i.e., equid hybrids) recorded in these texts are notable, and J. Zarins (2014) has summarized evidence for the capture and raising of the former and the breeding of the latter animal in Mesopotamian texts. He has argued that wild asses were regularly captured and kept in captivity, where they were eaten as well as crossbred with domestic donkeys to produce the valuable hybrid equid referred to as a *kunga*. This breeding required specialized personnel and a constant stream of new wild hemiones, since F1 hybrids of these taxa are sterile, and hemiones likely did not breed well in captivity.

Although the scale of wild animal populations moving through Puzrish-Dagan was small, compared to the hundreds of thousands of head of livestock, the movement of thousands of live wild animals through this settlement suggests that they represent the "tip of the iceberg" in regard to the scale of wild animal economies in Bronze Age Southwest Asia. Moreover, the range of wild taxa represented at Puzrish-Dagan, in addition to the presence of gamekeepers, suggests that wild animals were a regular part of urban life in the Bronze Age and that markets for them were robust enough to support the specialists needed to capture, transport, raise, and breed them on a continuous basis.

PROVISIONING BRONZE AGE ACEMHÖYÜK

The site of Acemhöyük represents the remains of a large (50+ ha) Early and Middle Bronze Age urban center and lower town located on the Aksaray plain in central Anatolia (modern Turkey) (figure 2.1) (Özgüç 1966, 2015). The large faunal assemblage from the site recovered during excavations led by Aliye Öztan from 1989 to 2019 provides a direct record of the animals and animal products used in this Bronze Age city and thus a unique window into the nature of provisioning systems in second- and third-millennia BC central Anatolia.

The Early Bronze Age (EBA) occupation of the city dates to the mid- to late third millennium BC (levels XI–IV) (table 2.1) (Arbuckle 2013; Özgüç 1966). At this

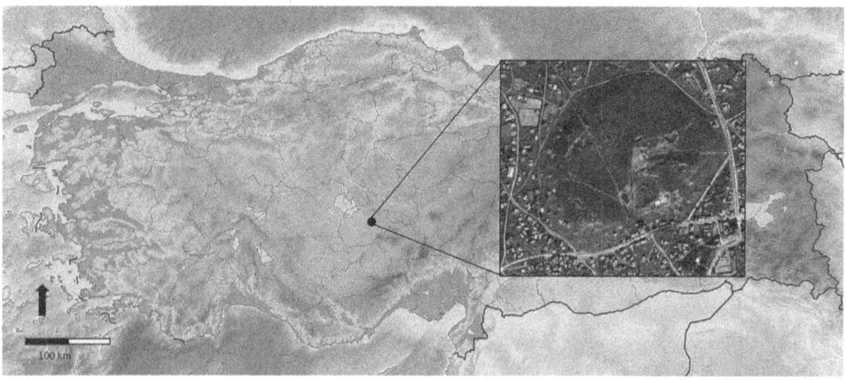

Figure 2.1. *Map showing the location of Acemhöyük. Inset image shows the main mound of Acemhöyük (image from Google Earth Pro 7.3.2.5491, 2018 DigitalGlobe; base map by Sémhur, Wikimedia Commons, CC-BY-SA-3.0).*

Table 2.1. Recent radiocarbon results from EBA and MBA Acemhöyük

Lab ID	*Specimen ID*	*Strat Level*	*Material*	*Conv. Age BP*	*2 Sigma Calibration (cal BC)*
BETA361835	AC13.VA52	II	Bone collagen	3480 ± 30	1890–1740/1710–1700
BETA402640	ACUA49	III	Charred material	3460 ± 30	1880–1690
BETA305371	AC9017	IV	Bone collagen	3560 ± 30	1970–1870
BETA305368	AC7900	IV	Bone collagen	3580 ± 30	2020–1880
BETA305370	AC8813	IV	Bone collagen	3650 ± 30	2130–2080/2060–1940
BETA305369	AC8609	IV	Bone collagen	3650 ± 30	2130–2080/2060–1940
BETA423304	ACFB48	VII	Charred material	3800 ± 30	2335–2325/2300–2190/2180–2140
BETA402638	AC13540	XI	Bone collagen	3670 ± 30	2140–1955
BETA402639	ACFB50	XI	Bone collagen	3770 ± 30	2285–2130/2080–2060
UBA-30288	AC13346	XI	Bone collagen	3782 ± 41	2345–2119/2096–2040
BETA402641	ACDB50	XI	Charred material	3870 ± 30	2465–2275/2250–2210
BETA422493	AC14405	XI	Bone collagen	3880 ± 30	2465–2280/2245–2230
BETA422494	DB50	XI	Charred material	3900 ± 30	2470–2290
BETA422492	AC14396	XI	Bone collagen	3940 ± 30	2550–2535/2490–2395/2385–2345
BETA342026	ACCB5011_1	XI?	Charred material	4030 ± 30	2620–2470
BETA361837	AC13.DB50	XI	Bone collagen	4080 ± 30	2740–2720/2700–2570/2520–2500
BETA342028	ACCB5011_3	XI?	Bone collagen	4220 ± 30	2810–2760/2720–2700
BETA342027	ACCB5011_2	XI?	Bone collagen	4130 ± 30	2870–2580
BETA422495	DB50	XI	Charred material	4300 ± 30	2925–2885

time, the city center was surrounded by a monumental mudbrick wall with evidence suggesting that the settlement was intimately involved in the competitive

Table 2.2. Faunal remains identified in the Bronze Age levels of Acemhöyük

Taxon/Level	*Common name*	*MBA II+III*	*EBA/MBA IV+V*	*EBA VI–XI*	*Total*
Small mammal		5	0	0	5
Small-medium		5	2	1	8
Medium		73	28	31	132
Med-large		2	0	0	2
Large mammal		152	85	67	304
Med artiodactyl		161	65	12	238
Large artiodactyl		211	21	9	241
Ovis/Capra	Sheep/goat	3,107	709	295	4,111
Ovis aries/orientalis	Sheep	1,496	243	173	1,912
Capra hircus	Goat	859	74	51	984
Bovid/cervid		292	0	9	301
Bos spp.	Cattle/aurochs	1,265	609	388	2,262
Capreolus capreolus	Roe deer	8	2	0	10
Dama	Fallow deer	10	6	0	16
Cervus elaphus	Red deer	24	1	15	40
Sus scrofa	Pig	752	225	57	1,034
Equus asinus/hydruntinus	"Ass"	93	92	104	289
Equus caballus/ferus	Horse	21	15	2	38
Equus sp.	Equid	4	10	4	18
Small carnivore		4	0	0	4
Medium carnivore		2	1	0	3
Large carnivore		2	0	0	2
Canis spp.	Dog/wolf	267	45	36	348
Vulpes	Fox	28	2	4	34
Ursus arctos	Bear	17	1	1	19
Lepus	Hare	74	10	0	84
Osteichthyes	Fish	1	0	1	2
Aves	Bird	10	14	0	24
Total		8,945	2,260	1,260	12,465

and fragmentary political landscape of third-millennium central Anatolia and greater Mesopotamia (Kamış 2017). The Middle Bronze Age (MBA; levels III–II; 2000–1750 BC) at Acemhöyük is better documented. At this time, the settlement was the center of a wealthy kingdom, perhaps known as the city of Purushanda (or perhaps Uluma) in Old Assyrian texts (Barjamovic 2011; Özgüç 2015). Excavations have uncovered administrative buildings, including a monumental palace destroyed by fire. Excavation of this "Sarıkaya Palace" by Nimet Özgüç, and of other administrative buildings by Aliye Öztan, have revealed a complex and hierarchical political and economic system with evidence for craft production; concentrations of exotic, high-status trade goods; a small number of cuneiform texts; and seals and sealings indicating extensive connections with northern Mesopotamian kingdoms (Kuzuoğlu 2016; Özgüç 1966, 2015; Öztan 2007).

Analysis of the faunal remains from the EBA and MBA levels have revealed an animal economy dominated by domestic sheep and goats (62% of mammal remains identified to genus), and cattle (21%), followed by smaller numbers of pigs (8.8%), dogs (3%), and equids (2.9%) (Arbuckle 2013; Deniz 1985; Nicola and Glew 1999) (table 2.2). These domestic animals represent 90% of the total faunal assemblage and show signs of butchery and intentional fragmentation, indicating that they represent the core animal economy providing the inhabitants of the city with both primary and secondary animal resources. Although most of the faunal remains derive from pits and room fill deposits, in some cases, animal remains were recovered within and near burials, which suggests that livestock played important roles in both economic and ritual contexts.

PROVISIONING ACEMHÖYÜK WITH WILD MAMMALS

In addition to domestic taxa, a range of wild species are consistently found in the Acemhöyük faunal assemblage. These remains support evidence from texts and iconography showing that urban centers were regularly provisioned with wild animals. These wild species are relatively rare (<2% number of identified specimens [NISP]) but likely played important roles in the functioning of this Bronze Age urban community—an interpretation supported by their presence in virtually all contemporary urban faunal assemblages in the region.

Cervidae

Deer are the most numerous wild taxa identified in the faunal assemblages at Acemhöyük but still represent less than 1% of the identified mammalian remains in the EBA and MBA levels. Cervids have been identified in faunal samples at Acemhöyük analyzed by Deniz (1985; $NISP_{cervid} = 13$), Nicola and Glew (1999; $NISP_{cervid} = 10$) and Arbuckle ($NISP_{cervid} = 66$), with red deer (*Cervus elaphus*) being the most abundant. The remains of fallow deer (*Dama dama*) and roe deer (*Capreolus capreolus*) are found in smaller numbers (Arbuckle data: $NISP_{Cervus} = 40$, $NISP_{Dama} = 16$; $NISP_{Capreolus} = 10$). Antler is the most abundant cervid element recovered ($NISP_{antler} = 27$), often from contexts within buildings; saw marks and cut marks indicate an antler industry was located within the city in both the EBA and MBA periods. However, the remains of upper limb bones (scapula, humerus, femur—some with cut marks) and lower limb bones (tibia, radius, ulna), as well as autopodia (metapodials, phalanges), have also been recovered from within structures and trash pits both on the mound and within the lower town, suggesting that complete carcasses were brought to the site, butchered, consumed, and disposed of in middens. It is likely that deer were available in the forested hills surrounding the Aksaray plain or in the Melendiz Mountains, although red deer may have also ventured down onto the Aksaray plain drawn by extensive grasslands as well as salt deposits in the Tuz Gölü (Salt Lake) basin.

Aurochs (*Bos primigenius*)

Domestic taurine cattle (*Bos taurus*) are an important component of the faunal assemblages at Acemhöyük, where they represent 10–35% of the identified mammal remains depending on archaeological context ($NISP_{Bos}$ = 2,262). The body size of domestic cattle at Acemhöyük varied widely, reflecting the presence of small-sized cows as well as larger bulls and/or oxen. However, biometric data indicate that a few cattle specimens represent animals of extraordinary size that fall outside of the range of sexual dimorphism of local domestic cattle (figure 2.2). These outliers likely represent the remains of wild aurochs (*Bos primigenius*), which were frequently hunted in the marshes and grasslands of central Anatolia in the Neolithic and Chalcolithic periods and likely persisted in the region well into the Bronze Age.

Biometric evidence for the presence of wild and domestic cattle at Acemhöyük are presented in figure 2.2. Here length and proximal breadth measurements for the first phalanx of Acemhöyük bovines are plotted along with those representing a wild aurochs population from the early Neolithic site of Mureybet on the Syrian Euphrates. Clusters representing smaller and larger domestic cattle are notably smaller than the Neolithic aurochs from Mureybet. However, six specimens from Acemhöyük fall outside of the range of the domestic cattle and fall within the range of the Neolithic aurochs (GL ≥67.7 mm; Bd≥ 35.1 mm). Five of these specimens group with aurochs cows, while the sixth (specimen AC13285) falls within the size range of bull aurochs. Biometric data from other skeletal elements exhibit parallel patterns, showing the consistent presence of a few individuals that overlap in size with (mostly female) aurochs.

It is likely that these aurochs-like specimens represent the remains of wild aurochs that were hunted on the nearby Aksaray plain and adjacent marshlands surrounding the Tuz Gölü and were consumed and disposed of within the elite portions of the settlement. It is also possible that aurochs were occasionally captured alive and incorporated into domestic herds, resulting in the presence of large-sized individuals (including wild-born animals as well as F1 crossbreeds) within herds.

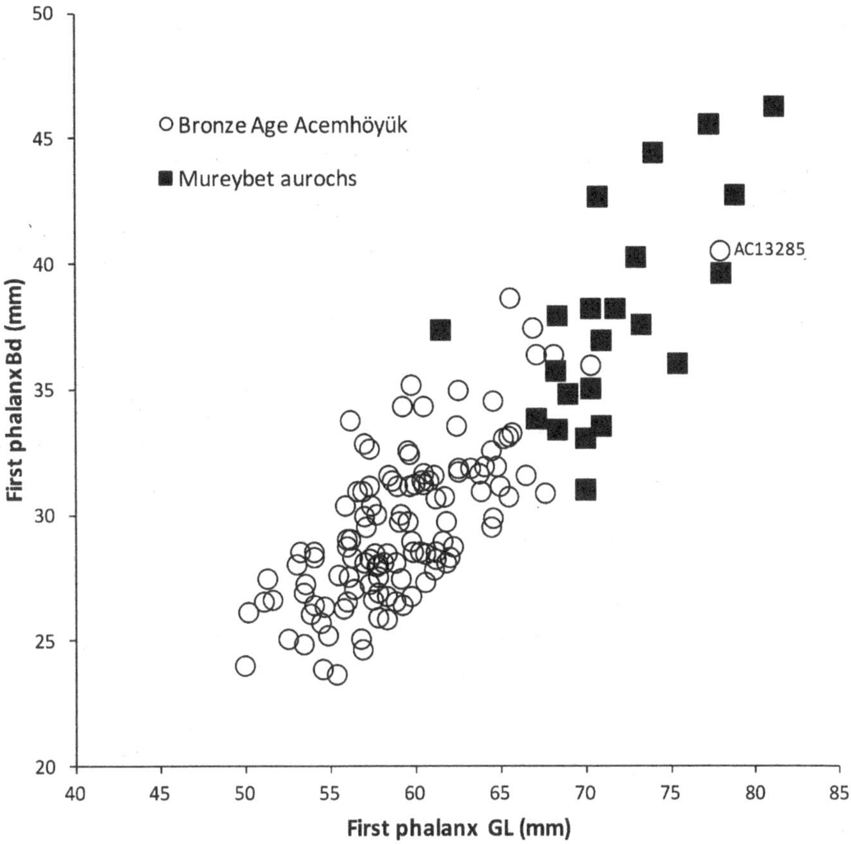

Figure 2.2. *Bivariate plot of distal breadth and greatest length of the first phalanx for Acemhöyük* Bos *and aurochs (*Bos primigenius*) from the site of Mureybet (Gourichon and Helmer 2008).*

Mouflon (*Ovis orientalis*)

Domestic sheep (*Ovis aries*) is the most abundant taxon at Acemhöyük in both EBA and MBA periods ($NISP_{Ovis}$ = 1,912; $NISP_{caprine}$ = 4,111). Among the ovine remains, a small number of specimens exhibit characteristics of wild sheep, the mouflon (*Ovis orientalis*). The Bronze Age domestic sheep population at Acemhöyük was characterized by large body size, with biometric distributions reflecting the presence of large numbers of adult males suggestive of a herding economy focused on the production of wool (Arbuckle 2012). These large-sized males are comparable in size to wild mouflon making it difficult to distinguish hunted from domestic animals based on biometric characteristics alone. However, domestic sheep at Acemhöyük and other Bronze Age sites are characterized by horn-core morphologies, which distinguish them from their wild relatives. In most cases, domestic rams exhibit significant reductions in horn size compared to wild rams—a feature that is quantifiable through measuring the basal anterior-posterior diameter of horn-cores. In addition, cross-sectional shape differs between domestic rams more likely to exhibit horn-cores with rounded cross-sections (and generally higher variability in shape) and those of mouflon, which are often quadrilateral in cross section with a flattened anterior margin (Bökönyi 1977; Hole et al. 1969:283, fig. 121; Reed 1983).

Among the sheep horn-cores at Acemhöyük representing both the EBA and MBA levels, fifteen specimens exhibit wild-type mouflon characteristics, including large basal diameters and the wide, flat anterior surface typical of wild rams. In previous work on the Acemhöyük faunal assemblage, J. Nicola and C. Glew (1999:fig. 1b) also identified these wild-type sheep horn-cores from the MBA Hatıplar Palace.

These large mouflon-like specimens range in basal diameter from 70 to 45.5 mm, measurements that overlap in size with recent wild rams reported by C. Reed (1983) (56 and 51 mm respectively) and with those from prehistoric Asiab (western Iran) reported by Bökönyi (1977) (65–78 mm for wild rams). The smaller of these specimens from Acemhöyük overlap with those of large domestic rams and are comparable to the presumably domestic rams from the Bronze Age sites of Lidar Höyük and Demircihöyük, the measurements of which range from 48 to 58 mm (Kussinger 1988; Rauh 1981). However, the largest horn-core specimens at Acemhöyük (>60 mm) are clearly within the size range of wild mouflon and are larger than expected for Bronze Age domestic sheep in Turkey. Some of these large specimens (for example AC13870), exhibit cut marks just above the base, suggesting that hornworking industry was present within the city center in both the EBA and MBA.

Wild mouflon are endemic to the central Anatolian plateau and were frequently hunted in the region in the early Holocene. Wild sheep were hunted in the nearby Taurus mountains into the nineteenth century and an extant population of wild mouflon (*Ovis orientalis anatolica*) are still present in the region at the Konya-Bozdağ Wildlife Development Area (Kaya et al. 2004). It would not be surprising, therefore, if wild mouflon were hunted in the hills and plains around Acemhöyük in the Bronze Age. As was the case with the interpretation of aurochs-like cattle specimens, multiple interpretations for mouflon-like sheep are possible. In addition to hunting, it is also possible that mouflon were captured and kept near or even within the settlement where their large size, sleek and characteristically colored coat, and prominent horns would have provided a strong visual contrast with multicolored, small-horned, and wooly domestic sheep.

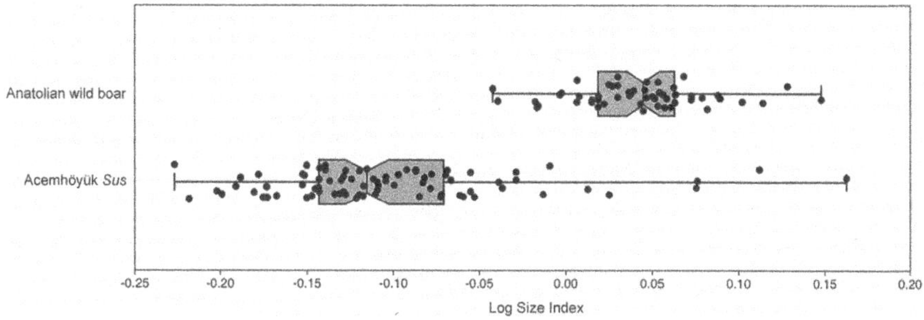

Figure 2.3. *Box and whisker and jitters plots of* Sus *LSI values from EBA and MBA Acemhöyük and those from central Anatolian wild boar from the sites Aşıklı Höyük, Çatalhöyük, and Köşk Höyük. Notch represents the location of the mean values.*

Boar (*Sus scrofa*)

Suids are present in low frequencies in the EBA assemblages (ca. 5%) at Acemhöyük and increase up to 11% of the fauna in the MBA levels (Arbuckle 2013) ($NISP_{Sus}$ = 1,034). The vast majority of these remains represent domestic pigs (*Sus scrofa domesticus*) exhibiting small-body size and reduced jaw and tooth sizes characteristic of Bronze Age domestic populations. However, a few specimens from both EBA and MBA contexts reflect much larger animals and are interpreted as wild boar. These larger specimens include limb bones (ulna, humerus, metacarpal III, calcaneus) and well as jaw bones with some exhibiting cut marks indicating that boar were butchered, consumed, and disposed of within the administrative portions of the settlement.

In order to assess the biometric evidence for the presence of boar, articular breadth measurements of common long bones including ulna (BPC), metacarpal III (Bp), and humerus (Bd) were compared to a modern Anatolian boar using the log size index (LSI) method (Meadow 1999). The LSI represents the difference between log transformed measurements from an archaeological specimen and comparable measurements from a standard animal; positive LSI values represent specimens larger than the standard, whereas negative values reflect specimens smaller than the standard. In this case, the standard is a modern female Anatolian wild boar (after Hongo 1996).

Of the 82 specimens examined, 76 (92.7%) are smaller than the wild boar standard (many are much smaller) and plausibly represent domestic pigs (figure 2.3). Six specimens (7.3% of the sample), however, are located in the tail of the distribution and are larger than the wild boar standard (LSI values > 0.0); four of these specimens are much larger than the standard and represent particularly robust animals. These large-sized suids likely represent wild boar (Deniz 1985 also reported the presence of wild boar at Acemhöyük)—an animal that is still common in the marshy areas of the central Anatolian plateau. A boar-hunting scene is depicted on a stone vessel found in the MBA palace at Acemhöyük, supporting the interpretation that boar were, in fact, hunted in nearby marshes (Türker 2008:pl. 50).

Wild Equids (*Equus hydruntinus* and *Equus ferus*)

Equids, including primarily domestic donkeys (*Equus asinus*) and horses (*Equus caballus*), represent 1–9% of the faunal remains from EBA and MBA contexts at Acemhöyük ($NISP_{equid}$ = 345). Among these remains, six specimens have been identified as a wild Anatolian hemione known as a "hydruntine" (*Equus hydruntinus*)—an extinct taxon closely related to the extant Iranian onager (*Equus hemionus onager*), central Asia kulan (*Equus hemionus kulan*), and the extinct Syrian wild ass (*Equus hemionus hemippus*) (Bennett et al. 2017). Although this taxon is well known in central Anatolia from Neolithic and Chalcolithic sites, its presence in second- and third-millennium BC contexts at Acemhöyük represents a rare identification of this species in a Bronze Age context in Anatolia.

Although the skeletal and dental remains of hemiones are difficult to distinguish from those of donkeys, five dental specimens display distinctive enamel morphologies characteristic of the Anatolian hydruntine, including extreme penetration of the buccal sulcus in mandibular molars (figure 2.4) (Geigl and Grange 2012). Due to the difficulty in distinguishing hemione and donkey postcranial remains, it is likely that hemiones are underidentified in the assemblage. Previously, E. Deniz (1985) also identified several equid remains from MBA Acemhöyük as representing wild hemiones, though the morphological basis of these identifications is unclear.

Hemione remains were recovered from a variety of contexts, and one mandible is likely associated with an intentional burial of a complete equid individual. Although it is possible that wild hemiones were hunted and eaten at Acemhöyük, as they were in contemporary Mesopotamia and in previous periods in central Anatolia, it is also possible that these animals were captured and bred in captivity with domestic donkeys to produce the high-status kunga hybrid (Zarins 2014). This hybrid was popular among elites in Greater Mesopotamia in the third millennium, when it was used to pull wheeled vehicles, and breeding centers are recorded in northern Mesopotamian cities known to have connections with Acemhöyük's MBA palace. Given the likelihood that wild hydruntines were present locally on the Konya-Ereğli-Aksaray plain, as well as evidence for the burial of a small equid with dental characteristics of a hydruntine, it is possible that local wild hydruntines were captured and bred with donkeys to produce hybrids at Acemhöyük (also Bennett et al. 2022; Weber 2008).

In the Acemhöyük faunal assemblage, thirty-eight specimens were identified by the author as horse (Deniz [1985] identified thirty additional specimens as horse as well). Although most of these specimens likely represent domestic

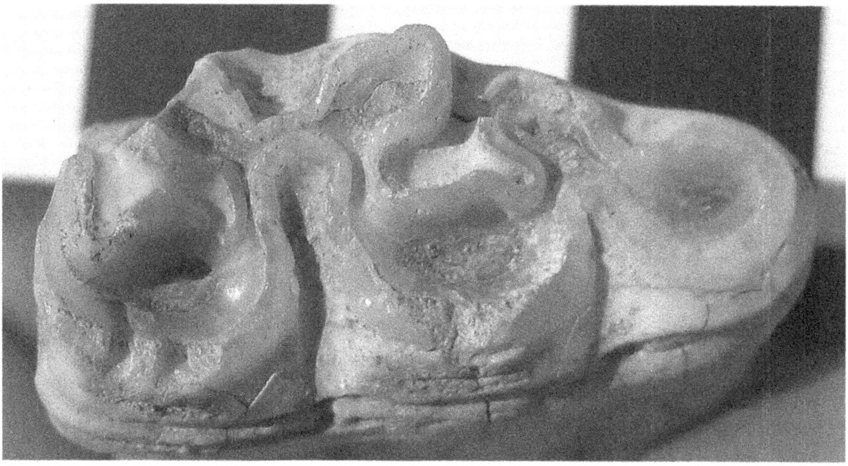

Figure 2.4. *Left lower third molar displaying typical* Equus hydruntinus *morphology (Acemhöyük level V, specimen AC12216).*

horses, it is possible that wild horse (*Equus ferus*) is also represented. Wild horses are well documented on the Anatolian plateau in the Neolithic and Chalcolithic, and it is likely that wild horses survived in the region at least until the fourth millennium BC (Arbuckle and Öztan 2018; Librado et al. 2021; Steadman et al. 2015).

Because of the lack of diagnostic characteristics for distinguishing between the remains of wild and domestic horses, it is very difficult to evaluate the status of horse remains in the third and second millennia BC. Although it is generally assumed that all Bronze Age horses in Anatolia represent domestic animals, the presence of wild individuals cannot be excluded and it seems quite likely that, rather than being hunted (as they were in the Neolithic), wild Anatolian mares may have been captured and incorporated into local domestic herds.

Bear (*Ursus arctos*)

The bones and teeth of brown bear are regularly found in small numbers at Bronze Age sites in SW Asia. At Acemhöyük, nineteen bear specimens (and two large carnivore metapodial fragments that are also likely bear) have been identified, most coming from MBA levels where they are found within buildings, in trash pits, and even in the lower town's Arıbaş cemetery. More than half of these remains represent foot bones (metapodial and phalanges), suggesting that they were associated with skins or dismembered paws. In addition, three specimens—including a tibia, astragalus, and metacarpal I—exhibit cut marks likely related to skinning. The two specimens that derive from the Arıbaş cemetery are both foot bones, suggesting that a portion of a bear paw may have been used as a funerary offering. However, the presence of limb elements—including radius, pelvis, tibia, and ankle bones such as the astragalus and calcaneus, recovered from loci mixed with the remains of livestock—suggest that bear carcasses (and perhaps live bears) were present at the site.

Wolf (*Canis lupus*)

Specimens representing the family Canidae are common at Acemhöyük ($NISP_{Canidae}$ = 382; $NISP_{Canis}$ = 348). These include a small number of fox remains ($NISP_{Vulpes}$ = 34), primarily representing jaws and teeth probably linked to pelts, and larger numbers of large canids. These large canids fall into the size category of domestic dogs (*Canis familiaris*) and frequently exhibit cut marks, indicating that they were regularly butchered and perhaps consumed at the site, particularly during the MBA occupation.

In their analysis of fauna from MBA level III at Acemhöyük, Nicola and Glew (1999) identified seventy specimens from the genus *Canis* and identified one specimen as a wolf—a large first cervical vertebra. Deniz (1985) also identified wolf at Acemhöyük. In the current study, among more than 300 *Canis* remains, several specimens stand out for their large size and may represent Anatolian wolves (*Canis lupus*). Measurements of the breadth of the distal humerus for Acemhöyük *Canis* specimens are shown in figure 2.5A, where they are compared to dogs from other sites in the region. Most of the Acemhöyük specimens fall within the range of prehistoric and early historic dogs from Southwest Asia, while two specimens (AC11098 and AC12255) are outside of the range of the dog sample. With measurements of 38.1 and 36.9 mm, these specimens fall within the lower end of the size range of modern wolves from the Iberian Peninsula (mean = 41.8, range 32.5–48.9 mm [Detry and Cardosa 2010]) and archaeological wolves from Italy (mean = 42.5mm; range 37.4–44.7 mm [Salari et al. 2017]), which are likely reasonable proxies for Bronze Age Anatolian wolves.

A similar pattern is evident in measurements of the distal breadth and length of the metatarsals (figure 2.5B). Most of the *Canis* hind foot specimens from Acemhöyük are similar in size to those from a dog burial from third-millennium BC Umm el-Marra, Syria, and are somewhat smaller than comparable measurements from Chalcolithic Köşk Höyük and Iron Age Çadır Höyük (Weber 2006). The Acemhöyük *Canis* specimens are similar in dimensions to modern standard poodle and Rottweiler breeds, with the exception of one particularly large specimen (AC12688). This specimen is a notable outlier among the Acemhöyük *Canis* remains and falls in the size range of large modern dog breeds such as German shepherd and husky, as well as Late Pleistocene and Holocene Italian wolves and may represent an Anatolian wolf.

Moreover, this specimen (a metatarsal II) is highly pathological, with the dorsal and medial surfaces of the diaphysis and proximal epiphysis encased in spongy and highly porous osseous lesions (figure 2.6). Although there is no

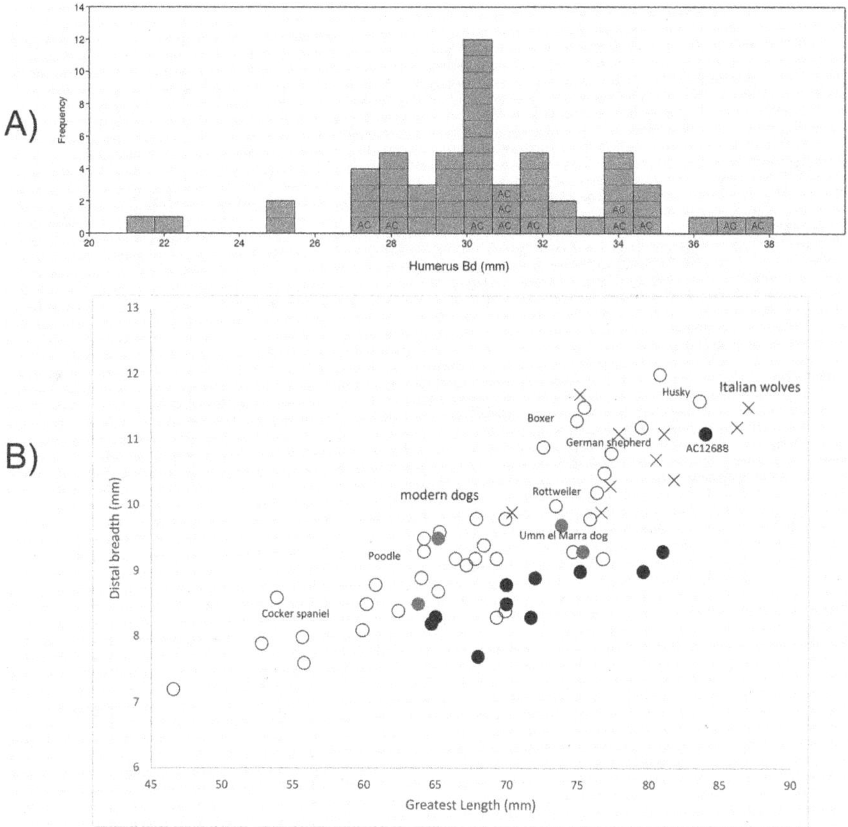

Figure 2.5. *(A) Measurements of the distal breadth of the humerus for* Canis *specimens from Acemhöyük as well as* Canis familiaris *specimens from Çadır Höyük, Köşk Höyük, Kaman-Kalehöyük, Lidar Höyük, Demircihöyük, Shaar Hagolan, Umm el-Marra, and Manching (Boessneck et al. 1971; Hongo 1996; Kussinger 1988; Marom 2011; Rauh 1981; Weber 2006). (B) Bivariate plot of distal breadth and greatest length measurements of metatarsals II–IV from Acemhöyük (black circles) compared to modern dog breeds (open circles, MTII only), archaeological specimens from Umm el-Marra (gray circles), and late Pleistocene and Holocene Italian wolves (black x's) (Salari et al. 2017; Weber 2006).*

obvious evidence for a fracture, this exostosis, which has resulted in a doubling of the diameter of the shaft of the metatarsal, suggests a major infection or trauma that would have likely affected the animal's mobility and gait. If this specimen does, in fact, represent a wolf, this pathology might suggest that this lame animal was under human care. Together, the faunal remains suggest that although dogs would have been a common sight at Acemhöyük, it is possible that a few wolves were also kept within the Bronze Age settlement.

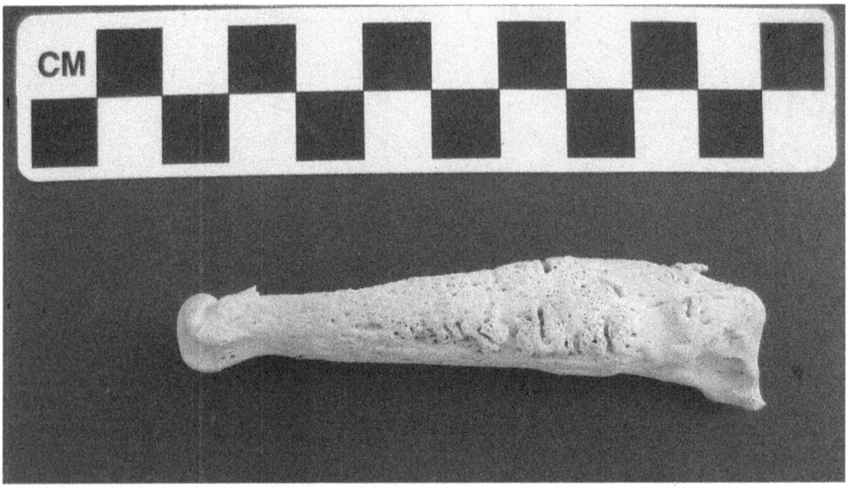

Figure 2.6. *Medial view of metatarsal IV specimen AC12688 (*Canis *cf.* lupus*).*

Hippopotamus (*Hippopotamus amphibious*) **and elephant** (*Elephas maximus*)

Both hippopotamus and elephant are represented at Acemhöyük exclusively in the form of ivory. During the excavation of the Sarıkaya Palace, several pieces of worked and unworked ivory were recovered from an MBA context interpreted as a storage room (Özgüç 1966). The worked pieces include an elaborate ivory box, fragments of gaming boards, and plaques, as well as carved figures interpreted as parts of elaborate furniture with parallels in the George Pratt collection in Metropolitan Museum of Art in New York City, which are thought to derive from illicit excavations at Acemhöyük in the early twentieth century (Özgüç 1966:42–44). These exquisitely carved, painted, and gilded ivories are thought to derive from hippopotamus ivory likely imported from the southern Levant (Aruz 2008).

In addition, unworked elephant ivory has also been recovered at the MBA palace at Acemhöyük. A section of an elephant tusk, 49 cm in length and weighing 13 kg, was recovered from excavations in 1982, indicating that workshops in the palace were involved in the production of ivory objects (Deniz et al. 1990). This unworked but sawn tusk fragment likely derives from an Asian elephant (*Elephas maximus*), the remains of which are known in Turkey and northern Syria in the second and early first millennia BC, where they were occasionally hunted by elites (Çakırlar and Ikram 2016).

DISCUSSION

Although the remains of wild taxa represent a small portion of the faunal assemblage at Acemhöyük, they represent important and valuable resources that were intentionally and repeatedly incorporated into this Bronze Age provisioning system. Much of the evidence for the use of wild mammals at Acemhöyük is associated with symbols of power, suggesting their exploitation by elites functioned as markers of status or was involved in ritual practices, whereas there is little to suggest that wild game played a significant role in the urban diet. For example, hares, tortoises, and wild birds are poorly represented in the faunal assemblage at Acemhöyük, indicating that three of the most abundant wild animals in the region were not regularly consumed within urban contexts.

However, large game—including red deer, aurochs, mouflon, and boar—were hunted and consumed at Acemhöyük, probably primarily by elites. The presence of postcranial remains of red deer (and to a lesser extent fallow deer) indicates that this symbolically potent animal was the target of hunting expeditions, and carcasses were brought back to the city, where they were consumed and their antlers (and perhaps hides) were incorporated into palace workshops. Given evidence from the contemporaneous Drehem texts for the capture and movement of live deer through that animal-processing center, it is also possible that Acemhöyük's palace maintained captive deer populations, or that live animals were occasionally paraded through the city associated with rituals and feasting events. This use is supported by the prominent role of deer symbolism in Bronze Age central Anatolia (e.g., Emre and Çınaroğlu 1993).

The presence of the remains of very large cattle, presumably representing wild aurochs, combined with abundant textual references to bull hunting as a symbolically important elite activity, suggests that Acemhöyük's ruling elite engaged in bull hunts, just like their contemporaries in Egypt and Mesopotamia. Given the lack of evidence for the widespread use of horses for riding or chariots in the late third millennium BC in Southwest Asia, it is likely that bull hunting took place on foot in the marshy basins on the margins of the Aksaray plain with the aid of a large royal retinue likely including hunting dogs as depicted in local imagery (Türker 2008:pl. 50). The resulting spectacle likely played an important role in the projection and negotiation of status among elites of the royal court (Allsen 2006). Aurochs remains are found associated with those of red deer as well as large numbers of livestock from loci within the EBA city walls, suggesting that they were consumed in feasting events within the exclusive social contexts of the administrative center.

Small numbers of wild mouflon and boar were also regularly hunted and perhaps also captured and brought to the city. In the case of these taxa, it is less clear who would have engaged in these activities. The Anitta text records that boar were hunted by the king himself and brought back to his capital, but it could also have been professional hunters or gamekeepers who acquired boar in nearby marshes or traveled to the margins of the Taurus Mountains to acquire mouflon, whose horns seem to have been incorporated into a palace horn industry. The single boar-hunting image recovered from the MBA levels of Acemhöyük does not seem to depict an elite hunter, suggesting that boar hunting may have been carried out by nonelites, perhaps soldiers, as a way to control this agricultural pest (Türker 2008:pl. 50). However, later Hittite iconography at sites such as Alacahöyük does suggest that boar hunting was an elite activity in Bronze Age Anatolia and may have been associated with elite ritual practices (Collins 2002).

Wild equids were also probably targeted exclusively by and for elites. Although it is not clear if wild horses were still present on the Aksaray plain the late third millennium BC, or whether they had been extirpated or incorporated into domestic herds at this time, it is certain that local wild hemiones were exploited. It is possible that these animals were not only regularly hunted, but were also captured, managed, and bred with domestic donkeys to produce high-status equid hybrids. This process was likely tightly controlled by the palace and required highly specialized resources, personnel, and knowledge in order to maintain supplies of wild equids and successfully raise, train, and produce hybrids. Like elite bull hunting, the production and use of hybrids likely comprised a shared feature of courtly culture, linking central Anatolian and Mesopotamian elites in the late EBA.

In addition to the hunt, it is clear that some wild animal resources were acquired at Acemhöyük via trade and exchange and were destined primarily for use by artisans or other craftspeople. Although the animals that produced antler and horn were hunted in the vicinity of the site, the presence of ivory at Acemhöyük reflects exchange networks devoted to the movement of these high-status animal products. In this case, hippopotamus and elephant ivory has only been found in the Sarıkaya Palace, indicating that these materials were exclusively available to the palace through specialized relationships with elites or traders from distant locales, most likely from cities along the upper Euphrates with which Acemhöyük was in close contact (e.g., Carchemish [Özgüç 2015]). The presence of raw elephant ivory, as well as the unique style of the hippopotamus ivory decorative elements (Aruz 2008), indicates that local palace workshops were likely engaged in local manufacture of ostentatious luxury goods from these high-value imports.

Finally, the presence of carnivores—including bears, foxes, and possibly wolves—indicates another range of uses for wild animals in Bronze Age urban contexts. Fox pelts may have been used as personal decorations or incorporated into decorative furnishing. Wolves may have been captured and tamed and kept in the city as a curiosity. The presence of a very large canid with a serious foot pathology may represent one of these captive wild individuals. As seen in the dowry of Eblaite princess Kesh-dut, bears were kept by Mesopotamian and perhaps also Anatolian elites. The presence of bear postcranial remains including limb bones at Acemhöyük indicates that live animals may have been present at the site and that bear skins were a regular part of the decor within the city. The recovery of a bear paw from the lower town Arıbaş cemetery suggests that bears had important ritual value to nonelite members of society as well.

CONCLUSION

Although livestock was the focus of urban animal economies in Bronze Age Southwest Asia, wild game played important roles in early urban communities, and specialized provisioning systems developed specifically for acquiring these valuable resources. The fauna and iconography from Acemhöyük suggest that instead of being involved in feeding cities, these specialized provisioning systems were primarily geared toward providing elites with symbolically potent wild animals and animal products that could be used to showcase and reify their social and political positions. As a result, wild animal provisioning systems developed a high degree of specialization, and significant resources were devoted to providing regular access to a range of wild animals, their products, and progeny. Although only representing a small part of urban animal economies, wild animal resources commanded disproportionate attention among urban elites and played vital and varied roles in the complex and hierarchical urban environments in the ancient Near East.

Acknowledgments. The research described in this chapter was conducted with the permission and support of Prof. Dr. Aliye Öztan and the Republic of Turkey's Kültür Varlıkları ve Müzeler Genel Müdürlüğü. Financial support for this research was received from the National Science Foundation (BCS-0530699; BCS-1311551), the American Research Institute in Turkey, the National Geographic Society, the Office of the Vice Provost for Research, Baylor University, and the Office of the Provost, University of North Carolina at Chapel Hill.

WORKS CITED

Albenda, P. 2008. "Assyrian Royal Hunts: Antlered and Horned Animals from Distant Lands." *Bulletin of the American Schools of Oriental Research* 350: 61–78.

Allsen, T. T. 2006. *The Royal Hunt in Eurasian History*. Cambridge: Cambridge University Press.

Arbuckle, B. S. 2012. "Pastoralism, Provisioning, and Power at Bronze Age Acemhöyük, Turkey." *American Anthropologist* 114: 462–476.

Arbuckle, B. S. 2013. "Zooarchaeology at Acemhöyük." *Anadolu/Anatolia* 39: 55–68.

Arbuckle, B. S., and A. Öztan. 2018. "Horse and Hemione Hunting at Late Neolithic/Chalcolithic Köşk Höyük, Central Turkey." In *Archaeozoology of the Near East XII*, edited by C. Çakırlar, J. Chahoud, Remi Berthon, and Suzanne E. Pilaar, 42–59. Groningen, Netherlands: Barkhuis Publishing.

Archi, A. 1987. "Gifts for a Princess." *Eblaitica* 1: 115–124.

Aruz, J. 2008. "Central Anatolian Ivories." In *Beyond Babylon: Art, Trade, and Diplomacy in the Second Millennium B.C.*, edited by J. Aruz, K. Benzel and J. M. Evans, 82–92. New Haven, CT: Yale University Press.

Atici, L. 2014. "The Secondary Products Revolution in Light of Textual Evidence from Kültepe/Kanesh, Central Turkey." In *New Approaches to Secondary Products Revolution*, edited by H. J. Greenfield, 233–252. Oxford: Oxbow.

Baltacıoğlu, H. 1993. "Four Reliefs from Alacahöyük." In *Nimet Özgüç'e Armağan: Aspects of Art and Iconography*, edited by M. Mellink, E. Porada, and T. Özgüç, 55–60. Ankara: Türk Tarih Kurumu.

Barjamovic, G. 2011. *A Historical Geography of Anatolia in the Old Assyrian Colony Period*. Copenhagen: Museum Tusculanum Press.

Beckman, G., P. Goedegebuure, J. Hazenbos, and Y. Cohen. 2007. "Hittite Historical Texts I." In *The Ancient Near East: Historical Sources in Translation*, edited by M. W. Chavalas, 215–252. Oxford: Blackwell.

Bennett, E. A., S. Champlot, J. Peters, B. S. Arbuckle, S. Guimaraes, M. Pruvost, S. Bar-David, et al. 2017. "Taming the Late Quaternary Phylogeography of the Eurasiatic Wild Ass through Ancient and Modern DNA." *PLOS One* 12:e0174216.

Bennett, E. Andrew, Jill Weber, Wejden Bendhafer, Sophie Champlot, Joris Peters, Glenn M. Schwartz, Thierry Grange, and Eva-Maria Geigl. 2022. "The Genetic Identity of the Earliest Human-Made Hybrid Animals, the Kungas of Syro-Mesopotamia." *Science Advances* 8:eabm0218. DOI: 10.1126/sciadv.abm0218.

Berthon, R. 2014. "Small but Varied: The Role of Rural Settlements in the Diversification of Subsistence Practices as Evidenced in the Upper Tigris River Area (Southeastern Turkey) during the Second and First Millennia BCE." *Journal of Eastern Mediterranean Archaeology and Heritage Studies* 2: 317–329.

Bökönyi, S. 1977. *Animal Remains from the Kermanshah Valley, Iran*. Oxford: BAR Supplement Series 34.

Boessneck, J., A. von den Driesch, U. Meyer-Lemppenau, and E. Wechsler von Ohlen. 1971. *Die Tierknochenfunde aus dem Oppidum von Manching. Ausgrabungen in Manching Band*. 6. Wiesbaden: F. Steiner.

Çakırlar, C., and S. Ikram. 2016. "'When Elephants Battle, the Grass Suffers.' Power, Ivory and the Syrian Elephant." *Levant* 48: 167–183.

Campbell, R. 2015. "Animal, Human, God: Pathways of Shang Animality and Divinity." In *Animals and Inequality in the Ancient World*, edited by B. S. Arbuckle and S. A. McCarty, 251–274. Boulder: University Press of Colorado.

Collins, B. J., ed. 2002. *A History of the Animal World in the Ancient Near East*. Leiden, Netherlands: Brill Academic Publishers.

Crabtree, P. J. 1990. "Zooarchaeology and Complex Societies: Some Uses of Faunal Analysis for the Study of Trade, Social Status, and Ethnicity." *Archaeological Method and Theory* 2: 155–205.

Defrance, S. 2009. "Zooarchaeology in Complex Societies: Political Economy, Status, and Ideology." *Journal of Archaeological Research* 17: 105–168.

Deniz, E. 1985. "Acemhöyük Saray Kazılarında Çikan Kemik Kalıntıları Üzerinde Arkeobiyolojik Araştırmalar." *Arkeometri Sonuçları Toplantısı* 1: 75–91.

Deniz, E., K. Sunguroğlu, O. Canpolat, and M. Akpoyraz. 1990. "Acemhöyük Kazılarında Çıkan Ve Türü Tükenmekte Olan Bir Hint Fili (*Elephus Maxima*) Dişi Üzerinde Arkeobiyolojik-Arkeometrik Erüdler." *Arkeometri Sonuçları Toplantısı* 6: 13–20.

Detry, C., and J. L. Cardosa. 2010. "On Some Remains of Dog (*Canis Familiaris*) from the Mesolithic Shell-Middens of Muge, Portugal." *Journal of Archaeological Science* 37: 2762–2774.

Emre, K., and A. Çınaroğlu. 1993. "A Group of Metal Hittite Vessels from Kınık-Kastamonu." In *Nimet Özgüç'e Armağan: Aspects of Art and Iconography*, edited by M. Mellink, E. Porada, and T. Özgüç, 675–713. Ankara: Türk Tarih Kurumu.

Foster, B. R. 2002. "Animals in Mesopotamian Literature." In *A History of the Animal World in the Ancient Near East*, edited by B. J. Collins, 271–288. Leiden, Netherlands: Brill.

Geigl, E.-M., and T. Grange. 2012. "Eurasian Wild Asses in Time and Space: Morphological versus Genetic Diversity." *Annals of Anatomy* 194: 88–102.

George, A. 2002. *The Epic of Gilgamesh: The Babylonian Epic Poem and Other Texts in Akkadian and Sumerian*. New York: Penguin.

Gourichon, L., and D. Helmer. 2008. "Étude archéozoologique de Mureybet." In *Le site néolithique de Tell Mureybet (Syrie du Nord)*, edited by J. J. Ibáñez, 115–228. Oxford: BAR International Series 1843.

Grayson, A. K. 1976. *Assyrian Royal Inscriptions*. Part 2, *From Tiglath-Pileser I to Ashur-Nasir-Apli II*. Wiesbaden, Germany: Harrassowitz.

Heimpel, W. 1968. *Tierbilder in der Sumerischen Literatur*. Vol. 2. Rome: Pontificium Institutum Biblicum.

Hole, F., K. V. Flannery, and J. A. Neely. 1969. *Prehistory and Human Ecology on the Deh Luran Plain*. Ann Arbor: Museum of Anthropology, University of Michigan, Memoir No. 1.

Hongo, H. 1996. "Patterns of Animal Husbandry in Central Anatolia from the Second Millennium BC through the Middle Ages: Faunal Remains from Kaman-Kalehöyük, Turkey." PhD diss., Harvard University, Cambridge, MA.

Kamış, Y. 2018. "Erken Tunç Çagı'nda Acemhöyük Ve Konya Ovası." In *Samsat'tan Acemhöyük'e Eski Uygarlıkların Izinde Aliye Öztan'a Armağan*, edited by S. Özkan, H. Hüryılmaz, and A. Türker, 165–176. Izmir, Turkey: Ege Üniversitesi Basımevi.

Kaya, M. A., T. D. Bunch, and M. Konuk. 2004. "On Konya Wild Sheep, *Ovis Orientalis Anatolica*, in the Bozdağ Protected Area." *Mammalia* 68: 229–232.

Kussinger, S. 1988. "Tierknochenfunde vom Lidar Höyük (Südostanatolien)." PhD diss., University of Munich.

Kuzuoğlu, R. 2016. "Two Cuneiform Texts Found in Acemhöyük from the Old Assyrian Period." *Belleten* 79: 685–699.

Lambert, W. G. 1960. *Babylonian Wisdom Literature*. Oxford: Oxford University Press.

Landon, D. B. 1997. "Interpreting Urban Food Supply and Distribution Systems from Faunal Assemblages: An Example from Colonial Massachusetts." *International Journal of Osteoarchaeology* 7: 51–64.

Lewis, S., and L. Llewellyn-Jones. 2018. *The Culture of Animals in Antiquity: A Sourcebook with Commentaries*. New York: Routledge.

Librado, Pablo, Naveed Khan, Antoine Fages, Mariya A. Kusliy, Tomasz Suchan, Laure Tonasso-Calvière, Stéphanie Schiavinato, Duha Alioglu, Aurore Fromentier, and Aude Perdereau. 2021. "The Origins and Spread of Domestic Horses from the Western Eurasian Steppes." *Nature* 598: 634–640.

Lion, B. 1992. "La circulation des animaux exotiques au Proche-Orient Antique." In *La circulation des biens, des personnes et des idées dans le Proche-Orient Ancient*, edited by D. Charpin and F. Joannes, 357–365. Paris: Éditions Recherche sur les Civilisations.

Maltby, M. 1979. *Faunal Studies on Urban Sites: The Animal Bones from Exeter, 1971–5*. Sheffield, UK: Exeter Archaeological Report 2.

Marom, N. 2011. "Animals and Society in the Neolithic Settlement at Sha'ar Hagolan." PhD diss., University of Haifa.

Mattick, L. 2015. *Finding Winnie: The True Story of the World's Most Famous Bear*. New York: Little, Brown Books for Young Readers.

Meadow, R. H. 1999. "The Use of Size Index Scaling Techniques for Research on Archaeozoological Collections from the Middle East." In *Historia Animalium ex Ossibus*, edited by C. Becker, H. Manhart, J. Peters, and J. Schibler, 285–300. Rahden, Germany: Verlag Marie Leidorf.

Miller, N. F., Zeder, M. A., and Arter, S. R. 2009. "From Food and Fuel to Farms and Flocks: The Integration of Plant and Animal Remains in the Study of the Agropastoral Economy at Gordion, Turkey." *Current Anthropology* 50: 915–924.

Nicola, J., and C. Glew. 1999. "Assyrian Colony Period Fauna from Acemhöyük Level III: A Preliminary Analysis." In *Essays on Ancient Anatolia*, edited by H. I. H. P. T. Mikasa, 93–148. Wiesbaden, Germany: Harrassowitz Verlag.

Oates, J., and D. Oates. 2001. *Nimrud: An Assyrian Imperial City Revealed*. London: British School of Archaeology in Iraq.

Özgüç, N. 1966. "Acemhöyük Kazıları." *Anadolu* 10: 29–52.

Özgüç, N. 2015. *Acemhöyük-Burushaddum I. Silindir Mühürler ve Mühür Baskılı Bullalar*. Ankara: Türk Tarih Kurumu.

Öztan, A. 2007. "Acemhöyük'den Assur Ticaret Kolonileri Çağı'na Ait İki Ender Buluntu." In *Belkıs Dinçol ve Ali Dinçol'e Armağan*, edited by M. Alparslan, M. Doğan-Alparslan, and H. Peker, 610–621. Istanbul: Ege Yayınları.

Price, M., K. Grossman, and T. Paulette. 2017. "Pigs and the Pastoral Bias: The Other Animal Economy in Northern Mesopotamia (3000–2000 BCE)." *Journal of Anthropological Archaeology* 48: 46–62.

Rauh, H. 1981. "Knochenfunde von Säugetieren aus dem Demircihüyük (Nordwestanatolien)." PhD diss., University of Munich.

Reed, C. A. 1983. "Archeozoological Studies in the Near East: a Short History (1960–1980)." In *Prehistoric Archaeology along the Zagros Flanks*, edited by L. S. Braidwood, R. J. Braidwood, B. Howe, C. A. Reed, and P. J. Watson, 511–536. Chicago: University of Chicago Oriental Institute Publications Volume 105.

Safar, F. 1951. "A Further Text of Shalmaneser III from Assur." *Sumer* 7: 3–21.

Salari, L., K. F. Achino, M. Gatta, C. Petronio, M. F. Rolfo, L. Silvestri, and L. Pandolfi. 2017. "The Wolf from Grotta Mora Cavorso (Simbruini Mountains, Latium) within the Evolution of *Canis Lupus* L., 1758 in the Quaternary of Italy." *Palaeogeography, Palaeoclimatology, Palaeoecology* 476: 90–105.

Sapir-Hen, L., Y. Gadot, and I. Finkelstein. 2016. "Animal Economy in a Temple City and Its Countryside: Iron Age Jerusalem as a Case Study." *Bulletin of the American Schools of Oriental Research* 375: 103–118.

Sherratt, A. 1983. "The Secondary Exploitation of Animals in the Old World." *World Archaeology* 15: 90–104.

Steadman, S., G. McMahon, J. C. Ross, M. Cassis, T. E. Şerifoğlu, B. S. Arbuckle, S. E. Adcock, S. Roodenberg, M. v. Baeyer, and A. J. Lauricella. 2015. "The 2013 and 2014 Excavation Seasons at Çadır Höyük on the Anatolian North Central Plateau." *Anatolica* 41: 87–124.

Steinkeller, P. 1987. "The Administrative and Economic Organization of the Ur III State: The Core and the Periphery." In *The Organization of Power and Aspects of Bureaucracy in the Ancient Near East*, edited by M. Gibson and R. Biggs, 19–41. Chicago: Oriental Institute Publication.

Sugiyama, N., G. Perez, B. Rodriguez, F. Torres, and R. Valadez. 2014. "Animals and the State: The Role of Animals in State-Level Rituals in Mesoamerica." In *Animals and Inequality in the Ancient World*, edited by B. S. Arbuckle and S. A. McCarty, 11–31. Boulder: University Press of Colorado.

Türker, A. 2008. "Assur Ticaret Kolonileri Çağı'nda Acemhöyük Çanak Çömleği." PhD diss., Ankara University.

van Buren, E. D. 1939. *The Fauna of Ancient Mesopotamia at Represented in Art*. Rome: Pontificium Institutum Biblicum.

van Delden, C. B. 1970. *The Large Commemorative Scarabs of Amenhotep III*. Leiden, Netherlands: Brill.

Vigne, J.-D., and D. Helmer. 2007. "Was Milk a 'Secondary Product' in the Old World Neolithisation Process? Its Role in the Domestication of Cattle, Sheep, and Goats." *Anthropozoologica* 42: 9–40.

Wapnish, P., and B. Hesse. 1988. "Urbanization and the Organization of Animal Production at Tell Jemmeh in the Middle Bronze Age Levant." *Journal of Near Eastern Studies* 47: 81–94.

Watanabe, C. E. 2002. *Animal Symbolism in Mesopotamia: A Contextual Approach*. Vienna: Institut für Orientalistik Universität Wien.

Weber, J. A. 2006. "Economic Developments of Urban Proportions: Evolving Systems of Animal-Product Consumption and Distribution in the Early and Middle Bronze Ages in Syro-Mesopotamia." PhD diss., University of Pennsylvania, Philadelphia.

Weber, J. A. 2008. "Elite Equids: Redefining Equid Burials of the Mid to Late 3rd Millennium BC from Umm El-Marra, Syria." In *Archaeozoology of the Near East VIII*, edited by E. Vila, L. Gourichon, A. Choyke, and H. Buitenhuis, 499–520. Lyon, France: Maison de l'Orient et de la Méditerranée.

Wu, Y. 2010. "The Anonymous Nasa and Nasa of the Animal Center during Šulgi 44–48 and the Wild Camel (gú-gur5), Hunchbacked Ox (gur8-gur8), ubi, habum and the Confusion of the Deer (lulim) with Donkey (anše) or šeg9." *Journal of Ancient Civilizations* 25: 1–20.

Zarins, J. 2014. *The Domestication of Equidae in Third-Millennium BCE Mesopotamia*. Ithaca, NY: Cornell University Studies in Assyriology and Sumerology, vol. 24.

Zeder, M. 1991. *Feeding Cities: Specialized Animal Economy in the Ancient Near East*. Washington, DC: Smithsonian Institute Press.

3

Distinguishing Palatial from Autonomous Subsistence Provisioning with Zooarchaeological and Isotopic Analyses at Petsas House, Mycenae

JACQUELINE S. MEIER, GYPSY C. PRICE, AND KIM S. SHELTON

Redistributive systems are central to classic models of local and regional economies that fueled complex societies in the Aegean during the Late Bronze Age (e.g., Gamble 1979; Halstead 1992a; Renfrew 1972). Knowledge of the production and distribution of animal resources within these systems is largely informed by faunal catalogues of administrative records recorded on clay tablets and sealings in Linear B script, which document variable systems of herd management among Mycenaean sites (Halstead 2003; Kyriakidis 2010). Yet, few tablets with Linear B text about animals have been recovered from Mycenae (Shelton 2002–2003; Varias Garcia 1999), a site with a central role in the extensive networks that traded animals, goods, and materials within and beyond the Aegean (Burns 2010). Although texts from other sites can highlight potential palatial interests in animals at Mycenae, the faunal record can provide a more nuanced picture of animal use across social strata. This record is needed to better clarify the roles of animals in wider redistributive systems as economies expanded and adapted across the Late Helladic (LH) IIIA, B and C periods (1420–1075 BC) (Cline 2010).

https://doi.org/10.5876/9781646422562.c003

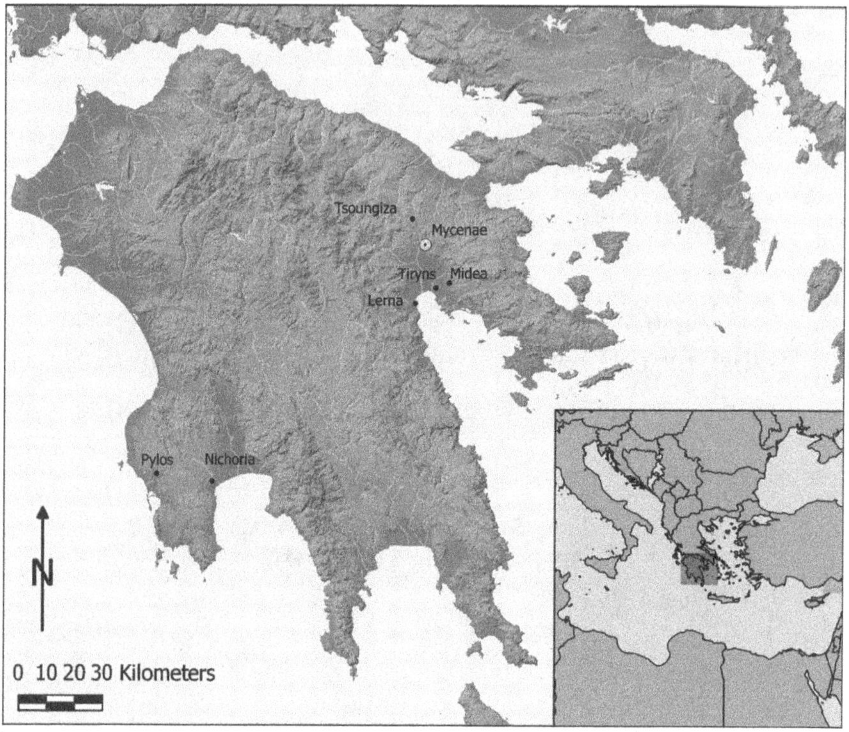

Figure 3.1. *Map of sites mentioned in the text including Mycenae (white circle), where Petsas House is located.*

During the LH IIIA2 period (1375–1300 BC) in the Peloponnese, craft production supplied palatial sites with commodities that could be mobilized through taxation and redistribution systems (Shelmerdine 2013). However, the strategies used to provision craft producers with animal resources are still unclear. Craft producers may have had access to animals from herds under the control of a central authority as Linear B texts suggest (Halstead 1999) or, rather, obtained animals raised at a smaller scale by more independent herders (Halstead 1992b; Redding 1981). Faunal remains offer an avenue to investigate the degree to which subsistence resources were regulated and mobilized by the palace to support specialized laborers, such as the craft producers who used the manufacturing and storage facilities uncovered within and around the citadel of Mycenae (Voutsaki 2010).

We investigate the provisioning of craft producers in one household located in the settlement of Mycenae. This building, Petsas House, was a domestic complex used for ceramic production and storage (Shelton 2015), and it yielded a large faunal assemblage dating to the LH IIIA2 period—the height of the palatial period at Mycenae (figure 3.1). The multistoried structure is located outside of the citadel walls of Mycenae and thus likely housed community members who ranked below the occupants of the citadel. By examining how this extrapalatial household was provisioned, we begin to address whether access to animals at palatial sites was asymmetrical across social strata, potentially reinforcing social inequalities during the palatial period.

We investigate whether the occupants of Petsas House were provisioned indirectly by a regulated source or directly through more self-sufficient means (Zeder 1988). To do this, we utilize zooarchaeological and isotopic methods to investigate animal selection and management evidence from a large faunal assemblage recovered from a LH IIIA2 well deposit within the structure. This combined approach is novel for the study of Mycenaean fauna in the Peloponnese. Furthermore, the well assemblage offers unique spatially and temporally refined evidence of animal access by extrapalatial craft producers. When combined with previous evidence of animal use from Linear B texts and prior faunal studies from the surrounding Peloponnese region, this analysis can elucidate a more nuanced picture of faunal economic systems during the LH periods.

THE FAUNAL ECONOMY OF THE LATE HELLADIC PALATIAL PERIOD

Records in Linear B script have yielded important information about strategies of animal management during the palatial phase of the LH period (c. 1420–1190 BC at Mycenae) (Iakovidis et al. 2003). This information includes palatial herd sizes; numbers of replenished, taxed, and sacrificed animals; and quantities of secondary products, such as wool (Halstead 2003). Although the texts reflect narrow periods of time, the evidence gleaned from Linear B writings suggests that redistribution of agricultural goods, such as animals supplied from flocks controlled by the palaces, served to create buffers against food shortages and/or functioned to build up surplus that could be exchanged for labor and goods or used in communal practices (Halstead 1992c). While some level of palatial control over herd animals at sites in the Peloponnese is implied by Linear B texts, descriptions of flock management practices vary across Mycenaean palaces in the wider Aegean region (Halstead 1998–1999). For example, tablets imply that an annual cull of flocks took place at Pylos (Halstead 2003), while at Knossos, young and old animals were gradually culled by local herders who replenished palatial stock using their own flocks (Halstead 2001). Texts from Pylos also suggest that palatial authorities culled animals to compensate some laborers, while other individuals received compensation in the form of land grants, which could have been used for autonomous food production (Nosch 1997; Palaima 1997; Shelmerdine 2011). Thus, the texts reveal that some Mycenaean extrapalatial workers exchanged services for palatial animal resources, while others were more independently provisioned.

Although Linear B tablets provide important details regarding animal management, they limit the study of the animal economy to elite palatial contexts at the time just before the tablets were accidentally burned and preserved (Halstead 2003). Discrepancies between textual and archaeological evidence of subsistence also highlight the need for better integration of this evidence (Halstead 1992a, 1992c). Records of animals in Linear B script mainly comprise accounts of sheep. For example, sheep comprise 74–83% of the total archive of Linear B writings on sealings from Thebes (Killen 1994). There are fewer references to other domesticates, such as pigs, goats, and cattle (Halstead 1999; Killen 1964a, 1964b; 1993a, 1993b, 1998; Palaima 1992a). Furthermore, only a few texts mention wild animals, such as the deer mentioned in texts from Pylos (Texts Cr 591, Cr 868, and Cr 875; Halstead 2003; Palaima 1992b). However, wild taxa are depicted in art, and their remains are regularly recovered from LH sites such as Tiryns, where wild boar, bear, and red, fallow, and roe deer remains were identified (von den Driesch and Boessneck 1990).

Previous zooarchaeological findings largely agree with the texts on the importance of sheep in the Mycenaean economy—caprines (sheep and goats) are typically the most common of the domesticated ungulates represented in LH faunal assemblages in the Peloponnese, comprising 41–47% of the total number of identifiable specimens (NISP) of cattle, caprines, and pigs at the palatial sites of Pylos and Tiryns (Halstead 1996; Nobis 1993; von den Driesch and Boessneck 1990). Long-term continuity in the proportions of these major domesticates was observed at Helladic sites by Paul Halstead (2003), who hypothesized that this may reflect stable animal husbandry practices in the region across periods of political change, from the prepalatial to palatial periods. Yet, recent studies of the ritual deposits dating to the palatial period at Ayios Konstantinos (LH IIIA-B) and Tsoungiza (LH IIIA2) differ from the typical caprine-dominated pattern, with higher abundances of pig (53.7% minimum number of anatomical units [MinAU]) and cattle remains (54% MinAU), respectively (Dabney et al. 2004; Hamilakis and Konsolaki 2004). This variation is likely due to the special nature of the consumption activities associated with these deposits. These examples highlight the need for more studies of faunal assemblages from different types of sites and contexts to better understand potential variation in animal economies over time in the region.

As isotopic analyses are able to detect the dietary and environmental drivers of inter- and intrataxonomic variation that are otherwise unobservable by macroscopic observations, they also have the potential to elucidate more nuanced details of the animal management strategies employed by Mycenaean agriculturalists than is possible from the texts alone (e.g., Balasse et al. 2002; Stevens et al. 2013). Beyond studies of Neolithic assemblages (e.g., Papathanasiou 2015; Vaiglova et al. 2014), isotopic surveys of faunal materials in the Peloponnese are scarce, relatively limited in sample size, and largely serve to provide baselines for the interpretation of human isotope data (e.g., Petroutsa and Manolis

2010; Petroutsa et al. 2009; Triantaphyllou et al. 2008). More integrative isotopic studies are needed to explore how variation in animal use relates to animal production and provisioning strategies for LH sites in the Peloponnese.

ANIMAL AND CRAFT PRODUCTION AT MYCENAE

Currently, the archaeological evidence of animal use at Mycenae is limited. To date, relatively few tablets have been recovered from the citadel at the site, especially when compared to the substantial tablet archives found at Pylos, Knossos, and Thebes (Aravantinos 1999; Bennet 1985, 1998). Of the few relevant textual records recovered from Mycenae, references are limited to mentions of animal products made of wool, hide, and boar's tusk (Killen 1964a). Furthermore, few texts predate the LH IIIB period (late/end thirteenth century BC) (Shelton 2002–2003). David Reese (2013) studied the assemblages of faunal remains recovered at Mycenae during the years ranging from 1966 to 1989, which largely date to the LH IIIB-C periods. He found that caprines were the most abundant species represented in Room Γ3A, a kitchen in the Southwest Slope area. Here, caprines comprised 49.8% of the 231 remains of ungulate livestock recovered from the floor deposit. Yet, interpretations of this faunal assemblage are limited by the size of the sample. Thus, more evidence is needed to understand the role of animals across the site of Mycenae (see also Trantalidou 2007-8).

The faunal assemblage from Petsas House provides new evidence of animal use from a structure located within the settlement of Mycenae (Shelton 2010, 2015). Petsas House was excavated as an Archaeological Society of Athens project that was initially under the direction of Papadimitriou and Petsas (1950–1951) and is currently under the field direction of Kim S. Shelton. The initial interpretation of Petsas House as a ceramic production facility was based on the discovery of stacks of complete fineware vessels on the ground floor (Shelton 2004, 2010). Additional evidence of ceramic production at the house includes clay deposits, misfired or malformed vessels, and a kiln (Shelton 2015). Furthermore, the presence of Linear B tablets suggests that craft activities in the house may have been associated with palatial economic record keeping (Shelton 2002–2003). Nevertheless, recent findings—including common types of ceramic cookware, remains of large ceramic food storage containers, or pithoi, set onto the bedrock of one room within a clay and plaster floor, and abundant fragments of highly decorated wall paintings originating from other, upper-story rooms in the house—indicate that it served dual domestic and industrial uses (Shelton 2010, 2015).

Daniel Pullen (2013) suggested that Petsas House was owned by wealthy individuals who may have engaged in a reciprocal relationship with the palace. This type of relationship is implied by the Linear B texts from Pylos (Nosch 1997), describing the exchange of specialized ceramic vessels with palatial authorities in return for land. Reciprocity may also have served as a mechanism of economic control (Parkinson and Galaty 2007), wherein herders supplied the palace with animals that were used in turn to support specialized labor (Hruby 2013). Therefore, the ceramic production evidenced at Petsas House may have been supported by authorities who granted indirect access to animal resources. Alternatively, Petsas House may have functioned more independently and had direct access to animals. Our combined zooarchaeological and isotopic investigation at Petsas House will explore the animals used at the site and their life histories to better understand the provisioning of craft producers at Mycenae.

ANALYTICAL FRAMEWORK

Multiple lines of faunal evidence were utilized to distinguish direct from indirect animal acquisition strategies at Petsas House, following the analytical model developed by Melinda Zeder (1988, 1991, 1998a). In this model, direct access reflects the use of straightforward channels to obtain animals, such as when the consumer is the animal producer or has an open exchange with a herder /producer. Animals are accessed indirectly when acquired through regulated exchange channels including those controlled by state institutions.

Directly and indirectly provisioned animals can be distinguished based on the amount of risk taken in their management (Zeder 1991). Remains of directly accessed animals often reflect management strategies that prioritized low-risk practices to promote food security at the local level, including diverse animal keeping, use of supplemental wild game, and use of highly fecund taxa—all of which can limit potential failure due to a catastrophic loss of individuals of any one species (Redding 1981; Zeder 1991, 1988). By contrast, animals accessed indirectly by the consumer often reflect more specialized management of select taxa to maximize the yield of animal products, though with a higher risk of failure (Zeder 1988, 1991). This type of specialized production likely characterizes the strategy used by palatial authorities to manage sheep for wool, given the Linear B text accounts of palatial herd records (Halstead 1999).

In an assemblage of faunal remains, the diversity and types of taxa represented should reflect the degree of risk taken in animal management. A comparison of the ratio of sheep to goats provides an additional proxy of the risk involved in herding caprines. A higher ratio of goats to sheep reflects a less risky herding strategy due to the differing behavioral and ecological characteristics of each species. Goats require less investment, as they are more intelligent and less selective in diet but lower in caloric value than sheep (Dahl and Hjort 1976; Redding 1984; Squires 1982). Alternatively, herds with a higher ratio of sheep to goats yield more calories and wool (Sen et al. 2004), but reflect a riskier production strategy due to the higher vulnerability of sheep to illnesses (Redding 1984). Thus, evidence of more diverse taxa with a higher ratio of goats overall is expected to reflect direct caprine access at Petsas House, while a narrower selection of taxa with a higher ratio of sheep is more likely to reflect indirect access to animals managed with a riskier production strategy.

Other faunal indicators can be used to determine the type of animal access based on whether they were managed locally or more distantly from the site. A greater abundance of domesticated animals, such as pigs, that are not easily regulated or moved over long distances (Zeder 1998b) should reflect more direct access to animals raised locally. In turn, assemblages dominated by animals that are more easily mobilized by authorities, namely caprines and cattle, should reflect more indirect access to potentially regulated herds (Zeder 1991). Remains of more juvenile animals and animals of a diverse range of ages are also expected if they were obtained directly from a local source, comprising individuals that were likely culled from nearby herds to manage the growth of the population (Zeder 1991). By contrast, indirectly accessed animals that are used more distantly from the place of management should represent more prime-aged animals or more uniform age groups, reflecting individuals that were culled to maximize the potential output of meat, wool and/or milk given the overall cost of labor and foddering (Payne 1973; Zeder 1991).

Given the disparate management strategies reflected in differently accessed herds, isotopic ratios should also vary for directly and indirectly accessed animals. Domestic ungulates accessed directly through local sources should reflect isotopic ratios that are relatively homogenous and exhibit limited intrataxonomic variation. By contrast, isotopic ratios of animals raised in more specialized herds and accessed indirectly are expected to reflect more diverse ingested resources from wider or more variable locales (Stevens et al. 2013), especially in light of the Linear B textual descriptions of mixed palatial and private stock keeping that likely brought together animals originating from diverse environments (Halstead 2001, 2003).

METHODS

To distinguish direct from indirect animal access at Petsas House, we began with zooarchaeological analysis of relative species abundances based on the %NISP of each taxon (Grayson 1979). The domestic status of pigs was also established based on the linear dimensions of pig lower third molars (Ervynck et al. 2001). The sheep-to-goat ratio was examined based on the minimum number of individuals (MNI) of each species (Redding 1984).

Next, we situate the provisioning of Petsas House within a regional context. Relative abundances of the major domesticated ungulates found in the region (caprines, pigs, and cattle) were calculated out of their total combined NISP. The relative abundance of livestock from the Petsas House well assemblage was compared to those from sizable assemblages (~200 specimens or more) dating to the LH III subphases from other sites in the Peloponnese. These included faunal assemblages from the palatial site of Tiryns (von den Driesch and Boessneck 1990), the citadel site of Midea (Walberg and Reese 2008), and the extrapalatial sites of Lerna and Nichoria (Reese 2008; Sloan and Duncan 1978). Data from Lerna are limited to the LH IIIA2–B1 sample reexamined by Reese (2008). Only tentative comparisons are made to Nichoria following previous cautions (see von den Driesch and Boessneck 1990 and Halstead 1996). We also make general comparisons to the feasting deposits recovered from Tsoungiza and the Palace of Nestor at Pylos (Dabney et al. 2004; Halstead and Isaakidou 2004), where species abundance is calculated using MinAU and minimum number of elements (MNE) values respectively. The larger assemblage of faunal remains from Pylos (analyzed by Nobis 1993) was excluded from this study on account of likely temporal aggregation (Stocker and Davis 2004).

The proportions of juvenile pigs and caprines at Petsas House were calculated as the ratio of lower deciduous fourth premolars (dp4) to lower third molars (M3) (Stiner 1990). This analysis established the representative proportion of caprines and pigs that died while young. The dp4 represents pigs of six months of age and under (Lemoine et al. 2014) and caprines of less than twelve months of age (Zeder 2006). Caprine dp4s were only counted if assigned to Sebastian Payne's (1973) tooth wear stages A–C to avoid double counting of teeth in the mandible at the same time. This overlap is uncommon in pigs.

Bone collagen and apatite isotopic data were utilized to examine domesticated animal management strategies by using carbon ($\delta^{13}C$), nitrogen ($\delta^{15}N$), and oxygen ($\delta^{18}O$) values to infer the environmental and dietary conditions of animals during life (e.g., Balasse et al. 2002; Finucane et al. 2006; Price et al. 2017). Variation in $\delta^{13}C$ values is largely determined by the photosynthetic pathway characteristic of primary producers, differentiating between C_3, C_4, and CAM plants (e.g., DeNiro and Epstein 1978; Farquhar et al. 1989; Kohn 2010; O'Leary 1988; Tieszen 1991; Tieszen and Boutton 1989). $\delta^{15}N$ values reflect trophic level differences within known ecosystems (e.g., Bocherens et al. 1994; Lee-Thorp et al. 1989; Schoeninger and DeNiro 1984), can distinguish between leguminous and nonleguminous dietary inputs (e.g., DeNiro and Epstein 1981), and vary in relation to aridity and temperature fluctuations (e.g., Hartman and Danin 2010). $\delta^{18}O$ values reflect the local physical environment and associated climate (e.g., Bryant et al. 1994; Longinelli 1984; Luz et al. 1984; Sponheimer and Lee-Thorp 1999). In purposefully managed species, these conditions are the direct result of decisions made by the human agents responsible for animal production and distribution. Expected sources of isotopic variation include consumed plants that constitute the bulk of domesticated ungulate diets (DeNiro and Epstein 1978; Farquhar et al. 1989), disparity in drinking water sources (Dansgaard 1964; Longinelli 1984), and variable access to human refuse (e.g., Minagawa and Wada 1984; Minagawa et al. 2005).

Data Collection

The faunal sample was collected from a vertical section of the northwest quadrant of an approximately 12.5 m deep well in Room Π at Petsas House and dates to the LH IIIA2 period. Faunal remains were likely deposited in the well when the house was cleaned following a seismic event. This interpretation is based on evidence of the destruction of the structure and observed ceramic sherds from various layers in the well that join with those found in the house (Shelton 2004). One excavation unit was sampled from each layer from the northwest quadrant to ensure that a full cross-section of the well sequence was represented. Sixty-five percent of the faunal remains from the sample were identified to taxon or body-size category ($n = 13{,}322$ identified specimens).

Isotopic proxies were used to inform dietary regimes of taxa from the Petsas House well assemblage (e.g., Bocherens et al. 1994; Ingvarsson-Sundstrom et al. 2009). Here, $\delta^{13}C$, $\delta^{15}N$, and $\delta^{18}O$ values from bone collagen and bone apatite samples recovered from goat ($n = 16$), sheep ($n = 19$), and pig ($n = 9$) individuals were assessed to identify intrataxonomic variation amongst Petsas House caprines and pigs (Price et al. 2017). Additionally, $\delta^{15}N$ values from Petsas House pigs were compared to previously reported human $\delta^{15}N$ data from Mycenae in order to assess whether pig diets were largely based on human refuse. Preparation, extraction, and analytical protocols are detailed in Gypsy C. Price (2015). The $\delta^{13}C$, $\delta^{15}N$, and $\delta^{18}O$ values shown were measured against relevant standards (see below).

RESULTS

Pigs are the most abundant species in the Petsas House assemblage (36% of the total NISP) followed by caprines (26%), and smaller proportions of cattle (7%), dog (7%), and equids (<0.1%) (table 3.1). The adult pig lower third molars are smaller (22–33 mm length, 13–15 mm breadth; $n = 11$) than those of wild pigs early in the process of domestication from Pre-Pottery Neolithic Çayönü in Turkey (34.75–48.5 mm length, 16.5–21.5 mm breadth) (Ervynck et al. 2001). They fall securely within the range for domesticated pigs from Bronze Age to Classical period sites in Turkey (23.5–39.5 mm length) (Flannery 1983; Rowley-Conwy et al. 2012) and below the documented range for modern wild boar from Turkey (37–44.5 mm length, 16–19.5 mm breadth) (Albarella et al. 2009). Additionally, of the specimens securely identified to species, sheep outnumber goats in a ratio of 2.2:1 (based on MNI).

A relatively high proportion of wild game is also present in the Petsas House assemblage (table 3.1). This includes small taxa such as hare (3%), songbirds (2%), waterbirds (0.3%) and fish (2%), as well as the remains of larger taxa including deer (0.6%). Some of these wild taxa—such as rodents and insectivores (0.2%)—may not have contributed to the meat diet, and others—such as mustelids (wild carnivores; 0.5%) and falconiformes (0.2%)—may have been targeted

Table 3.1. Identified faunal specimens from the sampled Petsas House well assemblage

Taxa		*NISP*	*%NISP*
Large Ungulates	Cattle (*Bos taurus*)	943	7.08
	Red deer (*Cervus elaphus*)	8	0.06
	Equids	3	0.02
Medium Ungulates	Fallow deer (*Dama dama*)	19	0.14
	Pigs (*Sus scrofa domesticus*)	4,871	36.56
	Goat (*Capra hircus*)	307	2.30
	Sheep (*Ovis aries*)	495	3.72
	Sheep/Goat	2,699	20.26
	Roe deer (*Capreolus capreolous*)	6	0.05
	Indt. deer	61	0.46
Small Ungulates	Indt. Ungulate	1,263	9.48
Small Mammals	Dog (*Canis familiaris*)	918	6.89
	Mustelids	66	0.50
	Hare (*Lepus* sp.)	401	3.01
	Rodents and insectivores	23	0.17
Birds			
	Songbirds	239	1.79
	Waterbirds	38	0.29
	Falconiformes	20	0.15
Fish		237	1.78
Shell fragments		705	5.29
Total		13,322	100.00

Note: %NISP is out of the total ungulate and small animal remains identified at least to taxonomic family.

for nonmeat products, such as feathers, skins, or claws for utilitarian or decorative functions. No remains of domestic fowl were present, though one has been identified in Helladic assemblages from the region (e.g., Tiryns; von den Driesch and Boessneck 1990).

The Petsas House well assemblage exhibits a relatively higher proportion of pigs and lower abundances of caprines and cattle than assemblages from other LH III sites in the Peloponnese (figure 3.2). Among the major livestock taxa, the relative abundance of pigs is highest at Petsas House (52.3%), followed by Midea (39.5–32.2%; LH IIIB–C), Nichoria (37.9–25.9%; LH IIIA2–B), Tiryns (32.5–20%, LH IIIB1–LH IIIC Late), and Lerna (30%; LH IIIA2–B1), whereas pigs are poorly represented at Tsoungiza (16% MinAU; LH IIIA2) and Pylos (5.6%; LH IIIB) (Dabney et al. 2004; Halstead and Isaakidou 2004; Reese 2008; Sloan and Duncan 1978; von den Driesch and Boessneck 1990). Caprine abundance is

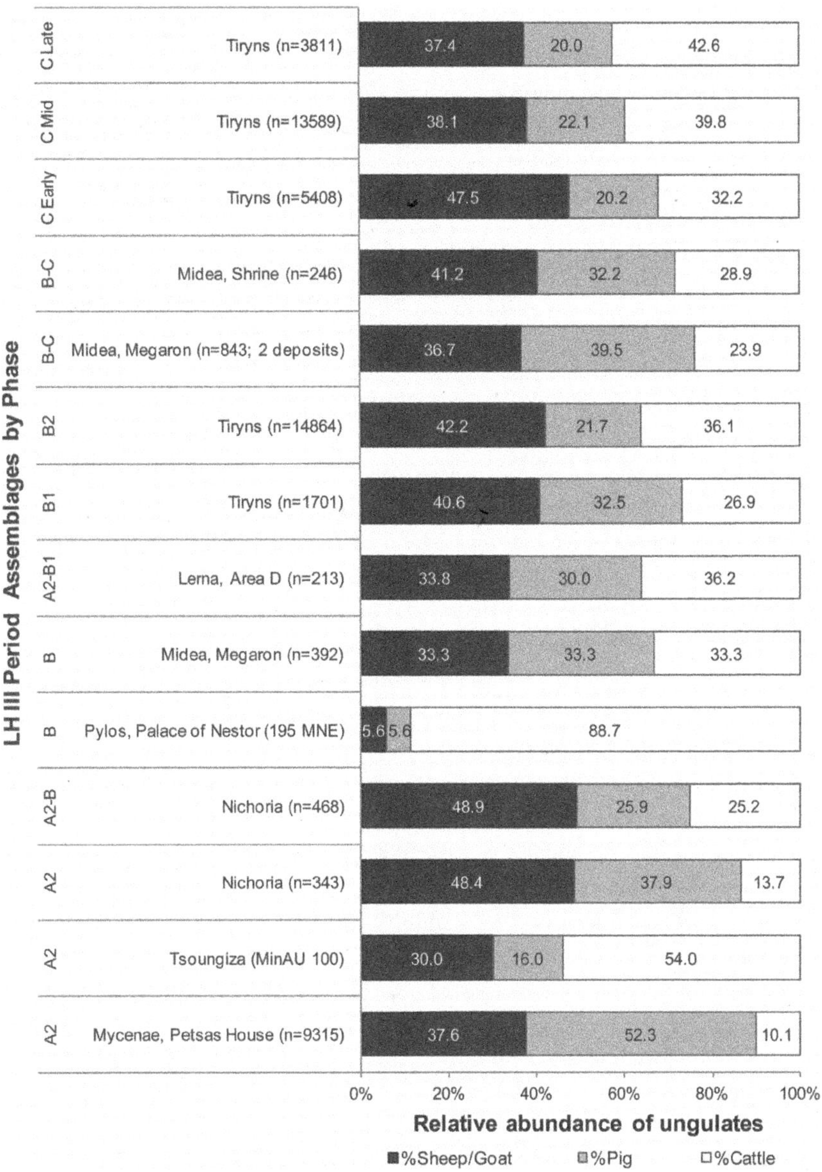

Figure 3.2. *Relative abundances of caprines, pigs, and cattle (%NISP of total livestock ungulates) limited to the LH III faunal assemblages from sites in the Peloponnese. Nichoria data include wild boar (Sloan and Duncan 1978). Lerna NISP counts were tallied from reanalyzed specimens from contexts limited to the LH IIIA2–B1 sample (Reese 2008). Data from Tiryns (von den Driesch and Boessneck 1990) and Midea (Walberg and Reese 2008) are also separated by area when possible. Tsoungiza data are in minimum animal units (MinAU; Dabney et al. 2004) and Pylos data are given in minimum number of element (MNE) values (Halstead and Isaakidou 2004).*

highest at Nichoria (48.9–48.4%) and Tiryns (47.5–37.4%), followed by the shrine area of Midea (41.2%), then Petsas House (37.6). Caprine abundances are lower from the megaron areas of Midea (36.7–33.3%), and at Lerna (33.8%), Tsoungiza (30%), and Pylos (5.6%). Cattle abundance is highest in the feasting deposits at Tsoungiza (54%) and Pylos (88.7%), followed by the assemblages from Tiryns (42.6–26.9%), Lerna (36.2%), Midea (33.3–23.9%), and Nichoria (13.7%), and is lowest at Petsas House (10.1%).

Toothwear-aging analysis focused on pigs and caprines from Petsas House. Based on the ratio of dp4 to M3, this analysis revealed a predominance of young pigs less than six months of age (90%; MNE = 61 of 68 total), the majority of which are very young newborns, less than one month of age (74% neonates; MNE = 50) based on wear of the dp4 (Hongo and Meadow 1998; Lemoine et al. 2014). In contrast, juvenile caprines killed off at/before one year of age are not as common (44%; MNE = 11 of 44 total), and only one newborn caprine dp4 is represented. When compared to the age structures of managed caprine populations modeled by Payne (1973), the proportion of culled juvenile caprines at Petsas House is most similar to that of a modern herd managed for meat or wool production (about 30% culled by one year of age).

The $\delta^{13}C_{co}$ and $\delta^{15}N$ values show no apparent structured variation amongst caprines exploited at Petsas House, revealing diets with similar proteinaceous input (figure 3.3). However, intrataxonomic subgroups are apparent when $\delta^{13}C_{ap}$ and $\delta^{18}O$ values are plotted against one another (figure 3.3). While one group exhibits relatively more negative $\delta^{18}O$ values and less negative $\delta^{13}C_{ap}$ values, the other exhibits relatively less negative $\delta^{18}O$ values and more negative $\delta^{13}C_{ap}$ values.

The $\delta^{13}C_{co}$ and $\delta^{15}N$ values from the pigs from Petsas House are consistent with those from other domesticated pigs from sites in the region (e.g., Vaiglova et al. 2014): $\delta^{13}C_{co}$ values are well within C_3 ranges (e.g., Farquhar et al. 1989) and exhibit more enriched $\delta^{15}N$ values than herbivorous ungulates at the site (figure 3.3). When compared to caprine apatite data, $\delta^{13}C_{ap}$ and $\delta^{18}O$ values from Petsas House pig bone apatite parse similarly into two groups, suggesting that a small proportion of them were also subject to a different set of environmental conditions.

DISCUSSION

Use of diverse taxa is evidenced by the Petsas House faunal assemblage, which primarily consists of domesticated livestock but also wild ungulates and some small game. The observed high levels of bone preservation and ceramic joins between sherds from many well layers and different rooms of the house suggest that the assemblage likely represents the remains of multiple consumption events that were first deposited in the house and then later moved to the well. Thus, the diverse taxa detected in the deposit may reflect not only the accumulation of

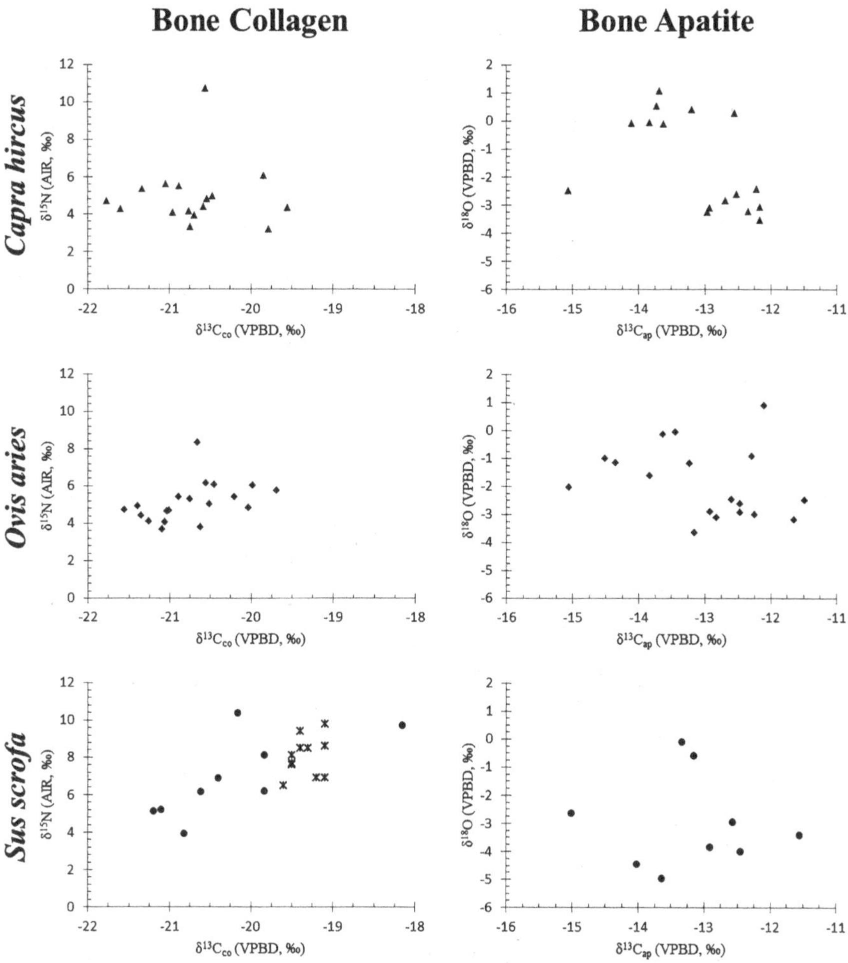

Figure 3.3. *Species-specific bone collagen (left column) and apatite (right column) isotope ratios recovered from Petsas House caprines and pigs (Price 2017). Human bone collagen isotope ratios from chamber tombs (Batsorachi, Loupouno, and Monastiraki) surrounding Mycenae (Richards and Hedges 2008) are indicated with the symbol* ж.

remains from animals used in different events or seasons, but also evidence how well the structure of the feature protected the assemblage from postdepositional loss, preserving the remains of a wide variety of taxa.

Petsas House is unique among LH III sites in the Peloponnese, with the highest pig representation among faunal assemblages in the region. The remainder of the Petsas House domesticated meat diet consisted mostly of caprine remains, which were similar in abundance to caprines in other ungulate assemblages in the region. Fewer cattle are represented in the well assemblage, and this differs significantly from most other sites with the exception of the LH IIIA2 assemblage from the site of Nichoria. The similarity between these assemblages hints that access to domesticated ungulates at Petsas House and other extrapalatial sites may have been influenced by the same larger regional systems of animal distribution during the LH IIIA2 period.

The regional faunal comparison also highlights variability in proportions of livestock taxa across the phases of the LH III period in the Peloponnese. By contrast, Halstead (2003) cited stable ungulate abundances over the Helladic periods at Tiryns (40.4–47.4% NISP caprines) and Nichoria (40.7–50.1% NISP caprines) (Sloan and Duncan 1978; von den Driesch and Boessneck 1990) as evidence of continuity in the relative proportions of domestic animals from the prepalatial to palatial periods, including across the rise and fall of the major Mycenaean palaces from the LH IIIA–C periods. While this continuity may largely hold true for caprines, we detect more variability in the abundances of pig and cattle across the region. For example, cattle abundance increases markedly from the LH IIIB1 to LH IIIC Late period at Tiryns (27% to 43%) (von den Driesch and Boessneck 1990). Additionally, high abundances of cattle were identified in the feasting deposits from Tsoungiza (Dabney et al. 2004) and Pylos (Halstead and Isaakidou 2004). Furthermore, pigs are more abundant from the smaller assemblage associated with cult activities at Ayios Konstantinos (LH IIIA–B) (Hamilakis and Konsolaki 2004). Together, this evidence highlights the need for further contextual studies of fauna to better understand how animal abundances may vary over time in relation to different social and economic activities at Mycenaean sites.

Access to Animals at Petsas House

The abundance of pigs at Petsas House points to a low-risk provisioning strategy, typical of small-scale subsistence production (Zeder 1998b). The small size of the adult pig teeth from Petsas House indicates that they represent domesticated individuals rather than hunted wild boar. Of the domesticated animals present at the site, pigs have the highest fecundity rate and attain a large body size earlier than other domesticates—ideal attributes for maintaining food security (Zeder 1998b). The evidence of a low-risk subsistence strategy based largely on pigs supports a scenario of mostly direct animal access at Petsas House.

Moreover, results of the aging analysis further suggest that the residents of Petsas House had direct access to locally managed pigs. More young pigs died by one month of age at Petsas House (74%) than typically found in modern wild boar populations (25–41.4% young; Herrero et al. 2008). This high proportion of young pig kill-off suggests local pig management, based on previous studies of managed pig demographics (e.g., Ervynck et al. 2001). This evidence likely supports a mix of naturally high newborn mortality and purposeful culling. Such a pattern is typical of pig populations managed to maintain an ample supply of meat and limit their potential damage to nearby agricultural fields (Redding 1991; Zeder 1998b).

In addition, the requirement of a constant local water source tethers pigs to a more sedentary lifestyle that is not ideal for transport over long distances through indirect channels (Wapnish and Hesse 1988; Zeder 1998b). The relatively more negative oxygen ratios exhibited by the majority of Petsas House pigs are consistent with imbibed standing water. This type of water would have been available to pigs raised and consumed in one location, such as in the area of Petsas House. Pigs compete for resources with humans and take up cultivable land (Redding 1991; Serjeantson 2007), yet they may have been managed as domestic scavengers by the occupants of Petsas House, effectively converting garbage into meaty calories for humans (Grigson 1982; Hesse 1986). Consumption of human refuse by domestic pigs may explain the relatively high nitrogen ratios exhibited by all but three of the pigs sampled from Petsas House. These predominant ratios align closely with those exhibited by human remains from chamber tombs around Mycenae (Richards and Hedges 2008) (figure 3.3), suggesting that the majority of the pigs had similar access to human food, perhaps in the form of refuse.

However, the evidence of caprine management and use reveals a more complex picture of access to animals at Petsas House. Caprines do not dominate the assemblage, and this is unexpected as they are the best represented species in other LH III assemblages. Still, caprine abundance is similar to other sites, and of the caprine specimens securely identified to species, sheep outnumber goats, indicating more potential risk in caprine management. This riskier strategy suggests that some caprines may have been obtained indirectly from herds managed for large-scale production (Zeder 1988). Still, the caprine aging results reflect the culling of a moderate proportion of young caprine individuals, suggesting some direct access to managed herds. Thus, the combination of evidence of direct and indirect access to caprines likely reflects a mix of household and palatial provisioning at Petsas House. Alternatively, the combined evidence of local management and a higher ratio of sheep may also point to a local production focus on sheep, possibly to replenish palatial herds in a similar manner to that suggested by Linear B texts from Knossos (Halstead 2003).

Isotopic analysis can further address the question of whether caprines were accessed from similar or disparate sources. Clustering of subgroups in caprine isotopic data further supports mixed access to caprines at Petsas House. Subgroups identified by $\delta^{13}C_{ap}$ and $\delta^{18}O$ values suggest that Petsas House caprines were raised under differing environmental and dietary conditions. These ratios may be explained by access to different sources of ingested water, such as rainwater, in contrast to groundwater potentially from the springs near Mycenae (Price 2015). It is also possible that the residents of Petsas House had access to both inland and coastal flocks, as the different $\delta^{18}O$ values in precipitation would account for the disparity in $\delta^{18}O$ values of Petsas House caprines (e.g., Price 2015; White et al. 1998).

In all, variation in the light isotope ratios hints that caprines accessed by Petsas House residents were raised under more than one set of environmental conditions and thus suggests access to animals from disparate herds. When considered with the high degree of palatial interest in caprine herd management in the Aegean, as implied by Linear B records (Halstead 2001, 2003), the diverse rearing conditions of caprines at Petsas House likely support some indirect access to specialized herds granted the use of a wide range of grazing areas and water resources by palatial authorities.

Thus, the combined zooarchaeological and isotopic evidence reveals complex access to caprines. Some young caprines were likely accessed and culled directly by residents, similarly to pigs. Further provisioning was likely gained through indirect channels that may have served to distribute caprines from palatial herds. Together, this evidence reflects how the subsistence strategy for this Mycenaean household was diverse not only due to local production and procurement of a rich variety of wild and domestic taxa, but also due to additional provisioning secured through relationships maintained with palatial authorities. In all, this diversified strategy likely minimized the risk involved in local subsistence production by the craft producers.

CONCLUSION

By combining zooarchaeological and isotopic analyses, this study enables a more robust understanding of access to animals by craft producers at Mycenae. The diverse types of access to herd animals at Petsas House highlight how the residents likely engaged in more than one of the informal, palatial, and possibly market exchange systems evidenced at Mycenae (Kvapil et al. 2019). Aging and isotopic results further reveal that types of animal exchange varied by taxa, likely due to the differing degrees of animal mobility, risk in animal production, and the greater suitability of some taxa for household use.

At Petsas House, the evidence for direct access to household pigs and some of the caprines may reflect a moderate degree of economic autonomy (Falconer 1995). Pigs are less easily regulated than caprines (Redding 1991), and the evidence of direct access to pigs at Petsas House points to largely independent provisioning. Similarly high proportions of pigs at other Bronze Age sites have been interpreted as evidence of reliance on animals that are not easily regulated by central authorities (Redding 2015). This may have led to later restrictions on pig rearing by authorities in urban settlements in the Near East and a consequential preference for more easily manageable and taxable animals with secondary products (Diener and Robkin 1978). Similarly, the high abundance of pigs at Petsas House may reflect the lax regulation of household pig management at Mycenae despite the presence of more easily taxable caprines and cattle. Additionally, the high percentage of wild game in the Petsas House assemblage suggests that some independent acquisition of supplementary animal resources occurred, which further highlights more lax regulations on access to some faunal resources (Zeder 1991). Wild game may have been especially important for offsetting periods of resource scarcity (Halstead 1992b; Redding and Rosenburg 1998). Finally, we hypothesize that the similarities between the relative abundances in the LH IIIA2 ungulate assemblages from Petsas House and Nichoria may possibly reflect similarly low levels of authoritative control over some subsistence channels accessed at two different extrapalatial sites during this subperiod. Yet, comparisons to Nichoria are tentative, and more studies of LH IIIA2 faunal assemblages are needed to investigate this potential pattern.

Evidence for independent provisioning by Petsas House residents implies that access to animals within the site of Mycenae may not have been highly asymmetrical. Rather, social inequalities between craft producers and palatial authorities at the site may have been reinforced through other means during the height of palatial development. The industrial role of the house in craft production possibly provided more unregulated opportunities for direct exchange of products for animals from local herders. This hypothesis merits further combined zooarchaeological and isotopic research of animal access across Mycenaean sites and social strata over time, as it may further clarify the role of animal resource provisioning in legitimizing and maintaining the sociopolitical environment during the LH period in the Aegean.

Acknowledgments. We would like to thank Levent Atici and Benjamin S. Arbuckle for organizing such an interesting International Council for Archaeozoology (ICAZ) session and for their dedication to creating this volume. This chapter benefited greatly from comments and suggestions by Natalie Munro. We also thank the Division of Research Implementation of the Ministry of Culture and Tourism General Directorship of Antiquities and Cultural Heritage of Greece for the permission to sample and transport materials to the United States for analyses and Nikos Katsoulieris at the Mycenae Museum. Many thanks to Maria Demopoulou and the many field school students who assisted with bone cleaning. Zooarchaeological research was supported by an American School of Classical Studies in Athens (ASCSA) Wiener Lab Short Term Grant and University of Connecticut Department of Anthropology Summer Research Fellowships to Meier. Isotopic research was supported by the ASCSA, University of Florida, and a Doctoral Dissertation Improvement Grant from the National Science Foundation to Price (#1435582). Thanks also to John Krigbaum of the Bone

Chemistry Laboratory in the Department of Anthropology and Jason Curtis of the Light Stable Isotopes Mass Spectroscopy Laboratory in the Department of Geological Sciences at the University of Florida. Travel to the 2014 ICAZ meeting was made possible by a Doctoral Student Travel Grant (UConn) to Meier. The excavation and study were made possible by the Archaeological Society of Athens and with funding from UC Berkeley, the Institute of Aegean Prehistory (INSTAP), and the Linda Witherill Foundation.

WORKS CITED

Albarella, Umberto, Keith Dobney, and Peter Rowley-Conwy. 2009. "Size and Shape of the Eurasian Wild Boar (*Sus Scrofa*), with a View to the Reconstruction of Its Holocene History." *Environmental Archaeology* 14 (2): 103–136.

Aravantinos, Vassilis. 1999. "Mycenaean Texts and Contexts at Thebes: The Discovery of New Linear B Archives on the Kadmeia." In *Floreant Studia Mycenaea, Akten des X. Internationalen Mykenologischen Colloquiums in Salzburg vom 1–5 Mai 1995*, edited by S. Hiller, S. Deger-Jalkotzy, and O. Panagl, 45–78. Vienna: Österreichische Akademie der Wissenschaften.

Balasse, Marie, Stanley H. Ambrose, Andrew B. Smith, and T. Douglas Price. 2002. "The Seasonal Mobility Model for Prehistoric Herders in the South-Western Cape of South Africa Assessed by Isotopic Analysis of Sheep Tooth Enamel." *Journal of Archaeological Science* 29 (9): 917–932.

Bennet, John. 1985. "The Structure of the Linear B Administration at Knossos." *American Journal of Archaeology* 89 (2): 231–249.

Bennet, John. 1998. "The Linear B Archives and the Kingdom of Nestor." In *Sandy Pylos: An Archaeological History from Nestor to Navarino*, edited by J. L. Davis, 111–133. Austin: University of Texas Press.

Bocherens, Hervé, Marc Fizet, and André Mariotti. 1994. "Diet, Physiology and Ecology of Fossil Mammals as Inferred from Stable Carbon and Nitrogen Isotope Biogeochemistry: Implications for Pleistocene Bears." *Palaeogeography, Palaeoclimatology, Palaeoecology* 107 (3–4): 213–225.

Bocherens, Hervé, Marilyn L. Fogel, Noreen Tuross, and Melinda Zeder. 1995. "Trophic Structure and Climatic Information from Isotopic Signatures in Pleistocene Cave Fauna of Southern England." *Journal of Archaeological Science* 22 (2): 327–340.

Bryant, J. Daniel, Boaz Luz, and Philip N. Froelich. 1994. "Oxygen Isotopic Composition of Fossil Horse Tooth Phosphate as a Record of Continental Paleoclimate." *Palaeogeography, Palaeoclimatology, Palaeoecology* 107 (3–4): 303–316.

Burns, Bryan. E. 2010. *Mycenaean Greece, Mediterranean Commerce, and the Formation of Identity*. New York: Cambridge University Press.

Cline, Eric H. 2010. *Oxford Handbook of the Aegean Bronze Age*. New York: Oxford University Press.

Dabney, Mary K., Paul Halstead, and Patrick Thomas. 2004. "Mycenaean Feasting on Tsoungiza at Ancient Nemea." *Hesperia: The Journal of the American School of Classical Studies at Athens* 73 (2): 197–215.

Dahl, Gudrun, and Anders Hjort. 1976. *Having Herds: Pastoral Herd Growth and Household Economy*. Stockholm: Studies in Social Anthropology 2, University of Stockholm.

Dansgaard, W. 1964. "Stable Isotopes in Precipitation." *Tellus* 16 (4): 436–468.

DeNiro, Michael J., and Samuel Epstein. 1978. "Influence of Diet on the Distribution of Carbon Isotopes in Animals." *Geochimica et Cosmochimica Acta* 42 (5): 495–506.

Diener, Paul, and Eugene E. Robkin. 1978. "Ecology, Evolution, and the Search for Cultural Origins: The Question of Islamic Pig Prohibition." *Current Anthropology* 19 (3): 493–540.

Ervynck, Anton, Hitomi Hongo, Keith M. Dobney, and Richard Meadow. 2001. "Born Free? New Evidence for the Status of '*Sus Scrofa*' at Neolithic Çayönü Tepesi (Southeastern Anatolia, Turkey)." *Paléorient* 27 (2): 47–73.

Falconer, Steven E. 1995. "Rural Responses to Early Urbanism: Bronze Age Household and Village Economy at Tell El-Hayyat, Jordan." *Journal of Field Archaeology* 22 (4): 399–419.

Farquhar, Graham. D., James R. Ehleringer, and Kerry T. Hubick. 1989. "Carbon Isotope Discrimination and Photosynthesis." *Annual Review of Plant Physiology and Plant Molecular Biology* 40 (1): 503–537.

Finucane, Brian, Agurto, Patricia Maita, and William H. Isbell. 2006. "Human and Animal Diet at Conchopata, Peru: Stable Isotope Evidence for Maize Agriculture and Animal Management Practices during the Middle Horizon." *Journal of Archaeological Science* 33 (12): 1766–1776.

Flannery, Kent V. 1983. "Early Pig Domestication in the Fertile Crescent: A Retrospective Look." In *The Hilly Flanks and Beyond: Essays on the Prehistory of Southwestern Asia Presented to Robert J. Braidwood*, edited by T. Cuyler Young, 163–188. Chicago: Oriental Institute of the University of Chicago.

Gamble, Clive S. 1979. "Surplus and Self-Sufficiency in the Cycladic Subsistence Economy." In *Papers in Cycladic Prehistory*, 14th edition, edited by Jack L. Davis and John F. Cherry, 122–134. Los Angeles: University of California, Institute of Archaeology.

Grayson, Donald K. 1979. "On the Quantification of Vertebrate Archaeofaunas." *Advances in Archaeological Method and Theory* 2: 199–237.

Grigson, Caroline. 1982. "Porridge and Pannage: Pig Husbandry in Neolithic England." In *Archaeological Aspects of Woodland Ecology*, edited by S. Limbrey and M. Bell, 297–313. Oxford: British Archaeological Reports Series 146.

Halstead, Paul. 1992a. "Agriculture in the Bronze Age Aegean: Toward a Model of Palatial Economy." In *Agriculture in Ancient Greece: Proceedings of the Seventh International Symposium at the Swedish Institute of Athens, 16–17 May 1990*, edited by Berit Wells, 104–117. Stockholm: P. Åströms förlag.

Halstead, Paul. 1992b. "From Reciprocity to Redistribution: Modeling the Exchange of Livestock in Neolithic Greece." *Anthropozoologica* 16: 19–30.

Halstead, Paul. 1992c. "The Mycenaean Palatial Economy: Making the Most of the Gaps in the Evidence." *Proceedings of the Cambridge Philological Society* 38: 57–86.

Halstead, Paul. 1996. "Pastoralism or Household Herding? Problems of Scale and Specialization in Early Greek Animal Husbandry." *World Archaeology* 28 (1): 20–42.

Halstead, Paul. 1998–1999. "Texts, Bones and Herders: Approaches to Animal Husbandry in Late Bronze Age Greece." *Minos* 33–34: 149–189.

Halstead, Paul. 1999. "Mycenaean Agriculture: The Nature of Palatial Intervention." *Bulletin of the Institute of Classical Studies* 43: 211–212.

Halstead, Paul. 2001. "Mycenaean Wheat, Flax, and Sheep: Palatial Intervention in Farming and Its Implications for Rural Society." In *Economy and Politics in the Mycenaean Palace States: Proceedings of a Conference Held on 1–3 July 1999 in the Faculty of Classics, Cambridge*, edited by Sofia Voutsaki and John T. Killen, 38–50. Cambridge: Cambridge Philological Society.

Halstead, Paul. 2003. "Texts and Bones: Contrasting Linear B and Archaeozoological Evidence for Animal Exploitation in Mycenaean Southern Greece." In *Zooarchaeology in Greece: Recent Advances*, edited by Eleni Kotjabopoulou, Yannis Hamilakis, Paul Halstead, Clive Gamble, and Paraskevi Elefanti, 257–261. London: British School at Athens Studies 9.

Halstead, Paul, and Valasia Isaakidou. 2004. "Faunal Evidence for Feasting: Burnt Offerings from the Palace of Nestor at Pylos." In *Food, Cuisine and Society in Prehistoric Greece*, edited by John F. Barrett and Paul Halstead, 136–154. Oxford: Oxbow.

Hamilakis, Yannis, and Eleni Konsolaki. 2004. "Pigs for the Gods: Burnt Animal Sacrifices as Embodied Rituals at Mycenaean Sanctuary." *Oxford Journal of Archaeology* 23 (2): 135–151.

Hartman, Gideon, and Avinoam Danin. 2010. "Isotopic Values of Plants in Relation to Water Availability in the Eastern Mediterranean Region." *Oecologia* 162 (4): 837–852. doi: 10.1007/s00442-009-1514-7.

Herrero, Juan, Alicia García-Serrano, and Ricardo García-González. 2008. "Reproductive and Demographic Parameters in Two Iberian Wild Boar *Sus scrofa* Populations." *Acta Theriologica* 53 (December): 355–364.

Hesse, Brian. 1986. "Animal Use at Tel Miqne-Ekron in the Bronze Age and Iron Age." *Bulletin of the American Schools of Oriental Research* 264 (November): 17–27.

Hongo, Hitomi, and Richard H. Meadow. 1998. "Pig Exploitation at Neolithic Çayönü Tepesi (Southeastern Anatolia)." In *MASCA Research Papers in Science and Archaeology*, edited by S. M. Nelson, 77–98. Philadelphia: MASCA.

Hruby, Julie. 2013. "Crafts, Specialists, and Markets in Mycenaean Greece: The Palace of Nestor, Craft Production, and Mechanisms for the Transfer of Goods." *American Journal of Archaeology* 117 (3): 423–427.

Iakovidis, Spyros, Elizabeth B. French, Kim Shelton, John Lavery, Anton G. Jansen, and Charalambos Ioannides. 2003. *Archaeological Atlas of Mycenae*. Archaeological Society at Athens Library, no. 299. Athens: The Archaeological Society at Athens; The British School at Athens.

Ingvarsson-Sundstrom, Anne, Mike P. Richards, and Sofia Voutsaki. 2009. "Stable Isotope Analysis of the Middle Helladic Population from Two Cemeteries at Asine: Barbouna and the East Cemetery." *Mediterranean Archaeology and Archaeometry* 9 (2): 1–14.

Killen, John T. 1964a. "Some Adjuncts to the SHEEP Ideogram on Knossos Tablets." *Eranos* 61: 69–93.

Killen, John T. 1964b. "The Wool Industry of Crete in the Late Bronze Age." *Annual of the British School at Athens* 59: 1–15.

Killen, John T. 1993a. "The Oxen's Name on the Knossos Ch Tablets." *Minos* 27–28: 101–107.

Killen, John T. 1993b. "Records of Sheep and Goats at Mycenaean Knossos and Pylos." *Bulletin on Sumerian Agriculture* 7: 209–218.

Killen, John T. 1994. "Thebes Sealings, Knossos Tablets and Mycenaean State Banquets." *Bulletin of the Institute of Classical Studies* 39 (1): 67–84.

Killen, John T. 1998. "The Role of the State in Wheat and Olive Production in Mycenaean Crete." *Aevum* 72: 19–23.

Kohn, Matthew. 2010. "Carbon Isotope Compositions of Terrestrial C3 Plants as Indicators of (Paleo)Ecology and (Paleo)Climate." *PNAS* 107 (46): 19691–19695.

Kvapil, Lynne A., Jacqueline S. Meier, Gypsy C. Price, and Kim Shelton. 2019. "Beyond City and Country at Mycenae: Urban and Rural Practices in a Subsistence Landscape." In *Country in the City: Forms and Functions of Agro-pastoral Activities in Mediterranean Pre-Classical Cities (Aegean and Western Mediterranean Protohistory)*, edited by Dominique Garcia, Raphaël Orgeolet, Maia Pomadère, and Julien Zurbach, 122–136. Oxford: Archaeopress.

Kyriakidis, Evangelos. 2010. "'Collectors' as Stakeholders in Mycenaean Governance: Property and the Relations between the Ruling Class and the State." *Cambridge Classical Journal* 56: 140–177.

Lee-Thorp, Julia A., Judith C. Sealy, and Nikolaas J. van der Merwe. 1989. "Stable Carbon Isotope Ratio Differences between Bone Collagen and Bone Apatite, and Their Relationship to Diet." *Journal of Archaeological Science* 16 (6): 585–599.

Lemoine, Ximena, Melinda A. Zeder, Katelyn J. Bishop, and Scott J. Rufolo. 2014. "A New System for Computing Dentition-Based Age Profiles in *Sus Scrofa*." *Journal of Archaeological Science* 47: 179–193.

Longinelli, Antonio. 1984. "Oxygen Isotopes in Mammal Bone Phosphate: A New Tool for Paleohydrological and Paleoclimatological Research?" *Geochimica et Cosmochimica Acta* 48 (2): 385–390.

Luz, Boaz, Yehoshua Kolodny, and Michal Horowitz. 1984. "Fractionation of Oxygen Isotopes between Mammalian Bone-Phosphate and Environmental Drinking Water." *Geochimica et Cosmochimica Acta* 48: 1689–1693.

Minagawa, Masao, and Eitaro Wada. 1984. "Stepwise Enrichment of ^{15}N along Food Chains: Further Evidence and the Relation between δ^{15}N and Animal Age." *Geochimica et Cosmochimica Acta* 48 (5): 1135–1140.

Minagawa, Masao, Akira Matsui, and Naotaka Ishiguro. 2005. "Patterns of Prehistoric Boar *Sus scrofa* Domestication, and Inter-islands Pig Trading across the East China Sea, as Determined by Carbon and Nitrogen Isotope Analysis." *Chemical Geology, In Search of Isotope Biosignatures In Search of Isotope Biosignatures* 218 (1–2): 91–102.

Nobis, Günter. 1993. "Archäozoologische Untersuchungen von Tierresten aus dem 'Palast des Nestor' bei Pylos in Messenien, SW-Peloponnes." *Zeitschrift für Archäologie* 27: 151–173.

Nosch, Marie-Louise B. 1997. "Pylian Craftsmen: Payment in Kind / Rations or Land?" In *Technē: Craftsmen, Craftswomen and Craftsmanship in the Aegean Bronze Age. Proceedings of the 6th International Aegean Conference*, edited by Robert Laffineur and Philip P. Betancourt, 397–406. Liège: Université de Liège, Histoire de l'art et archéologie de la Grèce antique.

O'Leary, Marion H. 1988. "Carbon Isotopes in Photosynthesis: Fractionation Techniques May Reveal New Aspects of Carbon Dynamics in Plants." *BioScience* 38 (5): 328–336.

Palaima, Thomas G. 1992a. "The Knossos Oxen Dossier: The Use of Oxen in Mycenaean Crete, I: General Background and Scribe 107." *Mykenaïka*. BCH Supplementary vol. 25: 463–474.

Palaima, Thomas G. 1992b. "Mycenaean Scribal Aesthetics." In *EIKON. Aegean Bronze Age Iconography: Shaping a Methodology*, edited by Robert Laffineur and Janice L. Crowley. Aegean 8, 63–74. Liège: Université de Liège, Histoire de l'art et archéologie de la Grèce antique.

Palaima, Thomas G. 1997. "Potter and Fuller: The Royal Craftsmen." In *Technē: Craftsmen, Craftswomen and Craftsmanship in the Aegean Bronze Age: Proceedings of the 6th International Aegean Conference*, edited by Robert Laffineur and Philip P. Betancourt, 407–412. Belgium: Université de Liège, Histoire de l'art et archéologie de la Grèce antique.

Papathanasiou, Anastasia. 2015. "Stable Isotope Analyses in Neolithic and Bronze Age Greece: An Overview." In *Archaeodiet in the Greek World from Stable Isotope Analysis*, edited by Anastasia Papathanasiou, Michael Richards, and Sherry Fox, 25–55. Hesperia Supplement 49. Princeton, NJ: American School of Classical Studies at Athens.

Parkinson, William A., and Michael L. Galaty. 2007. "Secondary States in Perspective: An Integrated Approach to State Formation in the Prehistoric Aegean." *American Anthropologist* 109 (1): 113–129.

Payne, Sebastian. 1973. "Kill-Off Patterns in Sheep and Goats: The Mandibles from Aşvan Kale." *Anatolian Studies* 23 (December): 281–303.

Petroutsa, Eirini I., and Sotiris K. Manolis. 2010. "Reconstructing Late Bronze Age Diet in Mainland Greece Using Stable Isotope Analysis." *Journal of Archaeological Science* 37 (3): 614–620.

Petroutsa, Eirini I., Michael P. Richards, Lazaros Kolonas, and Sotiris K. Manolis. 2009. "Isotope Paleodietary Analysis of Humans and Fauna from the Late Bronze Age Site of Voudeni." *Hesperia Supplements* 43: 237–243.

Price, Gypsy C. 2015. "Isotopic Contributions to Unpacking Political Economies: Human-Livestock Relations at Bronze Age Mycenae." PhD diss., University of Florida, Gainesville.

Price, Gypsy C., John Krigbaum, and Kim Shelton. 2017. "Stable Isotopes and Discriminating Tastes: Faunal Management Practices at the Late Bronze Age Settlement of Mycenae, Greece." *Journal of Archaeological Science: Reports* 14 (August): 116–126.

Pullen, Daniel J. 2013. "Crafts, Specialists, and Markets in Mycenaean Greece. Exchanging the Mycenaean Economy." *American Journal of Archaeology* 117 (3): 437–445.

Redding, Richard W. 1981. "Decision Making in Subsistence Herding of Sheep and Goats in the Middle East." PhD diss., University of Michigan, Ann Arbor.

Redding, Richard W. 1984. "Theoretical Determinants of a Herder's Decisions: Modeling Variation in the Sheep / Goat Ratio." *Animals and Archaeology* 3: *Early Herders and Their Flocks*. BAR S202: 223–240.

Redding, Richard W. 1991. "The Role of the Pig in the Subsistence System of Ancient Egypt: A Parable on the Potential of Faunal Data." In *Animal Use and Culture Change*, edited by P. J. Crabtree and K. Ryan, 20–30. MASCA Research Papers in Science and Archaeology, Supplement to Volume 8.

Redding, Richard W. 2015. "The Pig and the Chicken in the Middle East: Modeling Human Subsistence Behavior in the Archaeological Record Using Historical and Animal Husbandry Data." *Journal of Archaeological Research* 23 (December): 1–44.

Redding, Richard W., and M. Rosenberg. 1998. "Ancestral Pigs: A New (Guinea) Model for Pig Domestication in the Middle East." In *Ancestors for the Pigs: Pigs in Prehistory*, edited by Sarah M. Nelson, 64–76. Ann Arbor, MI: Cushing-Malloy, Inc.

Reese, David S. 2008. "Faunal Remains from Late Helladic Lerna (Argolid, Greece)." *Mediterranean Archaeology and Archaeometry* 8 (1): 5–25.

Reese, David S. 2013. "Appendix: Organic Remains from the Southwest Quarter, Mycenae." In *The Excavations of Mycenae III: The Southwest Quarter*, edited by Spiros E. Iakovidis, 475–493. Athens: Library of the Archaeological Society at Athens (no. 278).

Renfrew, Colin. 1972. *The Emergence of Civilisation: The Cyclades and the Aegean in the Third Millennium B.C.* London: Methuen.

Richards, Michael P., and Robert E. M. Hedges. 2008. "Stable Isotope Results from the Sites of Gerani, Armenoi and Mycenae." *Archaeology Meets Science: Biomolecular and Site Investigations in Bronze Age Greece*, edited by Yannis Tzedakis, Holley Martlew, and Martin Jones, 220–230. Oxford: Oxbow Books.

Rowley-Conwy, Peter, Umberto Albarella, and Keith M. Dobney. 2012. "Distinguishing Wild Boar from Domestic Pigs in Prehistory: A Review of Approaches and Recent Results." *Journal of World Prehistory* 25 (1): 1–44.

Schoeninger, Margaret J., and Michael J. DeNiro. 1984. "Nitrogen and Carbon Isotopic Composition of Bone Collagen from Marine and Terrestrial Animals." *Geochimica et Cosmochimica Acta* 48 (4): 625–639.

Sen, A. R., A. Santra, and S. A. Karim. 2004. "Carcass Yield, Composition and Meat Quality Attributes of Sheep and Goat Under Semiarid Conditions." *Meat Science* 66 (4): 757–763.

Serjeantson, Dale. 2007. "Intensification of Animal Husbandry in the Late Bronze Age? The Contribution of Sheep and Pigs." In *The Earlier Iron Age in Britain and the Near Continent*, edited by Colin Haselgrove and Rachel Pope, 80–93. Oxford: Oxbow Books.

Shelmerdine, Cynthia W. 2011. "The Individual and the State in Mycenaean Greece." *Bulletin of the Institute of Classical Studies* 54 (1): 19–28.

Shelmerdine, Cynthia W. 2013. "Crafts, Specialists, and Markets in Mycenaean Greece: Economic Interplay Among Households and States." *American Journal of Archaeology* 117 (3): 447–452.

Shelton, Kim. 2002–2003. "A New Linear B Tablet from Petsas House, Mycenae." *Minos* 37–38: 387–397.

Shelton, Kim. 2004. "Open and Ready for Business: The Excavations at Petsas House and the LH IIIA2 Period at Mycenae." *Mycenaean Seminar 2002/03: Bulletin of the Institute of Classical Studies* 47 (1): 175–190.

Shelton, Kim. 2010. "Citadel and Settlement: A Developing Economy at Mycenae, the Case of Petsas House." In *Political Economies of the Aegean Bronze Age: Papers from the Langford Conference, Florida State University, Tallahassee, 22–24 February 2007*, edited by Daniel. J. Pullen, 184–204. Oxford: Oxbow Books.

Shelton, Kim. 2015. "Pottery and Petsas House: Recent Research on LH IIIA 2 Mycenae." In *Mycenaeans up to Date: The Archaeology of the NE Peloponnese—Current Concepts and New Directions*, edited by A.-L. Schallin and I. Tournavitou, 27–36. Stockholm: Svenska institutet i Athen.

Sloan, Robert E., and Mary Ann Duncan. 1978. "Zooarchaeology of Nichoria." In *Excavations at Nichoria in Southwest Greece*. Vol. 1, edited by G. Rapp and S. E. Aschenbrenner, 60–77. Minneapolis: University of Minnesota Press.

Sponheimer, Matt, and Julia A. Lee-Thorp. 1999. "Isotopic Evidence for the Diet of an Early Hominid, *Australopithecus africanus*." *Science* 283 (5400): 368–370. doi: 10.1126/science.283.5400.368.

Squires, Victor R. 1982. "Dietary Overlap between Sheep, Cattle, and Goats When Grazing in Common." *Journal of Range Management* 35 (1): 116–119.

Stevens, Rhiannon E., Emma Lightfoot, Julie Hamilton, Barry W. Cunliffe, and Robert E.M. Hedges. 2013. "One for the Master and One for the Dame: Stable Isotope Investigations of Iron Age Animal Husbandry in the Danebury Environs." *Archaeological and Anthropological Sciences* 5 (2): 95–109.

Stiner, Mary C. 1990. "The Use of Mortality Patterns in Archaeological Studies of Hominid Predatory Adaptations." *Journal of Anthropological Archaeology* 9 (4): 305–351.

Stocker, Sharon R., and Jack L. Davis. 2004. "Animal Sacrifice, Archives, and Feasting at the Palace of Nestor." *Hesperia* 73(2): 179–195.

Tieszen, Larry L. 1991. "Natural Variations in the Carbon Isotope Values of Plants: Implications for Archaeology, Ecology, and Paleoecology." *Journal of Archaeological Science* 18 (3): 227–248.

Tieszen, Larry L., and T. W. Boutton. 1989. "Stable Carbon Isotopes in Terrestrial Ecosystem Research." In *Stable Isotopes in Ecological Research*, edited by P. W. Rundel, J. R. Ehleringer, and K. A. Nagy. Ecological Studies, vol. 68. New York: Springer. https://doi.org/10.1007/978-1-4612-3498-2_11.

Trantalidou Katerina. 2007–2008. "Nutritional choices and elements of the economy of Late Helladic Mycenae." *Athens Annals of Archaeology* 40–41: 115.

Triantaphyllou, Sevasti, Michael P. Richards, Carol Zerner, and Sofia Voutsaki. 2008. "Isotopic Dietary Reconstruction of Humans from Middle Bronze Age Lerna, Argolid, Greece." *Journal of Archaeological Science* 35 (11): 3028–3034.

Vaiglova, Petra, Amy Bogaard, Matthew Collins, William Cavanagh, Christopher Mee, Josette Renard, Angela Lamb, Armelle Gardeisen, and Rebecca Fraser. 2014. "An Integrated Stable Isotope Study of Plants and Animals from Kouphovouno, Southern Greece: A New Look at Neolithic Farming." *Journal of Archaeological Science* 42 (February): 201–215.

Varias Garcia, Carlos. 1999. "The Palace of Mycenae in LH IIIB2 According to the Documents in Linear B: A General Description," in *Floreant Studia Mycenaea*, edited by S. Deger-Jalkotzy, S. Hiller, and O. Panagl, 595–600. Vienna: Verlag der Österreichenischen Akademie der Wissenschaften.

von den Driesch, Angela, and Joachim Boessneck. 1990. "Die Tierreste Von Der Mykenischen Burg Tiryns Bei Nauplion/Peloponnes." In *Die Keramik von Talioti*, edited by Hans-Joachim Weisshaar, Ingrid Weber-Hiden, Angela von den Driesch-Karpf, Andreas Rieger, and Joachim Boessneck, 87–164. Mainz, Germany: P. von Zabern.

Voutsaki, Sofia. 2010. "From the Kinship Economy to the Palatial Economy: The Argolid in the Second Millennium BC." In *Political Economies of the Aegean Bronze Age: Papers from the Langford Conference*, Florida State University, Tallahassee, February 22–24, 2007, edited by D. J. Pullen, 86–111. Oxford: Oxbow.

Walberg, Gisela, and David S. Reese. 2008. "Feasting at Midea." In *DAIS: The Aegean Feast. Proceedings of the 12th International Aegean Conference University of Melbourne, Centre for Classics and Archaeology, 25–29 March 2008. Series Aegaeum, 29*, edited by Louise A. Hitchcock, Janice L. Crowley, and Robert Laffineur, 239–248. Liège, Belgium: Université de Liège Press.

Wapnish, Paula, and Brian Hesse. 1988. "Urbanization and the Organization of Animal Production at Tell Jemmeh in the Middle Bronze Age Levant." *Journal of Near Eastern Studies* 47 (2): 81–94.

White, Christine D., Michael W. Spence, Hilary Le Q. Stuart-Williams, and Henry P. Schwarcz. 1998. "Oxygen Isotopes and the Identification of Geographical Origins: The Valley of Oaxaca Versus the Valley of Mexico." *Journal of Archaeological Science* 25 (7): 643–655.

Zeder, Melinda A. 1988. "Understanding Urban Process through the Study of Specialized Subsistence Economy in the Near East." *Journal of Anthropological Archaeology* 7 (1): 1–55.

Zeder, Melinda A. 1991. *Feeding Cities: Specialized Animal Economy in the Ancient Near East.* Washington, DC: Smithsonian Institution Press.

Zeder, Melinda A. 1998a. "Environment, Economy, and Subsistence on the Threshold of Urban Emergence in Northern Mesopotamia." *Travaux de la Maison de l'Orient Méditerranée* 28 (1): 55–67.

Zeder, Melinda A. 1998b. "Pigs and Emergent Complexity in the Ancient Near East." In *Ancestors for the Pigs*, edited by Sarah Nelson, 109–122. MASCA Research Papers in Science and Archaeology. Philadelphia: MASCA, University Museum.

Zeder, Melinda A. 2006. "Reconciling Rates of Long Bone Fusion and Tooth Eruption and Wear in Sheep (*Ovis*) and Goat (*Capra*)." In *Recent Advances in Ageing and Sexing Animal Bones*, edited by Deborah Ruscillo, 87–118. Oxford: Oxbow Books.

4

The Fat of the Land

Meat and Dairy Products in Medieval Ireland

FIONA BEGLANE

The aim of this chapter is to examine the zooarchaeological evidence for variation in the quality and type of animal products in the diet of people in medieval Ireland, and specifically to investigate the potential dairy intake of the population. This study has been carried out by modeling the demographic profile and nutritional content represented by three archaeological case studies and comparing these results to historical and literary accounts. Medieval Ireland was a diverse and complex society, with chronological, geographical, and ethnic variations. The early medieval period (ca. AD 400–1100) was characterized by dispersed rural settlement, by some protourbanization around monastic sites, and in the later part of this early medieval period, by the introduction of true towns by the incoming Vikings (Ó Crónin 2005). The later medieval period (ca. AD 1100–1600) saw the arrival of the Anglo-Normans to eastern Ireland. They introduced European-style castles to Ireland and continued the process of urbanization. This period also saw the introduction of the European monastic orders such as the Cistercians, Franciscans, and Dominicans to Ireland (Cosgrove 1987). As a result of these variations, the amounts and types of food consumed and the

https://doi.org/10.5876/9781646422562.c004

species from which the food came could vary considerably. The causes of these differences included age, status and occupation of the individual, urban or rural location, season of the year, and chronological period.

Much of the twentieth-century scholarship examining the historical diet of Ireland focused on the importance of dairy products and of pork, and some authors have stressed a dearth of beef in the diet, particularly for lower-class individuals (Clarkson and Crawford 2001:25; Foley 1993; Lucas 1960; Nicholls 1987:413; Ó Corráin 2005:572). In his influential paper, Anthony Lucas (1960) attempted to collate historical and literary evidence for the Irish diet in the periods "before the potato." He argued that "by far the most important kind of flesh meat eaten in ancient, medieval and later times seems to have been pork or bacon" (Lucas 1960:15), that "no cattle were reared specifically for slaughter" (Lucas 1960:14), and that sheep were reared mainly for their wool and rarely eaten (Lucas 1960:15). Further, he argued that the diet was predominantly dairy products and grain (Lucas 1960:8). He particularly notes the twelfth-century Gaelic-Irish poem *The Vision of MacConglinne*, or *Aisling of MacConglinne*, which is replete with references to dairy products and to pork and bacon (Lucas 1960:14–15). He also notes early postmedieval accounts such as those of Spenser, writing in 1596, who discusses the Irish, saying "the kyen [cattle] are barren and without milke, which useth to be his onelye foode" (Spenser 1596). The traveler Fynes Moryson, writing in the early seventeenth century, similarly says of the Irish: "They feed most on whitemeates [dairy products] . . . and when they are almost starved yet they will not kill a Cow, except it bee old, and yeeld no milke" (Moryson [1617] 1908:iv, 200–201).

Lucas's work has been highly influential, especially in general archaeological and historical volumes (e.g., Clarkson and Crawford 2001; Mac Con Iomaire 2011; Sexton 1998:27–8). One obvious issue with this work, however, is that he treats the entire early, later, and postmedieval periods prior to the introduction of the potato as a single entity, regardless of any differences that might be expected due to land quality or, in the later medieval period, to whether Anglo-Norman or Gaelic Irish-held regions are being discussed. Indeed he opens with the claim that "Irish food presents a remarkable continuity of tradition from the time of the earliest documentary evidence down to the widespread adoption of the potato in the late 17th century" (Lucas 1960:8). However, work by other researchers has shown a diversity of results, indicating that this is an oversimplification (e.g., Beglane 2009; McCormick 1997; McCormick and Murray 2007), and by examining the zooarchaeological evidence in detail this chapter aims to gain a more complex perspective.

This chapter will examine some of these variations in diet by means of demographic modeling of three contrasting case studies from medieval Ireland. It should be noted that only the animal-based elements of the diet have been

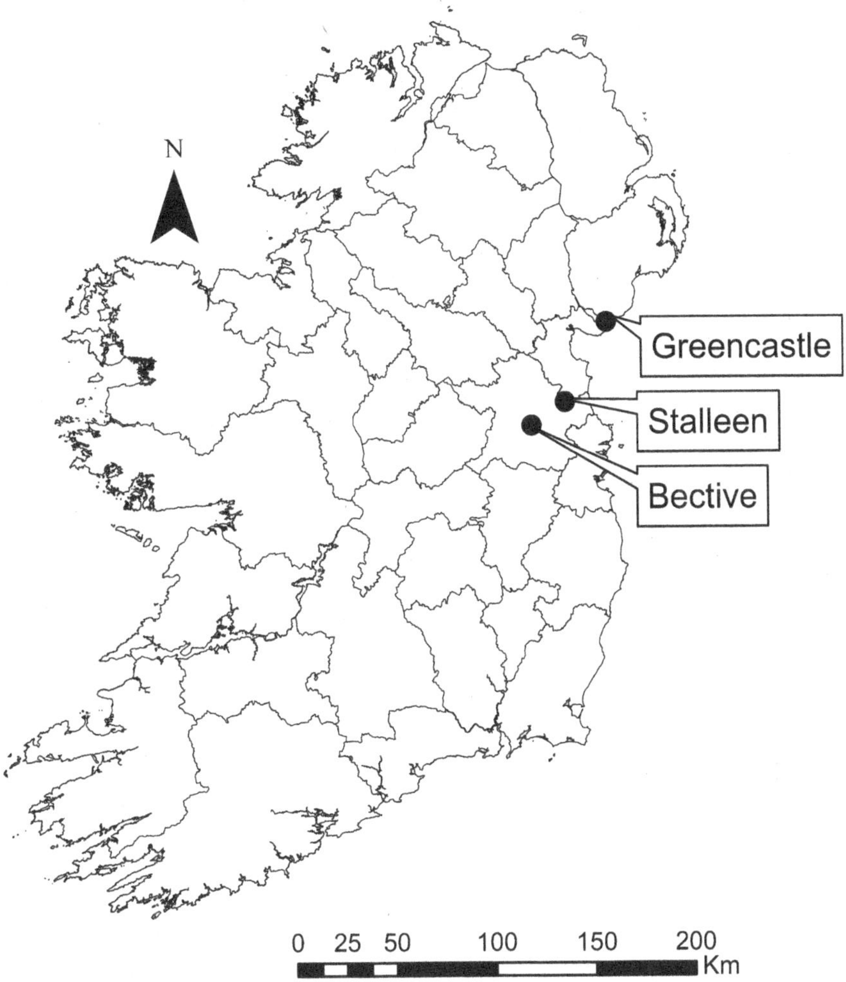

Figure 4.1. *Map showing the sites discussed in the text.*

considered, whereas a substantial proportion of the diet would also have been made up of cereals, fruits, and vegetables, which could potentially have made up a majority of the calorific intake. All three assemblages are from a relatively small geographical area in the east of Ireland, which, during the later medieval period, was in the heartland of Anglo-Norman control (figure 4.1).

The first site is at Stalleen, County Meath. In the early medieval period this was most probably a very early ecclesiastical foundation, although a prosperous secular settlement cannot be completely discounted (Beglane 2022; Stout and Stout 2022). For this chapter, data from Phase 2a (c. AD 540–660) are discussed. The next example is from Greencastle, County Down, where excavation trenches were located approximately 20 m southwest of the Anglo-Norman castle (Beglane 2007; Ó Baoill 2007). This chapter concentrates on the main occupation period of the castle, Phase 3, dated to the fourteenth century. The final site is Bective Abbey, County Meath, which was a Cistercian foundation (Beglane 2016; Stout and Stout 2016). This chapter discusses the late medieval Cistercian period, Phases 3–7 (ca. AD 1300–1537).

Remains were quantified using a method modified from that described by Simon Davis (1992), using selected skeletal elements where at least 50% of the diagnostic feature is present. This analysis has the benefit of rapid recording time but results in relatively low numbers of number of identifiable specimens (NISP) compared to the calculated minimum number of individuals (MNI) and to the total number of fragments (TNF). The analyses are based on the MNI values obtained for the three main domesticated species—cattle, sheep/goat, and pig—which were calculated taking into account the side of the body but not states of fusion, sizes of bones, and tooth wear. The age at slaughter was calculated using fusion data based on Ian Silver (1963) and Elizabeth Reitz and Elizabeth Wing (1999:76). For discussion of the role of minor species in the diet, the NISP has been used, since MNI is not appropriate for small numbers of specimens.

PROPORTIONS OF MEAT AND DAIRY IN THE DIET

Cattle Demographics and Meat Yields

In order to examine the relative proportions of dairy products and meat available in the diet, it is first necessary to consider the likely demographic profile and size of the herds available to medieval communities. The Maasai people of Kenya are pastoralists who subsist on relatively high proportions of milk and hold cattle as wealth in what could be argued to be analogous to early medieval Ireland. Their herds are predominantly female, at 65–70%, though this figure also includes female calves and heifers, so that there are averages of 36% adult cows in their herds and 34% males of all ages (de Leeuw et al. 1994). Similarly, across the entire modern Mexican cattle industry around 2010, 36% of 22 million cattle were adult females (Peel et al. 2010), and in Ireland in 2010, 37% of 7 million cattle were adult females (Central Statistics Office 2012). Gudrun Dahl and Anders Hjort (1976:28–33) conducted a detailed survey of cattle demographics in contemporary Africa and obtained figures of between 40% and 75% for the total number of females of all ages. On a macrolevel, therefore, herd structures are relatively constant whether one examines a modern commercial economy or a pastoral milk-based subsistence economy. It is therefore reasonable to take the Maasai herd structure of approximately 36% adult females, 30% juvenile females and 34% males, including bulls as well as castrated and juvenile males, as the basis for calculations.

The size of a herd of cattle depends on issues such as status, access to grazing, access to stock, and also on chronological period. Documentary sources suggest that agriculture in the early medieval period was primarily self-sufficient subsistence farming, and central to the lives of the majority of people (O'Sullivan et al. 2014:179). In the early medieval Irish laws an *ócaire*, a "young noble" or small farmer, who was the lowest grade of freeman, was expected to own seven cows (specifically female cattle), a bull and an ox, seven pigs and a brood sow, seven sheep, and a horse (MacNeill 1921–1924:286–291), whereas a strong farmer, or *bóaire*, "cow-lord," was expected to have at least twelve cows, two oxen, and two horses as well as other stock. Moving further up the scale, a prosperous "*bóaire* of adjudication" needed at least twenty cows and a commensurate number of other animals. It should be noted that juvenile animals are not included in these figures, which represent the breeding and working stock only. The early Irish laws describe how each year a heifer, in the case of an ócaire, or a steer, in the case of a bóaire, was payable as house custom to his lord, so either way, one animal from the herd would be given away each year, and, in addition, fines and dowries as well as rent on any additional land was paid for in cattle (MacNeill 1921–1924:288–289). Early sources indicate that cows were kept for both milk and breeding and that steers were trained as oxen. Furthermore, while cattle appear to have been selected for color and sometimes size, there is no indication of specialist dairy or beef breeds; instead, prior to the postmedieval period, all the indications are that general-purpose breeds were kept were kept (e.g., Kelly 1997:27–66).

For the purposes of calculation, this chapter will consider an individual between the ócaire and the bóaire in status, holding a herd of 30 cattle in total, and with his household self-sufficient in food production. Of the 30 cattle there would be an average of 10.8 cows, 9 juvenile females, and 10.2 male cattle of all ages, based on the Maasai herd structures described above (de Leeuw et al. 1994). For a wealthier individual, these figures would be multiplied up, but of course the number of family members, servants, and retainers that needed to be fed would also increase in a commensurate way, and the lord would also receive additional animals in house customs.

The following assumptions have been made: that 10 out of the 10.8 cows give birth to a calf each year. One of the cows is deliberately slaughtered or dies each year, being replaced in the breeding herd by one of the young heifers and with the beef from this old cow being consumed as subprime meat. On average, males are slaughtered in their fourth year, since most prime-meat animals will be slaughtered by the end of their third year but some will be retained indefinitely for breeding or as oxen for traction, before being slaughtered for subprime meat. Therefore, of a total of 10.2 males in the herd, 2.55 are available for meat each year, with excess females occasionally being slaughtered if, for example, insufficient males were available. Overall, this would leave the herd size relatively constant or slightly increasing in size and would allow for early deaths of calves, cattle gifted or given in taxes and fines, and other losses.

For this chapter the size of Irish cattle and the dressing-out proportions are estimated at 450 kg and 50% as cited by Finbar McCormick (2006:165). This 30-animal herd of cattle will therefore yield 2.55 males plus 1 old cow for meat each year. At an average of 225 kg per animal, this is equivalent to 799 kg of beef, which, at an average of 250 calories per 100 g, gives 1,996,875 calories/year in beef. However, as discussed below, depending on whether a site is self-sufficient, a producer site or a consumer site will affect how much of this meat is available for consumption by the inhabitants. It should be noted for clarity that in this chapter the word *meat* has been used for both muscle tissue and offal products, with *beef* referring to all products from cattle, *pork* used for all pig products, and *mutton* for all sheep/goat products.

Milk Yields

Medieval milk yields were not at the levels of modern cattle, which have been selectively bred. For example, the Kerry cow, which is an Irish traditional breed considered as an "all round" animal suitable for small farmers, is noted for its high milk yield on relatively poor fodder and provides about 3,300 l per year (Dept of Animal Science 1995–2015). Modern beef breeds are not bred for their milk yield, but, for example, in one study Hereford beef cows yielded approximately 8.5 l/day (Casebolt 1984), which would equate to approximately 2,600 l/yr. By contrast, a Holstein-Friesian cow, bred for milk production, will yield 7,600 l per year (Dept of Animal Science 1995–2015). Medieval yields are likely to have been much less, due to poorer nutrition levels especially in the winter and early spring, to the lack of selective breeding, and to the necessity of providing adequate nutrition to the calf. Thomson (2005:table 5) examined manorial accounts from thirteenth-century England and suggested that each cow could produce 214–442 l of milk per year, plus a weaned calf, which was allowed to suckle some of the milk. He compared this yield with Walter of Henley's treatise on agriculture, written approximately AD 1276–1290, which expected 567 l per cow per year, and the anonymous text known as the *Husbandry*, which suggested 509 l. Gregory Clark (1991:214–215), in his calculations for a "typical" English manor in the period AD 1300–1349, estimated 454 l per year, whereas Trow-Smith ([1957] 2006:122) estimated values of 546–682 l per year for well-managed English medieval demesne farms. These sources therefore cluster around 400–600 l per year.

Kenneth Nicholls (1987:415) noted that five gallons of butter would be expected from a cow in a single year, which, at a fat content of 3% and a density of 1,030 kg/l, equates to 573 liters of milk. By contrast, Fergus Kelly (1997:41) argues that the early medieval Irish *Corpus Iuris Hibernici* (ii 675.6–7) suggests that a cow should fill a standard 12 in. high bucket once, or more probably twice a day, as well as suckling her calf. This amount gives a yield of 5 or 10 l per day depending on the interpretation of the text. However, based on a 305-day lactation period, this would give either 1,525 or 3,050 l per year, which is far in excess of that found by other researchers and is on a par with a modern Kerry cow. Since milk yield is not constant over the course of the lactation period, it is most likely that the *Corpus* was referring to a good cow at the optimum point in the lactation cycle, but, even then, 5 l, or one bucket, is much more likely than two.

In summary, a figure of 500 l per year of surplus milk from each lactating cow at 580 calories/l has been taken for the calculations. Of the 10.8 cows in the herd, only those giving birth to a calf would yield milk in that year, so that these 10 cows would together produce 5,000 l of surplus milk, which is equivalent to 2.9 million calories/year.

SPECIES AND AGE DISTRIBUTIONS

Overall, therefore, a herd of 30 cattle would potentially provide almost 2 million calories/year of beef and 2.9 million calories/year of milk and milk products. However, beef is generally not the only meat consumed, and, although from smaller animals, both pork and mutton have a higher proportion of fat than beef. This means that even if eaten in relatively small quantities they would have contributed significantly to the diet both in calories and also in flavor and desirability. The meat from these species must also therefore be taken into consideration.

On Irish sites of all periods, cattle are usually the most common species when measured by MNI (e.g., Beglane 2009; McCormick 1997; McCormick and Murray 2007). Among the case study sites reported here, however, they range from an unusually low 28.0% of individuals at Bective Abbey to a high of 53.8% at Greencastle. Sheep vary between 23.1% at Greencastle up to 36% at Bective and pigs between a low of 23.1% at Greencastle and a high of 36.0% at Bective Abbey (table 4.1). When these MNI figures are converted from numbers of animals to weight of meat, this equates to 67–87% beef, with pork making up the majority of the rest at between 10% and 25% and mutton only supplying between 2.5% and 6% of the meat (figure 4.2). For pigs the live weight has been taken as 80 kg with a dressing-out proportion of 80% as cited by McCormick (2006:165) and for sheep a live weight of 30 kg with a 50% dressing-out proportion has been taken (Milner et al. 1999:table 2; Raines n.d.).

By examining the age at slaughter, it is possible to gain insights into the balance between meat production and secondary products and also the quality of the meat consumed (figure 4.3). At early medieval Stalleen, approximately half of the cattle were killed as adults at more than four years old, and approximately 38% were killed at two to three years. These figures suggest that females were being retained into adulthood for breeding and milk production, while the majority of males were reared for prime beef, with a few males retained for

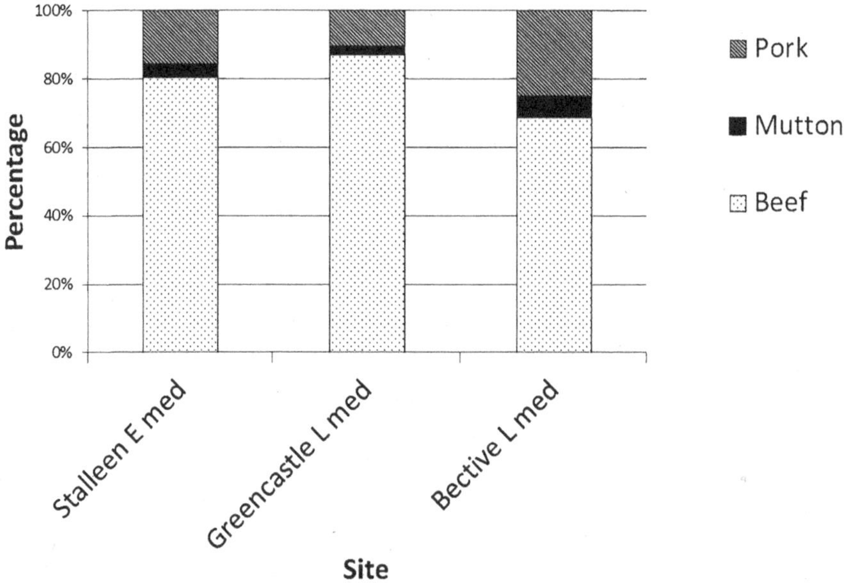

Figure 4.2. *Percentage meat weight for the three main species.*

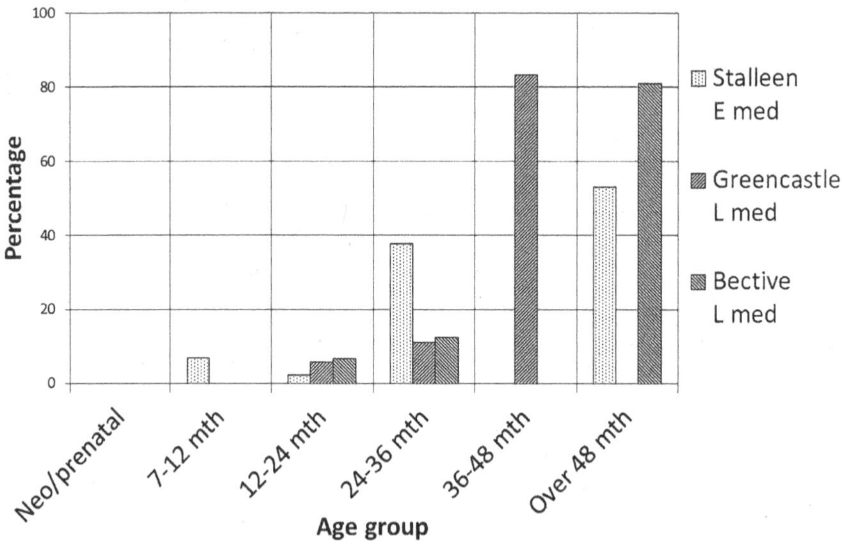

Figure 4.3. *Cattle age at slaughter based on fusion.*

breeding and traction. The cows would have been kept until they were no longer producing milk and calves, and, in the case of oxen, these would have been kept until they became too old to work. This signature can be interpreted as a self-sufficient food production/consumption site.

Table 4.1. Summary of zooarchaeological data

Site, Phase, and Chronological Period	*TNF*	*NISP* Cattle	*NISP* Sheep/Goat	*NISP* Pig	*MNI* Cattle	*MNI* Sheep/Goat	*MNI* Pig	*% MNI* Cattle	*% MNI* Sheep/Goat	*% MNI* Pig
Stalleen 2a, early medieval	4441	367	199	109	13	9	9	41.9	29.0	29.0
Greencastle 3, later medieval	n/a	169	54	42	7	3	3	53.8	23.1	23.1
Bective 3–7, late medieval	7378	210	212	179	7	9	9	28.0	36.0	36.0

Note: TNF—total number of fragments, NISP—number of identified specimens present, MNI—minimum number of individuals.

Table 4.2. Summary of calculations based on a herd of thirty animals

Site, Phase, and Chronological Period	*Meat %* Beef %	*Meat %* Mutton %	*Meat %* Pork %	*Meat Production* Beef kg	*Meat Production* Mutton kg	*Meat Production* Pork kg	*Calories / Year Produced* Beef Cal/yr	*Calories / Year Produced* Mutton Cal/yr	*Calories / Year Produced* Pork Cal/yr	*Calories / Year Produced* Dairy Cal/yr	*Calories / Year Produced* Total Cal/yr	*Percentage of Dietary Calories* Beef Cals%	*Percentage of Dietary Calories* Mutton Cals%	*Percentage of Dietary Calories* Pork Cals%	*Percentage of Dietary Calories* Dairy Cals%
Stalleen 2a, early medieval	80.5	3.7	15.8	799	37	157	1,996,875	110,138	533,029	2,900,000	5,540,042	36.0	2.0	9.6	52.3
Greencastle 3, later medieval	86.9	2.5	10.6	574	16	70	1,434,375	49,122	237,951	—	1,721,448	83.3	2.9	13.8	—
Bective 3–7, late medieval	68.9	5.9	25.2	282	24	103	705,938	72,540	351,145	2,900,000	4,029,623	17.5	1.8	8.7	72.0

The opposite extreme is found at Bective Abbey, where over 80% of cattle were adults, with a small proportion of prime-meat age animals being slaughtered. This suggests that at this site males were exported as prime-meat animals or to be trained elsewhere for traction. It further suggests that the females were retained for breeding and dairy production, with sufficient males kept for breeding and working stock. The age distributions indicate that this was a producer site rather than being a self-sufficient subsistence site. The alternative is that this was essentially a consumer site, supplied with aged animals as gifts of food; however, while dairy products were permitted foods, meat consumption was frowned upon by the Cistercians, so that this scenario is less likely than that the monks had their own dairy herds (Beglane 2016). By contrast, at Greencastle virtually all the animals were in the three-to-four-year age range. As this is a castle site, it is likely that these represent prime-age animals being used as renders (taxes due to the lord), to pay rents, and for payment of debts. Although rents were meant to be paid as money, there is evidence that payment as livestock did occur, for example, by the tenants of William FitzWarin at Pouloc, Ulster in AD 1282 (Beglane 2015a:75–76; Sweetman 1875–1886 ii, no. 1918).

For sheep/goat, at early medieval Stalleen and at later medieval Greencastle and Bective Abbey, between 35% and about 43% of sheep/goats were retained until they were adults (figure 4.4). In these three assemblages, about 40–50% of sheep were slaughtered for good-quality meat aged between 15 months to 42 months, with some younger deaths that may have been due to natural causes or to a desire for lamb meat. Overall, it appears that although mutton contributed only a small percentage of the meat in the diet (table 4.2; figure 4.5), it was often consumed while still relatively tender but having yielded several crops of wool.

Pigs are reared solely for meat and produce large litters, so few breeding animals are needed. This practice is reflected in these case studies, where no animals aged over forty-two months were found in any of the assemblages. Mature adults were therefore relatively uncommon, and pork was generally eaten as high-quality meat. At Stalleen in the early medieval period, 63% of animals were slaughtered between 30 and 42 months, similarly at Greencastle the peak (50%) was at 30–42 months, while at Bective there was a high rate of neo/prenatal death (31%), which could indicate consumption of suckling pig or poor husbandry, with a spread of slaughter ages after this, up to and including a small peak of 26% at 30–42 months.

A diverse diet gives a balance of nutrients, and greater diversity suggests better access to food choices and hence higher status (Beglane 2015b; Kuechelmann 2012; Pluskowski 2007). Table 4.3 shows deer, hare and rabbit, bird, and fish bones recovered from the various assemblages. One caveat with these results is the variability of excavation methodologies used. Bective Abbey was a research excavation, and much of the soil was sieved on-site, with extensive wet sieving

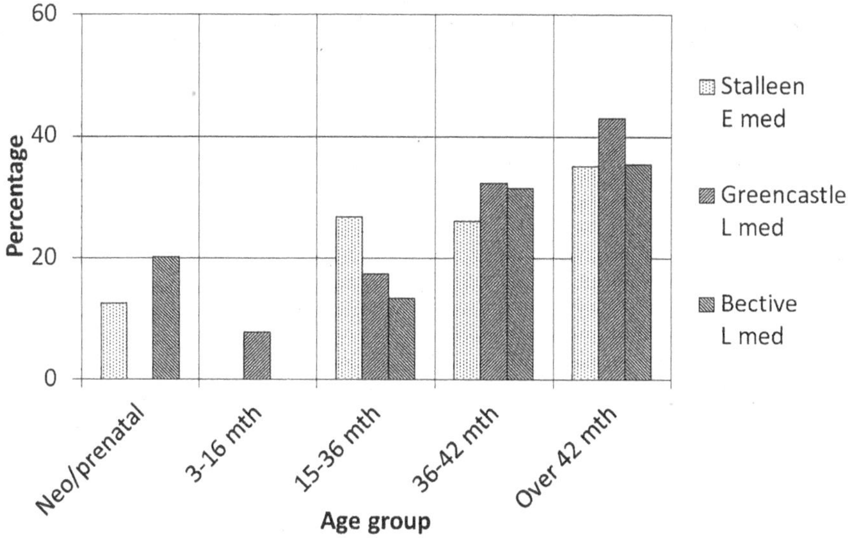

Figure 4.4. *Sheep/goat age at slaughter based on fusion.*

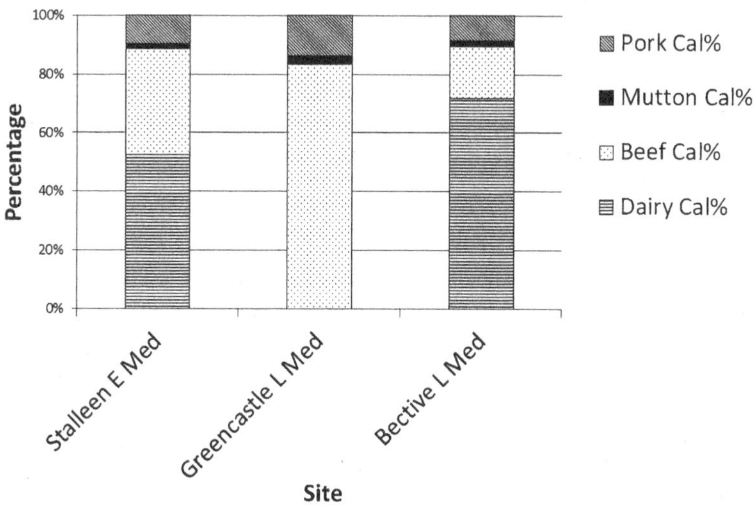

Figure 4.5. *Dietary contribution of various animal-based food products.*

of soil samples also taking place. As a result, high numbers of bird and fish bones were recovered compared to the other sites, which were both commercial excavations, where sieving and soil sampling was more limited. However, despite these limitations it is clear that the diet at Stalleen was the least diverse, with only ten bird bones and one fish bone identified. Greencastle was diverse, with relatively large numbers of deer bones, some birds, fish, and hare and rabbit. This

Table 4.3. Number of Identified Specimens Present (NISP) from minor food species

Site, Phase, and Chronological Period	*NISP from Minor Food Species*			
	Deer	Hare and rabbit	Bird	Fish
Stalleen 2a, early medieval	0	0	10	1
Greencastle 3, later medieval	19	5	10	5
Bective 3–7, late medieval	0	17	198	96

site also yielded a large assemblage of marine mollusk shells; however, as it has a coastal location, shells were expected (Beglane 2007). Bective Abbey yielded the largest numbers of the lesser species, and though undoubtedly skewed by the excavation methodology, this would fit with the monastic rule, which permitted poultry and fish to be consumed (de Venuto 2010; Ervynck 2004; Greene 1992:147), a point that is further reinforced by the presence of a significant number of marine mollusk shells at this inland site.

FOOD AVAILABILITY

Calculations for food availability on the case study sites are based on a cattle herd of thirty cattle as described above, with proportions of other species based on the percentage MNIs found archaeologically. The following assumptions have been made:

1. There is no historical or archaeological evidence for separate milk and beef breeds in Ireland until the postmedieval period. The assumption has therefore been made that all adult cows were put to the bull when they came into heat and that after having had a calf, any surplus milk was used for human consumption.
2. Due to their poor keeping and traveling qualities, milk and milk products were consumed on-site rather than exported.
3. For early medieval Stalleen, which is interpreted as a self-sufficient site, all meat has been consumed on-site.
4. For Bective Abbey, interpreted as a producer site, 90% of the males were exported for prime beef and 10% of males were retained for traction and breeding.
5. For Bective Abbey, interpreted as a producer site, all the meat from non-productive animals was consumed. This includes meat from old oxen, bulls, and cows that no longer were able to work, breed, or provide milk.
6. For Greencastle, the only consumer site, all meat was eaten.

7. Minor species such as deer, rabbit, hare, birds, fish, and mollusks have not been included in the calculations.

Early Medieval Stalleen

In the early medieval period, the evidence suggests, Stalleen operated as a self-sufficient agricultural site. Calculations are shown here in detail for this case study. The calculations for other phases and sites are similar so have not been shown; however, all the results are shown in table 4.2.

In this case study, a herd size of thirty cattle is assumed, with a self-sufficient demographic profile comprising 10.8 cows, 9 juvenile females (calves and heifers) and 10.2 males (calves, steers and bulls). Each year 10 cows give birth to 10 calves, and then 1 old cow and 25% of the males (2.55 males) are slaughtered. In this model, a total of 3.55 cattle are slaughtered each year, with each animal weighing 450 kg, and with a dressing-out proportion of 50%. This provides 799 kg/year of beef (3.55 × 450 × 50/100 = 798.75 kg/year). Since beef provides 2,500 Cal/kg, in one year beef yields provide 1,996,875 Cal/year (798.75 × 2,500 = 1,996,875 Cal/year).

The 10 cows that produce a calf each year also produce 500 liters of surplus milk available for human consumption, giving a total of 5,000 liters of surplus milk (10 × 500 = 5,000 liters). Milk has a calorific value of 580 Cal/liter, so the milk and any products produced from it provide 2,900,000 Cal/year (580 × 5000 = 2,900,000 Cal/year).

The archaeological results from early medieval Stalleen show that cattle contributed an MNI of 13 (41.9%) individuals, sheep/goat 9 (29%) individuals, and pig 9 (29%) individuals. These figures can be converted to meat percentages based on weights and dressing-out proportions of 450 kg and 50% for cattle, 30kg and 50% for sheep/goat, and 80 kg and 80% for pig. For cattle, this comes to 2,925 kg of beef [13 × (450 kg × 50/100)]; for sheep/goat this comes to 135 kg of mutton [9 × (30 × 50/100)]; for pigs this comes to 576 kg of pork [9 × (80 × 80/100)]. Calculation of the available meat weight results in a total of 3,636 kg (2,925 + 135 + 576). From this total, beef represents 80.5% of meat weight, mutton 3.7%, and pork 15.8%.

This 3,636 kg is the total meat weight for the entire archaeological assemblage and does not represent the livestock held at any one time; however, the meat proportions can then be scaled to the theoretical herd size being examined. In any one year cattle contributed 799 kg, which is equivalent to 80.5% by weight of the total meat available. So 100% of the meat is 799 × 100/80.5 = 992 kg/year. From this, figures for the contributions of mutton and pork can be calculated. Mutton contributes 3.7% of the meat weight. This is equivalent to 992 × 3.3/100 = 36.7 kg/year. Mutton is higher in calories than beef and has an average of 3,000 Cal/kg so this is equivalent to 3,000 × 36.7 = 110,138 Cal/year. Pork contributes

15.8% of the meat weight. This is equivalent to 992 × 15.8/100 = 156.8 kg/year. Pork is higher again in calories than beef or mutton and has an average of 3,400 Cal/kg so this is equivalent to 3,400 × 156.8 = 533,029 Cal/year.

The total calories available are therefore the total of the calories from dairy, beef, mutton, and pork. Total calories available = 2,900,000 + 1,996,875 + 110,138 + 533,029 = 5,540,042 Cal/year. As percentages of calories available, dairy equals 52.3% (= 2,900,000/5,540,042 × 100), beef represents 36.0% (= 1,996,875/5,540,042 × 100), mutton is 2.0% (= 110,138/5,540,042× 100), and pork equals 9.6% (= 533,029/5,540,042 × 100).

Early medieval Stalleen was a self-sufficient community that maximized its dairy produce and that needed to export some excess animals in taxes, rents, and other payments. In this case 52.3% of the animal-based calories in the diet are estimated to have come from milk products, which could, for example, be consumed as milk, cheese, and yogurt. In addition, each milking cow would have produced a weaned calf. Half of these would be female and could be reared for future dairy production and breeding, whereas the other half would be male, and while some of these would have been retained for traction or for breeding, most would have been reared to approaching full size and then slaughtered for meat.

Greencastle

By contrast, Greencastle had the highest proportion of beef (86.9%) and the lowest proportion of mutton (2.5%). The amount of pork eaten was a modest 10.6% by weight, equating to 13.8% in calories. This modest figure may seem surprising given the association between pigs and feasting; however, a castle was the center for a large manorial estate, with a high proportion of servants, artisans, and soldiers present, as well as the lordly classes. The elite diet can be identified through the presence of deer, hare and rabbit, birds, and fish, showing that there was a significant variety of foods available. In fact, although not included in the calculations given here, an estimated 6% of the meat eaten at Greencastle was venison, which would have been restricted to the upper levels of castle society (Beglane 2010). The age-at-slaughter data from Greencastle show that only prime beef of thirty-six to forty-eight months was present in the assemblage. These figures suggest that much of the beef may have been coming into the site as food renders and taxes. With no mature animals present, there is no direct evidence for herds of dairy cattle associated with the castle and hence no evidence for dairy-based foods. Nevertheless, although archaeologically invisible, some dairy foods are likely to have been consumed even if they were produced elsewhere and traded into the castle or given as renders and taxes. Overall, therefore, Greencastle was a consumer site, taking in prime beef produced in the wider landscape as well as consuming pork and a variety of high-status foods.

Bective Abbey

The Cistercians were among the strictest of the orders following the Rule of Saint Benedict. Up to the fourteenth century only the sick could eat meat, with the monks and lay visitors being limited to fish, dairy products, fowl, and vegetables (Greene 1992:147; de Venuto 2010; Ervynck 2004). The rule was gradually relaxed, and by the sixteenth century meat was commonly served. The assemblage discussed here dates to a later period, circa AD 1300–1537.

Performing similar calculations to those for the other sites shows that the animal-based calories in the diet would have been 72% dairy products and 28% meat, so despite the official stance, meat was evidently eaten at Bective. The age demographics show that cattle were slaughtered mainly as adults, indicating that the monks maintained dairy herds, with the majority of male animals exported elsewhere as livestock for sale (Beglane 2016:136). Possible local markets for these animals would have included the towns of Trim, 8 km to the southwest, and Navan, 9 km to the north. With mutton at 5.9% of the total meat, the monks ate a larger proportion of this meat than on all other sites. However, the mutton eaten by the monks tended to be from young, tender animals. This site also showed a diversity of diet, with birds and fish in evidence, and notably these diverse foods were those that were allowed under the Rule of Benedict.

The zooarchaeological evidence shows, therefore, that there was more emphasis on the consumption of dairy, fish, and birds at the abbey compared to the secular sites, but without strict adherence to the Rule of Saint Benedict. The practicalities of farming meant that eventually the older cattle had to be slaughtered, and the meat would have been too valuable to discard. As early as the twelfth century, Benedictine and Cistercian monks were allowed to eat *carnea*, which was processed meat, chopped meat, and offal, and after AD 1335, under certain circumstances, they were allowed to eat *carnis*, which was muscle meat and joints of meat (Beglane 2016:138). It can thus be suggested that when an old cow was killed, this tough, sinewy meat would have been chopped or minced into stews and broths. By doing this, the meat became *carnea*, and hence acceptable under the revised rule, but would have contributed fats, proteins, and minerals to the diet (Beglane 2016:139).

The relatively high proportion of pork (25.2% of meat, 8.7% of calories) at Bective Abbey is worthy of note, since this is a meat often associated with feasting. However, smoked or salted bacon would have been classified as *carnea* and so, as with processed beef, would have been considered an acceptable food. Today, bacon is generally considered the most palatable meat for preserving, and this flavor, coupled with its acceptable status as *carnea*, would have made it a desirable meat for the monks.

DISCUSSION

The data presented here have shown a diversity of diet at different settlement types in medieval Ireland depending on the social position of the inhabitants and the time at which they lived. These results contrast with the traditional view of the Irish diet of the past, which has been heavily influenced by Lucas (1960). He argued that the diet throughout the period "before the potato" was predominantly dairy products and grain, with pork being the most important meat, and as such he presented an oversimplified view of a complex situation.

The first case study is the early medieval self-sufficient subsistence site of Stalleen. This chronological period is often considered to be characterized by a focus on cattle rearing and on dairying (O'Sullivan et al. 2014:209). By contrast, agriculture during the later medieval period in this eastern region of the country is often considered, rightly or wrongly, to have been more diverse than during the early medieval period (Down 1987:476–482).

Interestingly, however, of the three case studies, early medieval Stalleen had lower levels of cattle as a percentage of MNI than Greencastle and lower dairy production than Bective Abbey. This example clearly demonstrates that dairying and beef production go hand in hand, with milk providing 57% of the cattle-based calories and beef 43%, but this is reduced to 52% of total calories when the consumption of pork and mutton are taken into consideration.

Lucas (1960) was much taken with the early postmedieval writings of Moryson ([1617] 1908), who stated that the Irish ate mostly dairy products and would not kill a cow, and interpreted this to mean that little beef was consumed. Looking more closely at the source, it is clear that it talks only about the Irish not slaughtering cows, but does not discuss the slaughter of the otherwise-superfluous males that would have made up half of all calves born. The cattle herds would have contained females of all ages plus juvenile males up to about three or four years old, most of which would then have been either eaten on a self-sufficient site such as early medieval Stalleen, or moved elsewhere for trade or consumption as demonstrated at Bective and Greencastle respectively.

The high-status Anglo-Norman later medieval castle of Greencastle was a consumer site, taking in prime meat produced in the wider landscape. Unfortunately it is not possible to determine the dairy element in the Greencastle diet, which was highest in terms of the proportion of beef to pork and mutton, and where the age, and hence quality of that meat, was optimum for consumption rather than being older, tougher animals. This finding demonstrates the importance of not only considering the species of meat served but also its likely quality in any discussion on the relative status of the diet.

The monks at Bective Abbey had the lowest proportion of calories from beef in their diet (17.5%), with the highest proportion of pork meat, and they also had small amounts of good-quality mutton; overall, however, their diet was dominated by dairy products, which made up an estimated 72% of their animal-based calories. The inhabitants of Bective, aiming to avoid joints of meat, did, however, have access to *carnea*, processed meat from the old dairy cattle, oxen, bulls, and sheep. Meat becomes tougher with age and more difficult to digest, so fewer of the nutrients can be extracted from it, but it also becomes higher in fat content, so the stews and broths made from these older animals would have been nutritious (Bouton et al. 1978; Swatland 1995:233–237). Notably, the presence of these older cattle in the assemblage and the lack of prime-aged animals clearly demonstrate that it is not possible to produce milk products without also producing meat that must then be either consumed, given away, or traded.

A discussion of status as it is reflected in food must also consider those foods consumed less often. The zooarchaeological evidence shows the diversity of wild mammals, birds, fish, and mollusks at Bective Abbey and at Greencastle, with venison, hare, and rabbit restricted to these two sites and absent from Stalleen. The presence of marine foods at Bective Abbey, some 35 km inland, is particularly significant, demonstrating the importance to the monks of these minor foods, which would have provided variety in the diet. Furthermore, restrictions on access to venison mean that the inclusion of poultry, as well as wild and marine foods, in the Bective and Greencastle assemblages act as direct indicators for high status (Beglane 2015a, 2015b).

Lucas (1960:13) argued on the basis of literary references that "by far the most important kind of flesh meat eaten in ancient, medieval, and later times seems to have been pork or bacon." Based on the evidence presented here, this was certainly not true; beef was the most important meat, both in terms of actual quantity and in terms of calories. This raises the question of why texts such as the *Vision of MacConglinne* focus on pork and bacon? And why was Lucas so badly misled in terms of the "most important" meat? There are three likely reasons for this: First, pork was a meat for holidays and for feasting. This means it had very positive associations and was much more likely to be recorded in poems, songs, and sagas than everyday foods. Second, as the data show, pigs were almost always slaughtered at the optimum age to maximize both quality and quantity, whereas other meats could be served well past their prime, which affected the ways in which they were cooked and presented. Finally, the relatively high fat content of pork would have made it a valuable and desirable food in the diet.

CONCLUSIONS

While traditional scholarship has seen the Irish diet as essentially uniform and unchanging, the zooarchaeological evidence shows that diet could vary greatly depending on the circumstances. The inhabitants of early medieval Stalleen had a self-sufficient diet, with a balance between meat and dairy products and with both older and prime animals represented in the meat. The other two sites could be considered "special cases." The monks of Bective Abbey had a diet low in mammal meat and high in dairy products, and their beef consisted of older animals, probably served in stews. However, pork was served relatively frequently, and both this and mutton were generally of good quality. Coupled with access to a diverse range of wild foods and poultry, this was a high-status diet. The castle site at Greencastle also had high diversity, with good-quality beef, pork, and mutton and access to a high-status range of wild foods and birds.

This chapter has demonstrated the range of approaches to diet that could occur within a relatively small geographical area. It has highlighted the importance of such factors as social status, religious proscription, and economics in determining access to dairy and to meat products and in determining the quantity, species, and quality of the meat available. Despite these differences, it is clear that beef was the most significant source of meat in medieval Ireland and that pork was less significant than has traditionally been assumed. Furthermore, while the documentary and literary sources stress the high levels of dairy consumption associated with early medieval settlements or with Gaelic settlements of the later medieval period, this study has shown that even in the Anglo-Norman and English-held areas of the east of Ireland, dairy could be central to the diet of particular communities.

Acknowledgments. I would like to thank Mandy Stephens (RIP) and Finola O'Carroll, both then of CRDS; Geraldine Stout of the National Monuments Service; and Ruairí Ó Baoill of Queens University Belfast, Centre for Archaeological Fieldwork for allowing me to use data from their excavations in this essay. Thank you to the reviewer, who provided very helpful comments and suggestions that have improved the chapter. I also acknowledge the generous financial assistance of the Centre for Environmental Research, Innovation and Sustainability, Atlantic Technological University, which has enabled me to conduct this research.

WORKS CITED

Beglane, Fiona. 2007. "Report on Faunal Material from Greencastle, Co. Down, 057:003, Licence No. AE/01/13." Unpublished report for Centre for Archaeological Fieldwork, Queens University.

Beglane, Fiona. 2009. "Meat and Craft in Medieval and Post-medieval Trim." In *Uncovering Medieval Trim: Archaeological Excavations in and around Trim, Co. Meath*, edited by Michael Potterton and Matthew Seaver, 346–370. Dublin: Four Courts Press.

Beglane, Fiona. 2010. "Deer and Identity in Medieval Ireland." In *Viavias 3. Animals as Material Culture in the Middle Ages: Bestial Mirrors: Using Animals to Construct Human Identities in Medieval Europe*, edited by Aleksander Pluskowski, Gunther Karl Kunst,

Matthias Kucera, Manfred Bietak, and Irmgard Hein, 77–84. Vienna: Vienna Institute of Archaeological Science.

Beglane, Fiona. 2015a. *Anglo-Norman Parks in Medieval Ireland*. Dublin: Four Courts Press.

Beglane, Fiona. 2015b. "The Social Significance of Game in the Diet of Later Medieval Ireland." *Proceedings of the Royal Irish Academy* 115C: 167–196.

Beglane, Fiona. 2016. "The Faunal Remains." In *The Bective Abbey Project: Archaeological Excavations 2009–12*, edited by Geraldine Stout and Matthew Stout, 106–153. Dublin: Wordwell.

Beglane, Fiona. 2022. "Mammalian Faunal Remains from Stalleen, Co. Meath." In *Excavation of a Multi-Period Site at Stalleen, Co. Meath, by Mandy Stephens: Research in the Brú na Bóinne World Heritage Site*, edited by Geraldine Stout and Matthew Stout, 74–106. Julianstown, Ireland: Chapel Press.

Bouton, P. E., A. L. Ford, P. V. Harris, W. R. Shorthose, D. Ratcliff, and J. H. Morgan. 1978. "Influence of Animal Age on the Tenderness of Beef: Muscle Differences." *Meat Science* 2 (4): 301–311.

Casebolt, David George. 1984. "Lactation Curves and Milk Production in Beef Cattle with Varying Degrees of Crossbred Influence." MSc thesis, Montana State University, Bozeman.

Central Statistics Office. 2012. *Census of Agriculture 2010: Preliminary Results*. Dublin: Stationery Office.

Clark, Gregory. 1991. "Labour Productivity in English Agriculture, 1300–1860." In *Land, Labour and Livestock: Historical Studies in European Agricultural Productivity*, edited by Bruce M.S. Campbell and Mark Overton, 211–235. Manchester, UK: Manchester University Press.

Clarkson, Leslie, and Margaret Crawford. 2001. *Feast and Famine: Food and Nutrition in Ireland 1500–1920*. Oxford: Oxford University Press.

Cosgrove, Art, ed. 1987. *A New History of Ireland: II: Medieval Ireland 1169–1534*. Oxford: Oxford University Press.

Dahl, Gudrun, and Anders Hjort. 1976. *Having Herds: Pastoral Herd Growth and Household Economy*. Stockholm: University of Stockholm.

Davis, Simon J.M. 1992. *A Rapid Method for Recording Information about Mammal Bones from Archaeological Sites*. London: Ancient Monuments Laboratory Report 19/92.

de Leeuw, P. N., Paterson P. Semenye, C. P. Peacock, and Barbara E. Grandin. 1994. "Chapter 7: Productivity of Cattle and Smallstock." In *Maasai Herding: An Analysis of the Livestock Production System of Maasai Pastoralists in Eastern Kajiado District, Kenya*, edited by S. Bekure, P. N. de Leeuw, B. E. Grandin, and P. J. H. Neate, 83–102. Addis Ababa: International Livestock Centre for Africa.

de Venuto, Giovanni. 2010. "To Eat and to Be in Medieval Southern Italy: The Zooarchaeological Contribution from Religious, Rural and Fortified Sites." In *Viavias 3. Animals as Material Culture in the Middle Ages: Bestial Mirrors: Using Animals to Construct*

Identity in Medieval Europe, edited by Aleksander Pluskowski, Gunther Karl Kunst, Matthias Kucera, Manfred Bietak, and Irmgard Hein, 55–61. Vienna: Vienna Institute of Archaeological Science.

Dept of Animal Science. 1995–2015. *Breeds of Livestock: Cattle*. Stillwater, OK: Department of Animal Sciences, Oklahoma State University. www.ansi.okstate.edu/breeds/cattle/.

Down, Kevin. 1987. "Colonial Society and Economy." In *A New History of Ireland*. Vol. 2, *Medieval Ireland 1169–1534*, edited by A. Cosgrove, 439–491. Oxford: Oxford University Press.

Ervynck, Anton. 2004. "*Orant, Pugnant, Laborant*. The Diet of the Three Orders in the Feudal Society of Medieval North-Western Europe." In *Behaviour behind Bones: The Zooarchaeology of Ritual, Religion, Status and Identity*, edited by Jones O'Day, Wim Van Neer, and Anton Ervynck, 215–223. Oxford: Oxbow Books.

Foley, John 1993. "The Irish Dairy Industry: A Historical Perspective." *Journal of the Society of Dairy Technology* 46 (4):124–138.

Greene, J. Patrick. 1992. *Medieval Monasteries*. London: Continuum.

Kelly, Fergus. 1997. *Early Irish Farming: A Study Based Mainly on the Law-Texts of the 7th and 8th Centuries AD*. Dublin: Early Irish Law Series Volume IV.

Kuechelmann, Hans Christian. 2012. "Noble Meals Instead of Abstinence? A Faunal Assemblage from the Dominican Monastery of Norden, Northern Germany." In *Proceedings of the General Session of the 11th International Council for Archaeozoology Conference*, edited by Christine Lefèvre, 87–97. Oxford: BAR International Series 2354.

Lucas, Anthony T. 1960. "Irish Food before the Potato." *Gwerin* 3 (2): 8–43.

Mac Con Iomaire, Máirtín. 2011. "Irish Corned Beef: A Culinary History." *Journal of Culinary Science and Technology* 9 (1): 27–43.

MacNeill, Eoin. 1921–1924. "Ancient Irish Law. The Law of Status or Franchise." *Proceedings of the Royal Irish Academy* 36: 265–316.

McCormick, Finbar. 1997. "Farming and Food in Medieval Lecale." In *Down: History and Society*, edited by L. Proudfoot and W. Nolan, 33–46. Dublin: Geography Publications.

McCormick, Finbar. 2006. "Animal Bone." In *Anatomy of an Iron Age Roundhouse: The Cnip Wheelhouse Excavations, Lewis*, edited by Ian Armit, 161–172. Edinburgh: Society of Antiquaries of Scotland.

McCormick, Finbar, and Emily Murray. 2007. *Knowth and the Zooarchaeology of Early Christian Ireland, Excavations at Knowth*. Dublin: Royal Irish Academy.

Milner, Jos M., Steve D. Albon, Andrew W. Illius, Josephine M. Pemberton, and Tim H. Clutton-Brock. 1999. "Repeated Selection of Morphometric Traits in the Soay Sheep on St Kilda." *Journal of Animal Ecology* 68: 472–488.

Moryson, Fynes. (1617) 1908. *An Itinerary*. Vol. 4. Glasgow: James MacLehose and Sons.

Nicholls, Kenneth W. 1987. "Gaelic Society and Economy in the High Middle Ages." In *A New History of Ireland*. Vol. 2, *Medieval Ireland, 1169–1534*, edited by A. Cosgrove, 397–438. Oxford: Clarendon Press.

Ó Baoill, Ruairí. 2007. "Excavations at Greencastle, County Down 057:003 AE/01/13." Unpublished data structure report for DOENI.

Ó Corráin, Donnchadh. 2005. "Ireland c.800: Aspects of Society." In *Early Medieval Ireland*, edited by Dáibhí O'Crónin, 549–608. London: Longman.

Ó Crónin, Dáibhí, ed. 2005. *A New History of Ireland*. Vol. 1, *Prehistoric and Early Ireland*. Oxford: Oxford University Press.

O'Sullivan, Aidan, Finbar McCormick, Thomas Kerr, and Lorcan Harney. 2014. *Early Medieval Ireland AD 400–1100: The Evidence from Archaeological Excavations*. Dublin: Royal Irish Academy.

Peel, Derrell S., Rachel J. Johnson, and Kenneth H. Mathews. 2010. "Cow-Calf Beef Production in Mexico: A Report from the Economic Research Service." Washington, DC: United States Department of Agriculture.

Pluskowski, Aleksander. 2007. "Who Ruled the Forests? An Interdisciplinary Approach towards Medieval Hunting Landscapes." In *Fauna and Flora in the Middle Ages*, edited by Sieglinde Hartman, 291–323. Frankfurt: Peter Lang.

Raines, Christopher R. n.d. *The Butcher Kept Your Meat?* University Park: Pennsylvania State University.

Reitz, Elizabeth J., and Elizabeth S. Wing. 1999. *Zooarchaeology*. Cambridge: Cambridge University Press.

Sexton, Regina. 1998. *A Little History of Irish Food*. Dublin: Gill and Macmillan.

Silver, Ian A. 1963. "The Ageing of Domestic Animals." In *Science in Archaeology*, edited by Don Brothwell and Eric Higgs, 250–268. London: Thames and Hudson.

Spenser, Edmund. 1596. *A View of the Present State of Ireland*. Accessed October 16, 2016. http://www.ucc.ie/celt/.

Stout, Geraldine, and Matthew Stout. 2022. *Excavation of a Multi-Period Site at Stalleen, Co. Meath, by Mandy Stephens: Research in the Brú na Bóinne World Heritage Site*. Julianstown, Ireland: Chapel Press.

Stout, Geraldine, and Matthew Stout. 2016. *The Bective Abbey Project: Archaeological Excavations 2009–12*. Dublin: Wordwell.

Swatland, H. J. 1995. *On-Line Evaluation of Meat*. Lancaster, PA: Technomic Publishing.

Sweetman, Henry Savage. 1875–1886. *Calendar of Documents Relating To Ireland, 1171–1307*. 5 vols. London: Longman.

Thomson, Mike. 2005. "Medieval Dairying in England: Prescription, Practice and Performance." In *The Zooarchaeology of Fats, Oils, Milk and Dairying*, edited by Jacqui Mulville and Alan Outram, 132–141. Oxford: Oxbow Books.

Trow-Smith, Robert. [1957] 2006. *History of British Livestock Husbandry, to 1700*. Abingdon, UK: Routledge.

5

Feeding the Great Settlement

Preliminary Notes on the Shang Animal Economy

RODERICK CAMPBELL

A basic set of questions confronting anyone interested in understanding an early complex polity concerns the polity's fundamental economic organization. How did the ancient city feed itself? Upon what base were its pyramids (real or figurative) built? Through what mechanisms were goods and services transacted such that workers were provisioned, elites privileged, and gods exulted? And yet, the question of provisioning is a more complex set of issues than, perhaps, it seems at first. On the one hand, and according to the hallowed traditions of zooarchaeology, the issue could be approached from the perspective of subsistence—the material base, the bare necessities of life—with the caveat that this is probably only an accurate representation of life in a concentration camp or among shipwrecked survivors. At best, a subsistence perspective frames a more complex set of questions; it provides a loose set of parameters within which specific social economies manifest their myriad ways of organizing human lives.

Approached from the other end of things, one might begin with the cultural logic of the complex society in question—its own etiologies of just distribution and world order—ideas as well as institutions that entangle people and things and

https://doi.org/10.5876/9781646422562.c005

generate the imaginary coherences of human collectives. If the first approach is quantitative and yields underspecified results, the second is necessarily qualitative and potentially problematically open-ended. While both qualitative and quantitative approaches have their merits, in combination they become more effective than either on their own—each potentially informing interpretations of the other.

Of the many aspects of food economy and social complexity that could be studied, the editors of this volume have chosen, as a means of imposing a certain degree of coherence on this collection of essays, the linked themes of centralization and bureaucratic control, inequality and the dynamics of production, and distribution and consumption. Framing these themes as a series of problems, then, they might be

1. How does the political economy of food actually work in the complex polity in question?
2. What was the relationship between polity organization, administration, and its (food) economy?
3. How do different social roles in the production, distribution, and consumption of food relate to wider sociopolitical distinctions or inequalities?

For the Great Settlement Shang (ca. 1250–1050 BC) and its wider, north China political networks, the answers to these questions can only be partial and tentative. Nevertheless, by estimating some of the fundamental quantitative parameters on the one hand, and sketching out the nature of the polity and its relevant institutions, on the other, an analytical framework can be constructed on which to hang what little evidence we currently possess concerning Shang provisioning.

BACKGROUND: THE SHANG POLITY

First of all, let us draw the outlines of the Shang polity. The Anyang period (1250–1050 BC) Shang kingdom was centered on the megacenter contemporaneously known as the Great Settlement Shang and located near the modern city of Anyang. This site, nearly continuously excavated since its discovery in 1928, has been divided into four phases of nearly equal length, collectively dating from circa 1250–1050 BC. Palatial rammed-earth courtyard structures, royal tombs, caches of tens of thousands of inscriptions (oracle-bones), and thousands of sacrificial deposits (many of them human) were discovered in the excavations of the 1920s and 1930s (Chang 1990). Since then, residential, mortuary, and industrial areas have been excavated, and the Great Settlement is now understood to be 3,000 ha in extent. It sat at the center of a web of alliances, subordinate polities, and royal lands stretching from the Yellow Sea in the east to Shaanxi in the west and from Beijing to the Yangzi in the south (Campbell 2014; ZSKY 2003) (figure 5.1). The degree to and means by which the more distant parts of this vast area

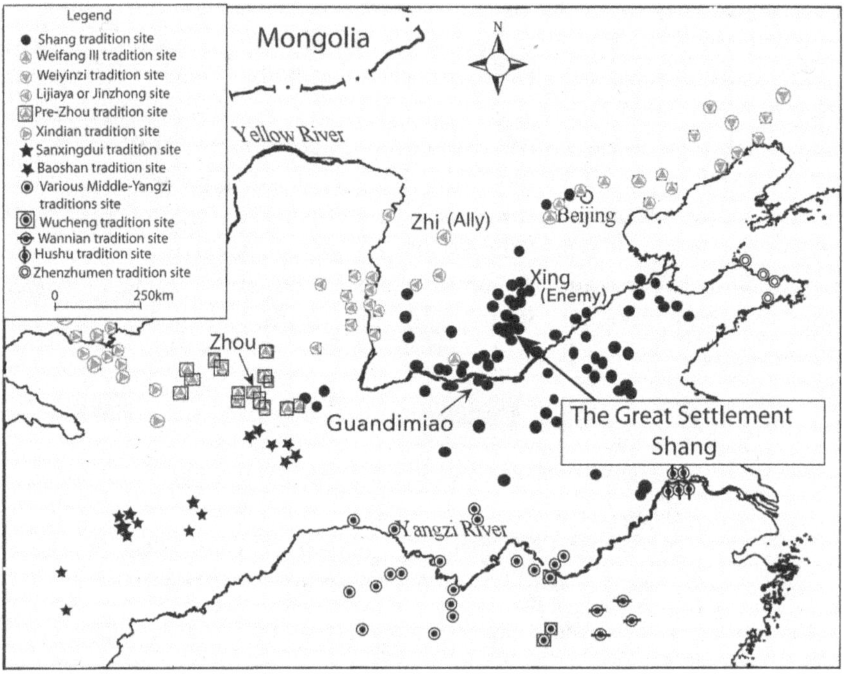

Figure 5.1. *Map showing the distribution of Anyang period material culture in North China.*

were integrated into the Shang polity remain matters of debate (Campbell 2009, 2018; Keightley 1983; Shaughnessy 1989), but in general terms the political networks for which the Great Settlement was the central hub can be divided into three types: the direct, intensive, royally administered flows of things; the links and nodes of indirectly controlled subordinate polities; and the web of independent allies (Campbell 2009, 2018).

Broadly speaking, and though there is continuing debate about the actual location of most Shang places, power and influence generally decline with distance, and so too the directly administered royal demesne is usually understood to cover most of northern Henan Province adjacent to Anyang, with subordinate *hou*-lords scattered beyond that, and independent *bo*-rulers generally still further afield (Campbell 2009, 2018; Chang 1980; Keightley 1983). The nature of the polity was also dynamic, and there is significant evidence of a fundamental reorganization roughly halfway through the Anyang period (phases III–IV ca. 1150–1050 BC). This reorganization can be characterized as a shift from an expansive kingdom based on alliance, and indirect control but frequent direct military intervention, to a more compact polity more tightly organized and directly administered (Campbell 2012, 2018; Keightley 1983). During this time, the Great Settlement Shang grew from a 1000 ha to a 3000 ha site, even as its population became increasingly homogeneous and its industries dramatically increased in scale (Campbell 2014; Campbell et al. 2011; Li 2003; Li Zhipeng et al. 2011; Tang Jigen and Jing Zhicun 2009).

At the level of the settlement itself and from the perspective of the social nature of Shang politics, north China in this period can be best understood as a vast network of lineage settlements—with no lexical distinction between the largest and the smallest other than the adjective "large/great"—and this despite a difference in size of three orders of magnitude between the largest and smallest settlements. Anyang itself was a collection of kin-based settlements surrounding the palace-temples, sacrificial grounds, and monumental tombs of the lineage leader of lineage leaders—the Shang king—with whom the lesser lineages were linked through real or fictitious kinship (Campbell 2018; Chang 1980; Keightley 2000; Zhu 1991). One additional factor that separated the capital supercluster from ordinary settlements—aside from population and political primacy—was the presence of large-scale workshops such as those for bronze and bone, which were able to fashion well-made things but also mass-produce for broad distribution (Campbell et al. 2011; Hou et al. 2018).

Looked at from the perspective of site size, a remarkable pattern emerges: Anyang is roughly a hundred times larger than the next-largest site known for its time, forming the apogee of a long tradition of strongly primate megacenters in the Central Plains and surrounding regions (Campbell 2014) (figure 5.2). Taken together, these things suggest that Shang kings were more concerned with the control of people than lands—especially skilled people. This fact is also reflected in the movable nature of Early Chinese polities, a corollary of the fact that the core of the polity was the ruling lineage and not the settlement or its lands. All of these facts—the massive concentration of population in the center, the combination of direct and indirect rule, and the changing nature of the polity and volatile geopolitical context, as well as the concentrated production of not only elite goods but also mass-produced ones—are factors that must be reckoned with in trying to reconstruct the Shang economic system and its management.

Beginning with Anyang's prodigious size—an obvious question when confronted with such a remarkable concentration of people and industry is, How was it provisioned? Yet before that question can be tackled, an even more basic problem must be resolved: How large was Anyang's population? Published estimates range from 300,000 to 30,000 people (Flad 2018; Song 1994) but do not take into account current understandings of the site. Ancient cities are generally estimated to have between 100 and 600 people per hectare—similar to North American suburban population densities at the low end of the scale (Modelski 2003). Simply multiplying the low estimate by 3,000 ha yields a population of 300,000. However, not all of parts of Anyang were residential. Using the site director's (Tang Jigen, personal communication, February 2015) estimate that

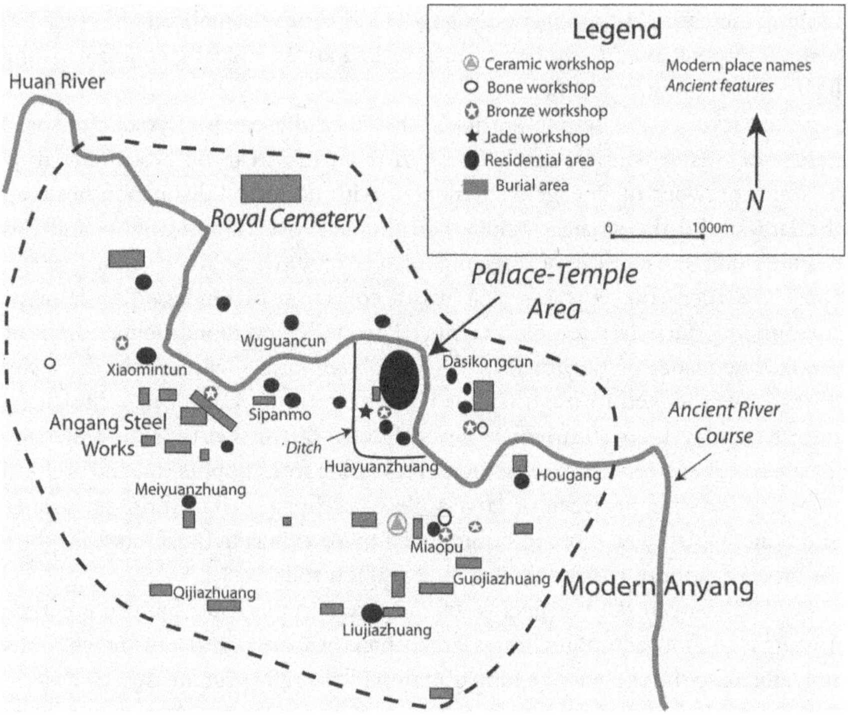

Figure 5.2. *Plan map of the site of Anyang.*

one-fourth of the site was residential and the lowest estimate for premodern urban population density multiplied over Anyang's 3000 ha, we would arrive at a minimum estimate of $(3000/4) \times 100 = 75{,}000$ people at its height (phases III–IV). Using this global method then, Anyang's peak population should be somewhere between 75,000 and 300,000.

Another, more direct method of estimating population would be to examine excavated areas and extrapolate from the number of houses and tombs discovered per ha. Unfortunately, there are few loci at Anyang where large exposures have been excavated and residential preservation has been good. One important exception is the locus of Xiaomintun (Yinxu Xiaomintun Team 2007), where a 6 ha area was excavated between 2001 and 2004. Currently, this locus is known to us from only a series of preliminary reports. Ninety residences and 1,200 tombs were discovered and reported in this area—the former belonging to phases I and II of the site whereas the tombs represented phases I–IV. The site map shows an area of surface structures that were not reported in the preliminary reports and so are not included in the total of ninety residences. Likewise, we do not currently possess full statistics on each of the houses that were reported, so the following calculations can only be taken as a minimum estimate. Assuming the houses were used for only one phase, we have 45 houses per phase, or (45/6) = 7.5 households per ha. These semisubterranean houses range from single room, 4–5 m^2 structures, to five-room structures 25 m^2 in surface area, with three-room structures (12–15 m^2) appearing to be the most common. Using the conservative assumption that each of these structures housed only one nuclear family, the minimum population density would be 37.5/ha.

From the mortuary side of things, assuming that four phases represent ten generations (roughly corroborated with the nine generations of kings that ruled at Anyang), there are 120 tombs per generation, or 20 tombs per hectare per generation. Assuming the coexistence of two generations at any one time (half of the previous plus half of the next) would yield a live person per hectare of 40. This, however, assumes that all of the dead were buried in the cemetery—an assumption we know to be incorrect. On the other hand, the cemetery may have served more than just the 6 ha area excavated. Using the residential number and multiplying over the 3,000 ha of Anyang would yield a minimum population of 112,500, while using the mortuary extrapolation would yield a population of 120,000 at Anyang's apogee.

One of the problems with using a single locus of a larger site to estimate population is that it is unclear what sort of sample it is. While neither the density of tombs nor residences at Xiaomintun appear to be peculiar for excavation loci at Anyang, it is possible that the 6 ha excavated at Xiaotun are not representative of the site as a whole. Another approach might be to examine a more delimited site. Guandimiao is a contemporaneous Shang village site that was nearly completely excavated (Henan Sheng Wenwu Kaogu Yanjiusuo 2008, 2009; Li et al. 2018). With a maximum population density of 50 people per hectare (Li et al. 2018), if Guandimiao could be used as a template for a Shang settlement, extrapolating over Anyang's 3,000 ha would yield a population estimate of 150,000 people.

Taking the various estimates together, a ballpark estimate of Anyang's maximum population should fall between 100,000 and 150,000 people. If this is correct, it would make the Great Settlement Shang one of, if not the, largest concentrations of population in the world in its time. This scale naturally creates a unique set of problems for provisioning when compared to smaller centers.

PROVISIONING THE "GREAT SETTLEMENT SHANG"

A full understanding of the Great Settlement's provisioning should involve everything from metal to meat and from fabric to fuel—especially if provisioning is understood to mean supplying with vital resources and ancient centers are understood to be more than a collection of human bodies. Thus, the provisioning of the capital's bronze foundries with the metals, molds, and charcoal that enabled the production of the ritual bronzes and weapons that were crucial mediators in the production of Shang civilization's order could be seen as just as fundamental to the functioning of the Great Settlement Shang as the meat and grain that fed its population. Nor were meat and grain simply physical sustenance; rather, they played roles as important as bronze in the maintenance of status and the mediation of ontological uncertainty—for not only the living but also the dead needed feeding, and not all foods were equal in significance (Campbell 2018). The royal ancestors, for instance, were offered humans as well as the more usual cattle, sheep, pig, dog, grain, and alcohol upon which the living, and perhaps the lesser dead, feasted. These concerns are clearly reflected in the records of royal divinations. For example:

> Dinghai day cracked, (diviner) Ke tested (the following charge): next Yiyou day perform an exorcism . . . Great Ding, Great Jia, Grandfather Yi, (using) one hundred (jars?) of millet beer, one hundred qiang-slaves, *mao*-cleave one hundred [specially reared sheep]. H 301
>
> Guihai day cracked, (unrecorded diviner) tested (the following charge): On Dinghai the King should offer one hundred (jars?) of millet beer, one hundred sheep, one hundred cattle. H32044+H32686

In these oracle-bone inscriptions, divinations are made on behalf of the king concerning the auspiciousness of particular offerings to the ancestors. The list of offerings for this major apotropaic ritual suggests a feast, while the fact that humans and other animal offerings were interchangeable in turn implies that humans were food for the ancestors.

Both inscriptions and sacrificial contexts at Anyang suggest that lesser elites (even Shang princes) offered less-prestigious offerings (in smaller amounts) to their ancestors (Schwartz 2013), a ranking that ran from humans and cattle down to chickens basically organized according to size (and presumably expense) of the animal. On the other hand, given the evidence that most of the nonhuman sacrificial offerings were consumed by the living, the midden deposits of residential areas cannot be considered separately from the sacrificial economy of the Great Settlement Shang (Li and Campbell 2019).

Interestingly, although pigs dominate Central Plains zooarchaeological assemblages in general, just as they did for thousands of years before the Shang, cattle (*Bos taurus*) became more and more common at Anyang, reaching over 30% of the mammalian assemblage by number of identifiable specimens (NISP) at the nonelite Xiaomintun locus by phase III (ca. 1150–1100 BCE) and surpassing pig as a meat source (Li 2009). That even nonelite areas of Anyang were consuming more beef than pork suggests some connection with royal or other elite sacrifice. Indeed, there is almost certainly a correlation between the size of the animal (and thus the need to share its meat) and feasting, which in the Shang context are productive of both ancestral blessings and social obligation.

In the royal oracle-bone divinatory inscriptions, cattle and human captive sacrificial resources were the most commonly divined "economic" topics (Campbell 2018), suggesting their signal importance to the king (who was also sacrificer-in-chief). The daily royal sacrifice of cattle, occasionally in the hundreds, would have meant considerable provisioning demands. When one considers that other members of the royal lineage and other lineages all had their own ancestral sacrifices, the scale becomes truly staggering.

Whether extrapolating the Xiaomintun cattle minimum number of individuals (MNI) of 324 (or 0.0120/m^2) across Anyang (360,000) or multiplying the extrapolated Tiesanlu bone workshop cattle MNI (113,367) by the three or four known major bone workshops at Anyang (300,000–400,000), the numbers of cattle consumed at Anyang are staggering. This is especially true if one considers that the workshop and Xiaomintun assemblages do not show a complementary element distribution, meaning that the bone workshop raw materials likely did not derive from loci such as Xiaomintun, and suggesting that the total quantity of cattle consumed at Anyang should be higher than either estimate alone. Conservative estimates of the total number of cattle sacrificed at Anyang, whether in royal or nonroyal lineage ritual, also amount to about 500,000 head of cattle over 200 years, suggesting that the prodigious consumption of cattle at the Great Settlement may have been mostly in the context of sacrificial feasting (Campbell 2018). While the same is not necessarily true for pigs or sheep (albeit the inscriptional evidence is nearly all for royal sacrifice), making the same kind of extrapolation for the Xiaomintun MNI across Anyang yields equally large numbers, including 710,000 pigs and 230,000 sheep (Campbell 2018).

ANIMAL PROVISIONING

Where did all these animals come from? Harvest profiles from Anyang not only confirm a primary products model for all three taxa, but the total absence of the youngest age stage suggests that the vast majority of sheep and cattle were not likely raised locally (Li 2009; Li et al. 2014). The harvest profiles for pigs at the Anyang loci of Xiaomintun and Baijiazhuang, on the other hand, do include all age classes for the first year, but these total no more than 10%, while nearly 50% of the pigs were harvested between a year and a half and two years of age—suggesting a predominantly market model and mostly external provisioning (Li 2009).

And yet, even if the majority of the large animals consumed at Anyang were not raised there (or at least not raised at the loci that have been analyzed), it does not mean that they came from the same places or arrived through the same provisioning networks. Pigs are much less likely to have come from distant locales, and those not raised in Anyang would likely have been raised by the surrounding agricultural communities that supplied the Great Settlement Shang with its grain. Cattle and sheep, on the other hand, came from a variety of places near and far. The oracle-bone inscriptions reflect this situation in a number of ways. Not only is there evidence for long distance tribute of cattle and captives from erstwhile enemy polities, but also for more regular flows of resources. Cattle and sheep, but not pigs, are "taken" (*qu*), "requested" (*qi*), and even "levied/raised" (*deng, gong*) like other mobile resources such as soldiers or workers (see Campbell 2018; Keightley 2012), as can be seen in the following Shang oracle-bone inscriptions:

> Cracked on Guihai day, (unnamed diviner) tested (the following charge): the cattle that the Wei Fang *(Shang enemies)* brought should be offered up (in sacrifice) on the coming Jiashen day. H32896
>
> Cracked on Wuwu day, Bin tested (the following charge): call upon (someone contextually understood) to take cattle, one hundred, and bring them. The King (then) read the cracks and said, "auspicious." "He will bring them, they should arrive." H93.
>
> Cracked on Jiawu day, Bin tested (the following charge): Command Zhou to request cattle, many . . . H4884
>
> Tested: levy cattle, one hundred. H9041
>
> . . . levy sheep, three hundred. H8959

While it should be kept in mind that divinatory inscriptions are, by their nature, a poor source for understanding routine flows of resources, one can still catch glimpses of at least a part of the system of royal resource acquisition. Conspicuously, however, all of the above inscriptions date to Anyang's first phases—when the Great Settlement was smaller (1000–2000 ha) and the Shang polity was characterized by an expansive but looser, more ad hoc governing apparatus. Nevertheless, if even in the early days of the Great Settlement the kings took, requested, or levied livestock from a variety of places (e.g., "the East," "the colonies," etc.), it is likely that as the provisioning requirements of the mega-center rose and its administration became more systematized, what were once sporadic extractions also became routinized. Indeed, both the Tiesanlu bone workshop (Campbell et al. 2011) and Xiaomintun residential (Li 2009) zooarchaeological assemblages show a massive increase in quantity between phase II and phase III correlating with the reorganization of the polity and the increasing size of Anyang (Campbell 2012, 2018; Keightley 1983). Given the range of places mentioned in the oracle-bones as sources of sheep and cattle, it is likely that the Great Settlement's enormous consumption (especially in its last two phases) was provisioned from a network of producers stretching across much of north China.

While more zooarchaeological (and especially isotopic) work at outlying Anyang period sites will enable a clearer understanding of the cattle network and its distribution, we can already make some generalizations. First of all, given the agricultural demands of such a large site, it is unlikely that there was much pastureland available in the area immediately adjacent to Anyang (though mixed agriculture with some cattle raising is possible). Even optimistically assuming maximally efficient pre-green-revolution agricultural outputs, Anyang's population would need at least 0.5 ha/person of land under cultivation (Bintliff 2002), and likely much more. Multiplied by the low estimate of 100,000 population at its apogee, Anyang would need at least 50,000 ha of farmland. Even assuming that some farming occurred between the lineage settlements at the Great Settlement and in the 5 km radius ($r = 8$ km, area $\doteq 200$ km^2 – 30 km^2 (Anyang's area) = 170 km^2 = 17,000 ha) that farmers might reasonably be expected to walk to fields (Bintliff 2002), at least 60% of the food consumed at Shang Anyang would have had to have come from somewhere else (50,000 ha – 17,000 ha = 33,000 ha = 60%).

Given that Shang sites are nearly always located near waterways, the remaining 330 km^2 of farmland should probably be imagined as a 5 × 65 km strip of river valley. Considering that probably no more than one-third of local agricultural production could be sustainably taken in taxes (in fact, agricultural taxes never reached these levels in imperial China), the total would be more like (minimally) 210 km of river valleys and likely much more. When one considers the amount of wood that would be required for Anyang's bronze and ceramic workshops, construction materials, and combustibles for heating (Campbell 2013), in addition to the substantial variety of other resources, the inescapable impression is a vortex of provisioning needs and a population and industrial center likely at the very limits of what could be sustained with contemporaneous transportation technology of dirt roads, oxcarts, and riverboats. Storage facilities, though not unambiguously archaeologically identified at present, are attested in the oracle-bone inscriptions and would surely have been necessary.

At this point it seems apropos to ask what system supplied the Great Settlement Shang with its vast resource needs. Although it is commonplace in the Western literature on ancient China to claim that the Shang lacked markets and had a relatively primitive economy (Chang 1989; Falkenhausen 2008), this view is predicated on an out-of-date understanding of Anyang as a "king's city"—a largely ceremonial center of a peripatetic royalty (Keightley 2000). The enormous population and industrial center that we now know the Great Settlement Shang to have been, however, could not possibly have been provisioned without markets and/or a redistributive economy far more encompassing than older scholarship dared imagine.

Several incomplete lines of evidence can be used to shed light on the nature of the Shang economy. The first is the royal oracle-bone inscriptions, which show Shang kings inquiring about the harvest of various places, as well as the levying of agricultural workers. In a study of agricultural place-names and their relationship to the Shang polity (Campbell 2018), I argued that not only are the places for which the harvest is divined mostly securely within the ambit of the king's zone of direct control, but also by far the most common subject of agricultural divination is "us" or "we" (see also Keightley 2012). While a Shang king (and again most of these harvest inscriptions date to the early reigns of the Anyang period) divining about "his" or "our" harvests, fields, and lands does not necessarily mean that all farmland in the royal demesne was directly administered, nevertheless, there is inscriptional evidence that suggests that at least some of it was. In the inscriptions that follow, the auspiciousness of having officials command the masses to plant millet was divined, implying at least some administered agriculture:

> Tested: It should be the Minor Servitors who command the masses to plant millet. H12
>
> . . . Order the masses to (plant) millet (for if we do we) may receive an abundant [harvest]. H14

Could the Great Settlement Shang, then, have been entirely provisioned with directly administered and organized agriculture as some argue (Keightley 2012)? In keeping with the new understanding of Anyang as a giant cluster of lineage settlements, and the widely accepted model of lineage occupation specialization, it is more likely that each lineage had its own lands and acquired its food from them, and/or traded for it. The king's lands seem to have been farmed by laborer forces levied in the same way as his armies, and thus at least some of the agricultural extractions supporting the governing apparatus came in the form of labor taxes.

Given the evidence of the levying of labor for agriculture, and the direct administration of at least some agricultural activity, the lack of references to the king's herds is striking. Indeed, given the widely divergent costs involved in the transportation of grain versus grass-eating bovids, it is far more cost effective for the latter to be raised afar and driven to the Great Settlement Shang than the former to be bulk-transported over great distances. This is most likely why we have inscriptions referring to Shang kings levying people for agriculture but not requisitioning grain itself, and at the same time inscriptions referring to the direct appropriation of cattle and sheep but nothing concerning their organized husbandry.

Our model of the Shang economy, then, involves both direct organization of labor for royal agricultural projects (not to mention construction and war) at a variety of different locations. Similar economies were likely reduplicated on a smaller scale in regional polities and perhaps within stratified lineages. In this way, Anyang's agricultural hinterland would likely have been a great patchwork tethered to the megacenter by a myriad of links—royal and otherwise. Pigs were likely to have been part of this regional agricultural economy, but there is no direct evidence to suggest they were raised on behalf of elites as opposed to raised and consumed or sold in markets (nor are these mutually exclusive possibilities). Cattle and sheep, but especially cattle, as high-prestige animals (Yuan and Flad 2005) central to elite sacrificial feasting at the core of the Shang ritual economy, seem to function something like captives as a resource, and, indeed, they show similar patterns in the inscriptions—as booty, tribute, and the object of requisition. In obtaining cattle and captives from other lands, the Shang kings and elite lineages of Anyang were both richly provisioning their ancestral rituals and, at the same time, depriving others of the very same key resources. This concentration of wealth, power, and sacrificial capital at the "pivot of the four quarters" was at the very core of the Shang polity's meaning and existence.

While zooarchaeological work on the Anyang period village site of Guandimiao is still ongoing, preliminary results are nonetheless startling and important to a fuller understanding of the Shang economy. Guandimiao is a nearly completely excavated village site. As mentioned above, its population was unlikely to have ever been more than 100 people, and it was located some 200 km from Anyang (Henan Sheng Wenwu Kaogu Yanjiusuo 2008, 2009; Li et al. 2018). From an economic standpoint, there are several remarkable things about this, the only well-documented Anyang period village. First of all, it appears to be a specialized craft production site with more kilns than houses—mostly producing fine ceramics that the producers did not themselves use, in quantities far beyond local needs (Li et al. 2018).

Second, hairpins recovered from Guandimiao have shown to have been mass-produced in large-scale bone workshops, the likes of which are only known from Anyang (Campbell et al. 2011; Hou et al. 2018). Third and finally, the Guandimiao assemblage compares with nonelite Anyang contexts (such as Xiaomintun) in interesting ways: the assemblage is less than one-tenth the size of that recovered from roughly equivalent excavation areas (20,000–30,000 m^2), and cattle was the most common taxon at Guandimiao by NISP (38%), but unlike Anyang loci, animals of all ages were present. An intriguing possibility that will have to be tested with isotopic work is that Guandimiao and sites like it were the sources of the cattle consumed at Anyang (Li et al. 2018).

The composite image of this tiny remote village, then, is one of relative poverty (whether seen from house size, recovered artifacts, tombs, or diet), yet it provides evidence of a hitherto-unsuspected degree of integration into regional (ceramic) and politywide (bone product) economic networks. The zooarchaeological assemblage suggests that the inhabitants ate little meat, but nonetheless had access to cattle for occasional ritual-feasting events—perhaps because cattle were being raised at the site for consumption at elite centers. At the same time, the near absence of weapons at Guandimiao (two small bronze knives and four arrowheads) contrasts utterly with their widespread distribution in even nonelite contexts at Anyang (Campbell 2009, 2018; Li et al. 2018).

If other Anyang period villages were similar to Guandimiao, then the overall picture of the Shang economy is of an entire landscape of specialized economic units, perhaps organized as hierarchical lineages and dependents, integrated into a vast network of political-economic interdependencies. Large domestic animals such as cattle, and to a lesser extent sheep and pigs, were central to the logic and functioning of this system. Although raised in different places and participating in different networks, massive flows of livestock made their way up the sociopolitical ladder to elite consumption sites—especially the megacluster of the Great Settlement Shang. At the Great Settlement, it was the lineage elites and the king most conspicuously of all, who disposed of the great quantities of livestock in ancestral sacrifice and feasting events—attempting to both avoid the wrath of the ancestral powers and to renew social bonds through the sharing of meat. At the Great settlement, even relatively low-ranking lineage members enjoyed the redistributed largesse of their leaders. At the other end of the polity's chains of provisioning, however, even relatively high-ranking members of rural communities apparently shared only a little in the abundance of the kingdom. This dominated and impoverished lifestyle can be intuited in comparison with nonelite residential and mortuary loci from Anyang—in terms of weapons, meat, ceramic sets, grave goods, and houses.

Notably, if there is evidence of high-status animals such as sacrificial cattle shared widely across the Great Settlement, wild taxa appear to show a different pattern. At the Anyang loci of Xiaomintun and Baijiazhuang, wild animals made up less than 3% of the mammal remains recovered (Li 2009), while at Guandimiao they appear to be even scarcer (less than 2%) (Li et al. 2018), yet the zooarchaeological assemblage recovered in the early twentieth century from the palace-temple area of Anyang was predominantly large wild taxa such as deer and buffalo, as well as more exotic taxa (de Chardin and Young 1936). The ritual and political roles of the Shang royal hunt and its association with high-elite status have been discussed in many places (Campbell 2018; Fiskesjö 2001; Keightley 2000), but far less attention has been paid to the distribution of the spoils of the hunt. The fact that even a relatively remote village such as Guandimiao—where one might expect more wild taxa than an urban site such as Anyang—shows almost no evidence of hunting, suggests a tight control over even hunting weapons, a restriction of hunting to the high elites, or both. While it remains difficult, if not impossible, to compare the zooarchaeological data sets of the early twentieth century with those of the early twenty-first, and we will likely never know the proportion of Shang high elites' diets composed by wild game, it nevertheless seems that the consumption of large game separated the rulers from the ruled in a manner that cut across even the urban-rural divide.

CONCLUSION

Returning to the issue of provisioning the Great Settlement Shang, one unanswered question is the degree to which writing played a role in the administration of its flows of resources. While there has been some argument over the role of writing in the Shang (Bagley 2004; Keightley 2006; Smith 2012), it remains a fact that the surviving texts pertain almost entirely to elite ancestral-ritual communication (whether the oracle-bone divinatory records, or the dedicatory inscriptions on bronze vessels) and had an extremely limited distribution. More than 99% of the inscribed oracle-bones found to date have been recovered from the palace-temple area of Anyang, whereas the inscribed Shang bronzes were likely all cast at Anyang. This concentration would argue against a widespread use of writing in the Shang polity. On the other hand, there is limited evidence for record keeping on certain media. Inscribed royal oracle-bones, for instance, are frequently inscribed with records of who contributed them and sometimes who prepared them. Some jades have been found with similar records written on them with a brush. It is possible, for at least royal provisioning, therefore, that written records were recorded on the goods themselves, as well as, perhaps, written on bamboo or wooden slips (冊).

Beyond the palaces at the center of the Great Settlement, there is precious little evidence of writing. Notably, the nonroyal, uninscribed oracle-bones that can be found in every Shang site from Anyang to Guandimiao never have the inventory records found on royal plastrons and scapulae. This finding suggests that significant portions of the Shang economy, including much of the provisioning of the Great Settlement Shang, were accomplished through myriad self-organized networks—with each major lineage either acquiring its own resources directly (or through subordinates), or trading for them. Given the evidence for significant occupational specialization, and in the absence of central government redistribution mechanisms (beyond its own self-provisioning needs), the most likely explanation is a well-developed system of exchange, including markets and traders of some kind.

WORKS CITED

Bagley, Robert. 2004. "Anyang Writing and the Origins of the Chinese Writing System." In *The First Writing: Script Invention as History and Process*, edited by Stephen Houston, 190–249. Cambridge: Cambridge University Press.

Bintliff, John. 2002. "Rethinking Early Mediterranean Urbanism." In *Mauerschau: Festschrift für Manfred Korfmann*, edited by R. Aslan and S. Blum, 153–177. Tübingen, Germany: Verlag Bernhard Albert Greiner.

Campbell, Roderick. 2009. "Toward a Networks and Boundaries Approach to Early Complex Polities: The Late Shang Case." *Current Anthropology* 50 (6): 821–848.

Campbell, Roderick. 2012. "Guo zhi da shi: Shangdai wanqi zhong de lizhi gailiang." In *Yinxu kexuefajue 80 nian xueshu jinianhui*, edited by Tang Jigen, 267–276. Beijing: Science Press.

Campbell, Roderick. 2013. "A Preliminary Estimation of Anyang Bronze Production." In *Kaoguxue shiye xia de chengshi, gongyi chuantong yu zhongwai jiaoliu—Liu Qingzhu xiansheng qishi huadan qingshou wenji* [Archaeological Perspectives on Cities, Craft Traditions and Sino-Foreign Interaction], edited by Liu Qingzhu, 160–172. Beijing: Science Press.

Campbell, Roderick. 2014. *Archaeology of Bronze Age China: From Erlitou to Anyang*. Los Angeles: Cotsen Institute of Archaeology Press.

Campbell, Roderick. 2018. *Violence, Kinship and the Early Chinese State: The Shang and Their World*. Cambridge: Cambridge University Press.

Campbell, Roderick, Li Zhipeng, He Yuling, and Yuan Jing. 2011. "Consumption, Exchange and Production at the Great Settlement Shang: Boneworking at Tiesanlu, Anyang." *Antiquity* 85: 1279–1297.

Chang, K. C. 1980. *Shang Civilization*. New Haven, CT: Yale University Press.

Chang, K. C. 1989. "Ancient China and its Anthropological Significance." In *Archaeological Thought in America*, edited by C. C. Lamberg-Karlovsky, 155–166. Cambridge: Cambridge University Press.

de Chardin, Teilhard P., and C. C. Young. 1936. *On the Mammalian Remains from the Archaeological Site of Anyang*. Nanjing: Geological Survey of China.

Falkenhausen, Lothar von. 2008. "Stages in the Development of 'Cities' in Pre-Imperial China." In *The Ancient City: New Perspectives on Urbanism in the Old and New World*, edited by Joyce Marcus and Jeremy Sabloff, 209–228. Santa Fe: School for Advanced Research.

Fiskesjö, Magnus. 2001. "Rising from Blood-Stained Fields: Royal Hunting and State Formation in Shang China." *Bulletin of the Museum of Far Eastern Antiquities* 73: 48–191.

Flad, Rowan. 2018. "Urbanism as Technology in Early China." *Archaeological Research in Asia* 14: 121–134.

Henan Sheng Wenwu Kaogu Yanjiusuo. 2008. "Henan Xingyangshi Guandimiao yizhi Shangdai wanqi yicun fajue jianbao." *Kaogu* 7: 32–46.

Henan Sheng Wenwu Kaogu Yanjiusuo. 2009. "Henan Xingyangshi Guandimiao yizhi kaogu faxian yu renshi." *Huaxia Kaogu* 3: 8–13.

Hou, Yanfeng, Roderick Campbell, Yan Zhang, Shuting Li, Zhipeng Li, and Yuling He. 2018. "The Guandimiao Bone Assemblage (and What It Says about the Shang Economy)." *Asian Perspectives* 57: 281–310.

Keightley, David. 1983. "The Late Shang State: When, Where, and What?" In *the Origins of Chinese Civilization*, edited by David Keightley, 523–564. Berkeley: University of California Press.

Keightley, David. 2000. *The Ancestral Landscape: Time, Space, and Community in Late Shang China*. Berkeley: Institute of East Asian Studies, University of California.

Keightley, David. 2006. "Marks and Labels: Early Writing in Neolithic and Shang China." In *Archaeology of Asia*, edited by Miriam Stark, 177–201. Malden, MA: Blackwell Publishing.

Keightley, David. 2012. *Working for His Majesty: Research Notes on Labor Mobilization in Late Shang China (ca. 1200–1045 B.C.)*. Berkeley: Institute of East Asian Studies, University of California.

Li, Shuting, Roderick Campbell, Hou Yanfeng. 2018. "Guandimiao: A Shang Village Site and its Significance." *Antiquity* 92: 1511–1529.

Li, Yung-ti. 2003. "The Anyang Bronze Foundries: Archaeological Remains, Casting Technology and Production Organization." PhD diss., Harvard University, Cambridge, MA.

Li, Zhipeng. 2009. "The Study of Faunal Remains from Anyang: The Capital Site of Late Shang." [In Chinese.] PhD diss., Department of Archaeology, Chinese Academy of Social Sciences.

Li, Zhipeng, and Roderick Campbell. 2019. "Puppies for the Ancestors: On the Many Roles of Shang Dogs." *Archaeological Research in Asia* 17 (March): 161–172.

Li, Zhipeng, Roderick Campbell, Katherine Brunson, Jie Yang, and Yang Tao. 2014. "The Exploitation of Domestic Animal Products from the Late Neolithic Age to the Early Bronze Age in the Heartland of Ancient China." In *New Perspectives on the Secondary Products Revolution*, edited by Haskel Greenfield, 56–79. Oxford: Oxbow.

Li, Zhipeng, He Yuling, and Jiang Yude (Roderick Campbell). 2011. "Yinxu Wan Shang zhigu zuofang yu zhigu shougongye de yanjiu huigu yu zai." *Sandai Kaogu* 4: 471–486.

Modelski, George. 2003. *World Cities: 3000 to 2000*. Washington, DC: Faros.

Schwartz, Adam. 2013. "Huayuanzhuang East I: An Annotated Study and Translation of the Oracle Bone Inscriptions." PhD diss., University of Chicago.

Shaughnessy, Edward. 1989. "Historical Geography and the Extent of the Earliest Chinese Kingdoms." *Asia Major* 2 (2): 1–22.

Smith, Adam. 2012. "Are Writing Systems Intelligently Designed." In *Agency in Ancient Writing*, edited by Joshua Englehardt, 71–94. Boulder: Colorado University Press.

Song, Zhenhao. 1994. *Xia Shang shehui shenghuoshi*. 2 vols. Beijing: Zhongguo shehuikexue chubanshe.

Tang, Jigen, and Jing, Zhicun. 2009. "Anyang de 'Shang yi' yu 'Da Yi Shang' 安阳的"商邑"与"大邑商." *Kaogu* 9: 70–80.

Yinxu Xiaomintun Team. 2007. "Henan Anyangshi Xiaomintun Shangdai Fangzhi 2003–2004 fajue jianbao." *Kaogu* 1: 3–13.

Yuan, Jing, and Rowan Flad. 2005. "New Zooarchaeological Evidence for Changes in Shang Dynasty Animal Sacrifice." *Journal of Anthropological Archaeology* 24 (3): 252–270.

Zhu, Fenghang. 1991. *A Study of the Family Patterns of Shang and Western Zhou China*. Reprint. Tianjin: Tianjin Guji Press.

ZSKY (Zhongguo Shehuikexue Kaogu Yanjiusuo). 2003. *Zhongguo kaoguxue: Xia, Shang juan*. Beijing: Zhongguo shehui kexue chubanshe.

6

Aksumite Foodways and Economic Strategies in the North Ethiopian Highland

HELINA S. WOLDEKIROS

Local and long-distance trade and productive agricultural systems contributed to the establishment of complex socioeconomic institutions in multiple regions of Africa, including the West African savanna, the Zimbabwe plateau, the Swahili coast, and northeastern Ethiopia (ancient Aksum) in prehistoric periods (LaViolette and Fleisher 2005; McIntosh et al. 1984; Phillipson 2012) (figure 6.1). Robust local and regional food-provisioning systems paved the way for life in urban centers and facilitated political centralization, stability, and specialist production of spectacular architecture, art, and religious centers. However, despite the important role of local and regional trade and in sourcing urban food supplies, such systems have received limited scholarly attention. Rather, academic discussions of food provisioning in Africa have been dominated by consideration of the present food insecurity and Africa's dependence on global food aid (Guyer 1987; Logan 2016). Thus, the way that food was supplied to prehistoric urban centers, as well as the larger provision systems in place to support this urban distribution, is not well understood.

https://doi.org/10.5876/9781646422562.c006

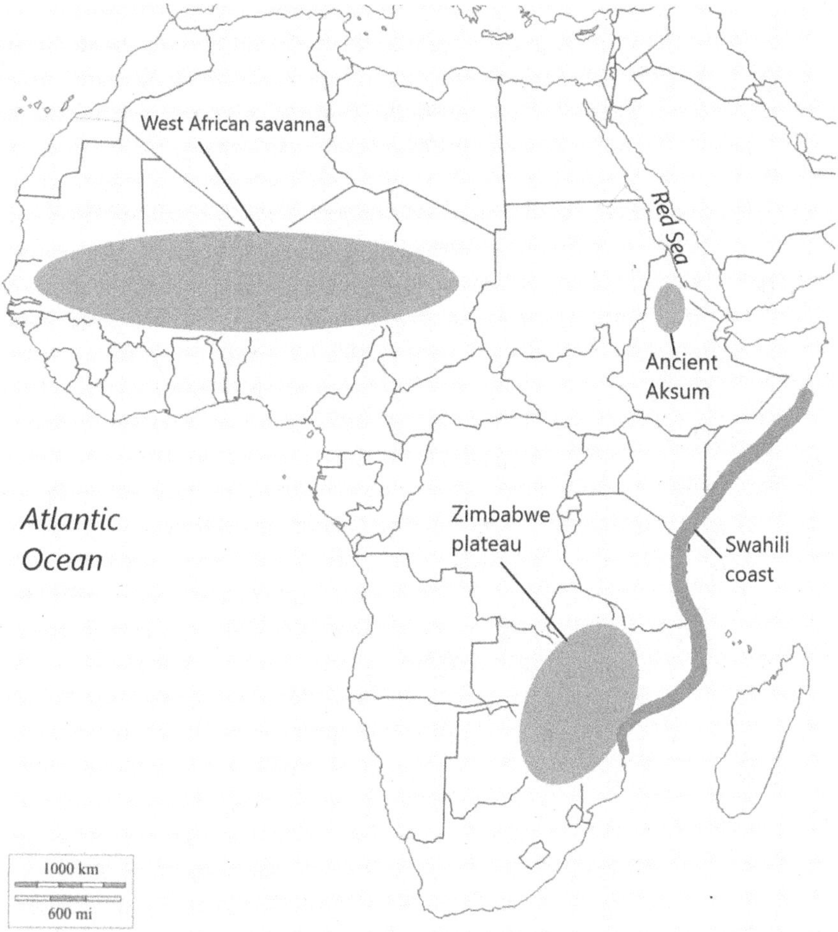

Figure 6.1. *Ancient Africa: historical states, kingdoms, and urban centers.*

Following a brief outline of the socioeconomic and political development of the Aksumites (50 BC–AD 800) of the North Ethiopian and Eritrean highlands (northern Horn of Africa), this chapter will draw on faunal data and evidence from the salt caravan trade to examine Aksumite food-provisioning strategies. The powerful Aksumite state controlled trade on the Red Sea and was considered a strong partner by the Romans. It is not surprising, therefore, that studies of external trade have dominated research. There has been little consideration of key local or regional food supply networks. I argue here that the Aksumite state had multiple food-provisioning systems in place, including market participation, indirect provisioning, local direct provisioning, and specialized provisioning by the state. Integrated historical and archaeological data regarding elite and nonelite Aksumite settlements, craft centers, and ritual sites allow for the examination of the role of domestic livestock distribution, consumption, and salt caravan activity. Together, the data paint a picture of the varied roles of local and government actors, individuals, Aksumite state institutions, and the environment (location of resources) in food networks.

AKSUMITE SOCIOECONOMIC AND POLITICAL DEVELOPMENT

The earliest evidence for complex polities in the northern Horn of Africa comes from the north Ethiopian and Eritrean highlands and dates back to the third millennium BC (Fattovich 2010; Finneran 2007; Phillipson 2012). Archaeologists have divided the time span in which these complex societies flourished into three major periods: pre-Aksumite (>800 BC–50 BC), Aksumite (50 BC–AD 800), and post-Aksumite (AD 800–1450) (Fattovich and Bard 2001; Harrower and D'Andrea 2014; Phillipson 2012). In addition to trade on the Red Sea, at the peak of its power, the Aksumite Empire controlled territories as far away as Yemen and Meroe in Sudan (Fattovich 2010; Munro-Hay 1991; Phillipson 2000).

Aksumite sociopolitical organization was hierarchical and controlled by the king. Bureaucratic administrative positions were held by the king's close family members, as well as subregional chiefs and kings. Some positions were reserved for military heads and possibly priests (Kobishchanov 1979). Power was created and maintained through a variety of mechanisms, including architectural display, control of trade and wealth, redistribution, and force (Phillipson 2012). Temples during the pre-Aksumite period and Christian churches during the Aksumite period might also have participated in power and economic relations. The city of Aksum (established ca. 50 BC) in the interior highlands was the capital of the Aksumite state and its main political center. Aksum lies at an elevation of 2,300 m above sea level and is connected by trade routes to the main Red Sea port of Adulis and the major urban centers of Kohaito, Tokonda, Kaskse, and Matara (Harrower and D'Andrea 2014) (figure 6.2).

The Aksum city center is much better known than the surrounding areas, but well-known sites near Aksum (e.g., Bieta Giyorgis hill, Addi Kilte, Mai Hejja, and Dungar) include monumental architecture, central palaces, elite tombs, monasteries, and administrative seals (Fattovich 2010; Fattovich and Bard 2001; Manzo 2003). During the Aksumite Empire, a prominent elite population lived in Aksum (Finneran 2007; Phillipson 2012), supported by an amalgamation of small farming settlements surrounding the city (Finneran 2007; Michels 2005). Archaeological evidence for the rural residences of these elites and the farming sites that supported them has been recently uncovered at Mezber (34 km from Aksum and 5 km from a major trade route), dating to the pre-Aksumite period (Harrower and D'Andrea 2014).

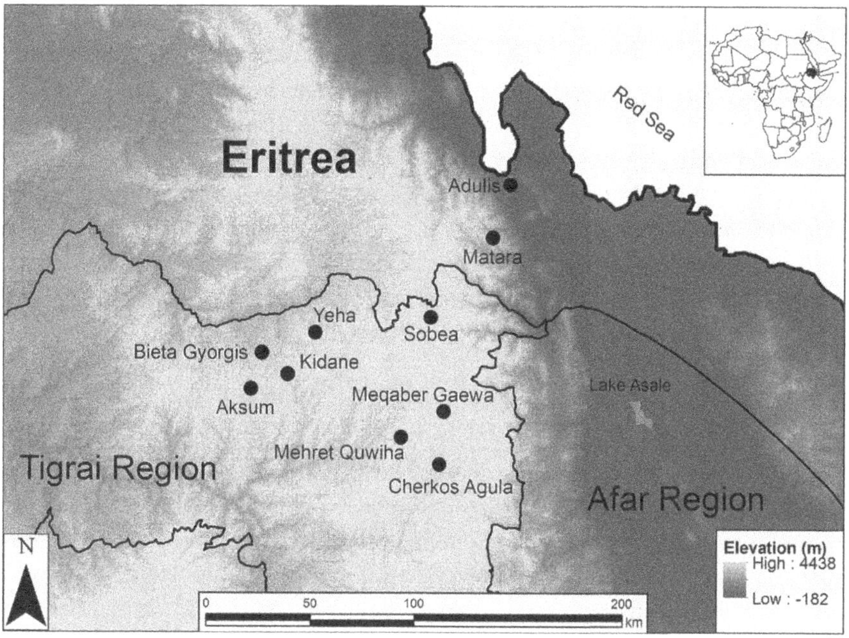

Figure 6.2. *Ancient Ethiopian and Eritrean highlands: sites mentioned in the text.*

The wealth and development of the Aksumite state have been tied to long-distance trade and agricultural products. The Aksumites enjoyed economic and political contact with the international world, engaging in extensive long-distance trade with the Red Sea and Indian Ocean territories. They also had contact with territories in the Mediterranean, Nile Valley, and South Arabia and received goods from as far away as India and China (Fattovich 2010; Munro-Hay 1991; Phillipson 2009). Administrative seals made of clay, stone, and metal attest to their bureaucratic control of political and economic systems. Textual evidence also exists for warriors and forces used to patrol trade routes and to control regional relationships (Kobishchanov 1979). There is less evidence regarding the roles of middlemen and local traders and producers in distribution systems and little discussion of the roles of formal and informal economies or diverse consumers.

Archaeological and textual studies in the northern Horn of Africa indicate a gradual change in economic organization and food provisioning. Household production and consumption were more common in the pre-Aksumite period, whereas specialized farming systems produced for the urban markets of the Aksumite state (Finneran 2007:153; Phillipson 2000). Archaeologically, this change is supported by faunal data and increases in crop diversity and cash crops during the Aksumite period. The integrated farming system included crops that originated in Africa and the Near East, including teff, barley, wheat, pulses, and the oilseed *noog* (D'Andrea 2008; D'Andrea et al. 1999).

Taken together, the Aksumite literature and faunal data analyzed to date suggest direct and indirect market-based provisioning of urban populations and an elite role in redistribution (Cain 2000a; Chaix 2013). Cattle were provisioned by the elite to their subjects; they were also preferred animals for ritual sacrifice (Kobishchanov 1979) and key to pulling plows (Barnett 1999; McCann 1995). Both inscriptions and faunal data also indicate that cattle were a form of wealth (Cain 2000b; Kobishchanov 1979).

ANIMAL RESOURCES AND THE AKSUMITE POLITICAL ECONOMY: AN ARCHAEOLOGICAL PERSPECTIVE

Today, domestic cattle are some of the most important domestic animals in Ethiopia, from the perspectives of economics, labor, food, and social values. For this reason, cattle are prized and kept by both agricultural and pastoral groups (Barnett 1999; Smith 1992). The introduction of cattle to the North Ethiopian and Eritrean highlands 3,000 years ago contributed to intensifying and developing specialized crop production systems (Barnett 1999). Later, increased reliance on donkeys, horses, and camels facilitated greater trade and transport in the highlands and between the highlands and lowlands.

Only a few archaeological studies have looked at food redistribution systems spanning production to consumption in the pre-Aksumite and Aksumite periods (Cain 2000a; Chaix 2013; Shoshani et al. 2008). It is, however, possible to piece together the nature of food production and distribution at this time from archaeological and historical data. Chester Cain's (1999, 2000a, 2000b) and Louis Chaix's (2013) analyses of faunal remains from pre-Aksumite and Aksumite contexts provided the first zooarchaeological insights into early food-provisioning strategies in the North Ethiopian highlands. The D and K sites, studied by Cain (2000a), are two nonelite settlements that were excavated in order to investigate the subsistence practices of pre-Aksumite and Aksumite societies (Phillipson 2000). The K site in Maleke Aksum is associated with craft production, and the D site at Kidane Mehret pertains to food production and processing (Harlow and Phillips 2000; Phillipson 2000). A high degree of craft specialization and technological sophistication was well established during the Aksumite period (Phillipson 2000), as evidenced by coin minting, metal, ivory, and glass-working specimens uncovered in these sites.

The D site is located outside the center of Aksum and dates to the pre-Aksumite and late Aksumite periods. It includes evidence of low- to middle-status groups engaged in farming and food processing, probably at a large scale (Phillipson and Phillips 2000). Domestic animals dominate the faunal assemblage, of which approximately 90% is made up of cattle, sheep, and goat specimens. Taxonomic and body part data suggest that people mostly occupied this site during the pre-Aksumite phase. The proportion of mutton and goat increased somewhat during the later Aksumite phase. At this time diets were more diverse, with fish and domestic chickens present. The remainder of the faunal assemblage (10%) comprises specimens from wild animals, including wild fowls, and Antilopinae, including bushbuck (*Tragelaphus scriptus*). Equids, canids, and hippopotamus ivory were also present (Cain 2000b).

The K site is located in the city of Aksum, itself, and is thought to have been occupied by middle-ranked (i.e., nonelite) groups engaged in craft production (Harlow and Philips 2000; Phillipson 2000). The faunal assemblage at this site shows a wider range of species than the D site (Cain 2000a), with cattle, sheep, goats, equids, chickens, suids, canids, felids, hippopotamus, elephants, fish, wild fowl, wild bovids, and rodents (Cain 2000a). Similar to the D site, the K site's faunal assemblage is dominated by specimens of domestic animals: cattle, sheep, and goats. At the K site about 35% more caprine meat was consumed than at the D site (Cain 2000a). Hippopotamus ivory is also present in the pre-Aksumite phase and elephant ivory in the Aksumite phase, consistent with production of high-status goods at Aksum. The increased presence of domestic chicken, cat, and rodent remains in the Aksumite phase also suggests increases in their populations at this time.

Complementary faunal data sets come from the sites of Ona Nagast (ON) and Ona Abo Zewge (OAZ), which lie in the Aksumite core on the hill of Bieta Giyorgis (Chaix 2013; Fattovich 2000). Bieta Giyorgis (AD 400 BC–800) is considered to have been the first settlement of the Aksumite kings (Bard et al. 2002). The ON site is a settlement with an assortment of residential stone buildings (Fattovich 2010). OAZ is a monumental funerary complex with fallen stelae and platforms (Chaix 2013; Fattovich 2010). As at the D and K sites at Aksum, the ON site faunal assemblage is dominated by domestic fauna—particularly cattle, followed by sheep and goats—in all major periods. Domestic chickens and dogs are present in very small numbers, as are wild animals in later Aksumite periods. At ON, beef is most common around AD 340–370 and thought to indicate population increase and trader diversity at this time.

Faunal remains from sites studied in the ancient city of Aksum reveal that the pre-Aksumite and Aksumite economies were dominated by domestic livestock—specifically cattle, sheep, and goats (Cain 2000a; Chaix 2013). Domestic herds were supplemented by a small percentage of domestic chicken and equids, as well as wild antelope, wild fowl, and some fish. As described above, at all sites and in all time periods studied, cattle outnumber caprines. This pattern is supported by recent research at the elite rural pre-Aksumite and Aksumite site of Mezber (D'Andrea et al. 2011; Woldekiros and D'Andrea 2016). Faunal data from Mezber confirm the significance of cattle for pre-Aksumite elites living in a farming settlement outside the urban context (D'Andrea et al. 2011; Woldekiros and D'Andrea 2016). As at other pre-Aksumite sites, sheep and goats were important at Mezber. This settlement also provided the first robust evidence for domestic chicken production through the pre-Aksumite and Aksumite periods (Woldekiros and D'Andrea 2016). Chickens account for 1.3% of the assemblage in less elite areas of the D site (Cain 2000) and 0.1% of the assemblage in the ON site (Chaix 2013), but 1.5% of the assemblage of Mezber. This finding suggests that chicken played an important role in the elite rural diet.

Taken together, data from these sites demonstrate that cattle made up a high proportion of all faunal assemblages. Herd managers culled young, adult, and aged individuals—suggesting that cattle were relied on for meat, and for milk, traction, and hides. Cattle were also significant in the material symbol systems of the Aksumite people, as suggested by their frequent depiction in engravings, on ceramic bowls, and on icons (Schmidt 2009). Sheep and goats are also common in sites but appear to have been primarily used for meat.

The formal and informal redistribution of meat and other animal products through markets, as well as through direct provisioning, were significant in pre-Aksumite and Aksumite food-provisioning systems (Cain 1999, 2000a:148; Chaix 2013). At the elite ON site, Chaix draws on the complete representation of anatomical units to argue that elites were directly provisioned by nonelite members of the community. He also suggests that hides were transported elsewhere for processing. This theory is significant, given that the Gaudit area of Aksum is well known for its high volumes of obsidian scrapers that are thought to have been used to prepare worked leather goods for international trade (Phillipson 2000).

In contrast, the nonelite D site outside the city center is considered to have had a specialized economic function within the broader political economy as an area of agricultural production (Cain 2000a:152). Archaeologists have argued that unprocessed plants and animals were brought from surrounding rural areas for consumption but that some animals were butchered at the D site and the meat transferred to urban areas. Over time, Aksum is thought to have developed more specialized animal provisioning. Although animals were consumed in the early phase, both high- and low-utility elements are missing from the D site in the later Aksumite phase. The later phases are dominated by medium utility elements. Cain (2000a) argues that this change reflects a shift from local animal production to more formal carcass and meat redistribution systems at Aksum.

Historical texts emphasize the role of animals in Aksumite trade. However, the first faunal-based evidence for a provisioned rather than producer-based settlement at Aksum comes from the K site (Cain 2000a). Here, craft specialists were supplied with young animals or calves. Similarly, at the K site, moderate utility anatomical units dominate. Cain (2000a) argues, following Zeder (1988,

1991), that the cattle age distribution and the representation of body parts indicate an indirect redistribution system. Household preference, market availability, or a bureaucracy that oversaw the distribution of meat for specialist groups may have played a role in carcass distribution.

Texts regarding the political and socioeconomic landscape of the Indian Ocean–trading Aksumites, and faunal data from the elite early settlement and funerary complex (ON and OAZ) on the hill at Aksum, the craft specialist settlement (site K) in the heart of the city, and the nonelite settlement outside the city (site D) suggest that the Aksumites employed both market-oriented and bureaucratically controlled food redistribution systems. State-controlled distribution is well documented in texts and inscriptions. A famous inscription by King Ezana I (ca. AD 330) mentions the provisioning of Beja mobile pastoralists who were being resettled to a new territory, by order of the king (Kobishchanov 1979). Daily food rations of meat and bread, as well as water and beer, were provided for the Beja and the soldiers who were accompanying them. The Beja were also supplied with live cattle, sheep, and goats. This undertaking would have required food provisioning by both the royal storehouse and by people along the route.

The royal livestock also provided food for state caravans. Cosmas Indicopleustes (ca. AD 540), a Greek author, wrote about Aksumite royal caravans going to Sasu, an important Ethiopian gold-bearing region, with salt, iron, and cattle (MacCrindle 1897; Wolska-Conus 1962). There, cattle were evidently traded for gold and used to provision the caravan (Kobishchanov 1979:159; MacCrindle 1897). Monumental inscriptions of both King Ezana I and King Ezana II (ca. AD 330–520), discovered in and around Aksum, indicate that the Aksumite kings kept a close record of their livestock through *sahāfē-lahm*—clerks of cows, or royal accountants (Kobishchanov 1979; Munro-Hay 1991). In addition to controlling the redistribution of food, the state is also thought to have played a major role in organizing caravans of people and pack animals to acquire and move essential foodstuffs, of which one of the most significant was salt (Kobishchanov 1979; MacCrindle 1897). Textual records mention that salt was an essential commodity in the Ethiopian highlands. Even today, all of the salt for the highlands originates in the salt trade from the Afar depression.

Survey and ethnoarchaeological research on the Afar salt trade route has documented that there was caravan activity on the routes to Afar during the Aksumite period (Woldekiros 2014). An important finding is that ancient towns and settlements were located near passes and coalescence points on the route and in transition zones between the highlands and lowlands. These locations were strategic for informal local participation in the trade and provisioning of caravanners. They also provided opportunities for formal state control, for which the location of ancient churches is significant. After the adoption of Christianity by King Ezana II, circa AD 340, churches were state sponsored. Temples and churches in the pre-Aksumite (Fattovich 1990) and Aksumite periods were at times located at the edge of the plateaus on the "Salt Route." The presence of churches along the route at Desi'a, Agula, and Haiki Meshail points to a role for the Aksumite state in organizing trade along the route (Woldekiros 2014). Furthermore, the orientation of these Aksumite churches toward the caravan trail indicates that they may have represented the interests of both the church and the state on the Salt Route. Aksumite churches are usually sited on inaccessible mountaintops, but the churches at in Desi'a (St. Georgis) and Agula (Cherkos) are located in the lowest elevation areas of the valley, facing the caravan routes (Woldekiros 2014). Ethnohistorical accounts document that Cherkos collected taxes from caravanners in the sixteenth century, during the time of Emperor Eyasu II (Crawford 1958; Huntingford and Pankhurst 1989). During the Aksumite period, it is likely, therefore, that some churches served as agents of the state. Settlements and towns along the route, however, indicate the participation of small-scale traders (Woldekiros 2014).

CONCLUSION

Settled agricultural towns, interregional trade, and complex polities first appear in the northern Horn of Africa (highland Ethiopia and Eritrea) during the pre-Aksumite and Aksumite periods. Historical and archaeological data demonstrate that food-provisioning practices underwent significant changes through time in the city of Aksum, moving from local animal production to more widespread carcass and meat redistribution during Aksumite times. Urban elites, such as those residing at the ON and OAZ sites, were directly provisioned, probably by nonelite members of the community. Nonelite sites outside the city center, such as the D site, functioned not only as places for agricultural production within the broader political economy, but also as areas where imported rural foodstuffs were consumed or prepared for distribution to city centers (e.g., the K site, where craft specialists resided).

Urban and rural residents of pre-Aksumite and Aksumite communities obtained meat from cattle, sheep, goats, and chickens, as well as some wild animals, including guinea fowl, francolin, antelope, and fish (Cain 2000a; Chaix 2013; D'Andrea et al. 2011; Woldekiros and D'Andrea 2016). Although cattle were predominantly relied on for food, they were also important work animals, and symbolically represented in both ritual and nonritual contexts (Finneran 2007). For this reason, they were a sign of wealth. Zooarchaeological studies at Aksumite sites indicate that meat was distributed to consumers from producers in or around Aksum. This finding suggests that there may have been markets, as well as household production and consumption. Textual data focus on larger-scale processes and attest to centralized state control over food provisioning—particularly the redistribution of meat and live cattle, sheep, and goats from royal herds to government agents on trade routes and to conquered peoples. Similarly, archaeological data on the organization of the salt trade show both local participation and state-scale control and centralization. Although the larger trade route was traversed by local caravanners, strategically located towns, villages, and Aksumite churches along transition zones between the highland and lowland portions of the route suggest state control or taxation on the route.

In this chapter, I have argued that food distribution in the Aksumite period operated at multiple scales including state-controlled distribution, formal market systems, and informal exchange between individuals and households. The distribution of food through markets was most common in urban areas. However, in rural areas (especially hard-to-reach areas)—where demand for salt, animals, and animal products was high—resources were provisioned by various individual agents. Some degree of bureaucratic control was also involved in salt trade, as evidenced by the location of temples and churches in the pre-Aksumite (Fattovich 1990) and Aksumite periods on the Salt Route. As was the case during the medieval period, it is likely that such churches were served by the state as points of taxation of trade goods as caravanners journeyed from the lowlands.

This study demonstrates the utility of understanding Aksumite food provisioning at different scales and through multiple agents, both inside and outside the state. Aksumite society—with its constituent members of different genders, statuses, and cultural affiliations—showed varied concerns with respect to food production, distribution, and consumption (Gumerman 1997; Zeder 1988). As shown by the pre-Aksumite and Aksumite data, elites were engaged in building labor-intensive, luxury monumental and residential structures, consumed high-quality meat, and led expensive caravan expeditions because they could afford to do so. In contrast, nonelites and middle-class members of society consumed low- or medium-utility food. Similarly, the ethnoarchaeology of the Afar salt trade reveals that small-scale caravanners participated in the trade on a subsistence scale, whereas high-status middlemen and agents of the Aksumite state participated for wealth and power.

The faunal and historical evidence, together with data on the salt caravan, contributes to our understanding of the ways in which ancient food-provisioning systems changed over time and space. The resettlement of entire communities (e.g., the Beja) and the seasonal movement of caravans created variability in large-scale food distribution systems in most ancient sub-Saharan African urban centers.

This study has illustrated the ways in which interrelated components—including environment, social, economic, and political, as well as belief systems—shaped the food-provisioning systems of the pre-Aksumite and Aksumite states. Economic specialization, seasonal trading, and formal/informal market distribution by nonelites, and the redistribution and participation in trade routes by elites, led to the distribution of staples and scarce resources by hierarchical and more heterarchical segments of society. The diversity of the members participating in these systems may have contributed to the resilience of the larger society, as well as the emergence and maintenance of early complex societies, more generally.

WORKS CITED

Bard, Kathryn A., Rodolfo Fattovich, Andrea Manzo, and Cinzia Perlingieri. 2002. "Aksum Origins, Kassala and Upper Nubia: New Evidence from Bieta Giyorgis, Aksum." *Archéologie du Nil moyen* 9 (3): 1–42.

Barnett, Tertia. 1999. *The Emergence of Food Production in Ethiopia*. Oxford: Archaeopress.

Cain, Chester. 1999. "Results from Zooarchaeological Analysis at Axum, Ethiopia." *ArchaeoZoologia* 10: 27–46.

Cain, Chester. 2000a. "Animals at Axum: Initial Zooarchaeological Research in the Later Prehistory of the Northern Ethiopian Highlands." PhD diss., Washington University, St. Louis.

Cain, Chester. 2000b. "Archaeozoology." In *Archaeology at Aksum, Ethiopia, 1993–97*. Vol. 2, edited by David Phillipson, 369–414. London: British Institute in Eastern Africa and Society of Antiquaries.

Chaix, Louis. 2013. "The Fauna from the UNO / BU Excavations at Bieta Giyorgis (Aksum) in Tigray, Northern Ethiopia: Campaigns 1995–2003: Pre-Aksumite, 700–400 BC to Late Aksumite, AD 800–1200." *Journal of African Archaeology* 11 (2): 211–241. https://doi.org/10.3213/2191-5784-10244.

Crawford, Osbert G. S. 1958. *Ethiopian Itineraries, circa 1400–1524*. Cambridge: Hakluyt Society.

D'Andrea, A. Catherine. 2008. "T'ef (*Eragrostis tef*) in Ancient Agricultural Systems of Highland Ethiopia." *Economic Botany* 62 (4): 547–566. https://doi.org/10.1007/s12231-008-9053-4.

D'Andrea, Catherine, Diane Lyons, Mitiku Haile, and Ann Butler. 1999. "Ethnoarchaeological Approaches to the Study of Prehistoric Agriculture in the Highlands of Ethiopia." In *The Exploitation of Plant Resources in Ancient Africa*, edited by Marijke van der Veen, 101–122. New York: Plenum Publishing Corporation.

D'Andrea, A. Catherine, Michael P. Richards, Laurence A. Pavlish, Shannon Wood, Andrea Manzo, and Helina S. Woldekiros. 2011. "Stable Isotopic Analysis of Human and Animal Diets from Two Pre-Aksumite / Proto-Aksumite Archaeological Sites in Northern Ethiopia." *Journal of Archaeological Science* 38 (2): 367–374. https://doi.org/10.1016/j.jas.2010.09.015.

Fattovich, Rodolfo. 1990. "Remarks on the Pre-Aksumite Period in Northern Ethiopia." *Journal of Ethiopian Studies* 23: 1–33.

Fattovich, Rodolfo. 2000. *The Aksum Archaeological Area: A Preliminary Assessment*. Naples: Istituto Universitario Orientale, Centro Interdipartimentale di Servizi per l'archeologia.

Fattovich, Rodolfo. 2010. "The Development of Ancient States in the Northern Horn of Africa, c. 3000 BC–AD 1000: An Archaeological Outline." *Journal of World Prehistory* 23 (3): 145–175. https://doi.org/10.1007/s10963-010-9035-1.

Fattovich, Rodolfo, and Kathryn A. Bard. 2001. "The Proto-Aksumite Period: An Overview." *Annales d'Ethiopie* 17: 3–24.

Finneran, Niall. 2007. *The Archaeology of Ethiopia*. London: Routledge.

Gumerman, George. 1997. "Food and Complex Societies." *Journal of Archaeological Method and Theory* 4 (2): 105–139. https://doi.org/10.1007/BF02428056.

Guyer, Jane I. 1987. *Feeding African Cities: Studies in Regional Social History*. Bloomington: Indiana University Press.

Harlow, Michael, and Jacke Phillips. 2000. "The K Site in Maleke Aksum." In *Archaeology at Aksum, Ethiopia, 1993–97*. Vol. 2, edited by David Phillipson, 267–280. London: British Institute in Eastern Africa and Society of Antiquaries.

Harrower, Michael J., and A. Catherine D'Andrea. 2014. "Landscapes of State Formation: Geospatial Analysis of Aksumite Settlement Patterns (Ethiopia)." *African Archaeological Review* 31 (3): 513–541. https://doi.org/10.1007/s10437-014-9165-4.

Huntingford, George Wynn Brereton, and Richard Pankhurst. 1989. *The Historical Geography of Ethiopia: From the First Century AD to 1704*. Oxford: Oxford University Press.

Kobishchanov, Illri M. 1979. *Axum*. Translated by Joseph W. Michels, and Lorraine T. Kapitanoff. University Park: Pennsylvania State University Press.

LaViolette, Adria, and Jeffrey Fleisher. 2005. "The Archaeology of Sub-Saharan Urbanism: Cities and their Countrysides." In *African Archaeology*, edited by Ann Brower Stahl, 327–353. Malden, MA: Blackwell.

Logan, Amanda L. 2016. "'Why Can't People Feed Themselves?': Archaeology as Alternative Archive of Food Security in Banda, Ghana." *American Anthropologist* 118 (3): 508–524. https://doi.org/10.1111/aman.12603.

MacCrindle, John W. 1897. *The Christian Topography of Cosmas, an Egyptian Monk*. London: Hakluyt Society.

Manzo, Andrea. 2003. "Note sulla più antica Fase Archeologica Aksumita." *Rassegna di Studi Etiopici* 2: 37–50.

McCann, James. 1995. *People of the Plow: An Agricultural History of Ethiopia, 1800–1990*. Madison: University of Wisconsin Press.

McIntosh, Susan Keech, and Roderick J. McIntosh. 1984. "The Early City in West Africa: Towards an Understanding." *African Archaeological Review* 2: 73–98. http://dx.doi.org/10.1007/BF01117226.

Michels, Joseph W. 2005. *Changing Settlement Patterns in the Aksum-Yeha Region of Ethiopia: 700 BC–AD 850*. Oxford: Archaeopress.

Munro-Hay, Stuart C. 1991. *Aksum: An African Civilisation of Late Antiquity*. Edinburgh: Edinburgh University Press.

Phillipson, David W. 2000. *Archaeology at Aksum, Ethiopia, 1993–97*. Vols. 1–2. London: British Institute in Eastern Africa and Society of Antiquaries.

Phillipson, David W. 2009. "The First Millennium BC in the Highlands of Northern Ethiopia and South-Central Eritrea: A Reassessment of Cultural and Political Development." *African Archaeological Review* 26 (4): 257–274. https://doi.org/10.1007/s10437-009-9064-2.

Phillipson, David W. 2012. *Foundations of an African Civilization: Aksum and the Northern Horn, 1000 BC–AD 1300*. Woodbridge, VA: James Currey.

Phillipson, David W., and Jacke Phillips. 2000. "The D Site at Kidane Mehret." In *Archaeology at Aksum, Ethiopia, 1993–97*. Vol. 2, edited by David Phillipson, 267–280. London: British Institute in Eastern Africa and Society of Antiquaries.

Schmidt, Peter R. 2009. "Variability in Eritrea and the Archaeology of the Northern Horn during the First Millennium BC: Subsistence, Ritual, and Gold Production." *African Archaeological Review* 26 (4): 305–325.

Shoshani, J., M. Ghebregiorgis, and P. R. Schmidt. 2008. "Interpretations of Faunal Remains from Archaeological Sites on the Asmara Plateau of Eritrea." In *The Archaeology of Ancient Eritrea*, edited by Peter R. Schmidt, Matthew C. Curtis, and Zelalem Teka, 217–233. Trenton, NJ: Red Sea Press.

Smith, Andrew B. 1992. *Pastoralism in Africa: Origins and Development Ecology*. London: Hurst and Co.

Woldekiros, Helina S. 2014. "The Afar Caravan Route Insights into Aksumite (50 BCE–CE 900) Trade and Exchange from the Low Deserts to the North Ethiopian Plateau." PhD diss., Washington University, St. Louis.

Woldekiros, Helina S., and Catherine A. D'Andrea. 2016. "Early Evidence for Domestic Chickens (*Gallus gallus domesticus*) in the Horn of Africa." *International Journal of Osteoarchaeology*. https://doi.org/10.1002/oa.2540.

Wolska-Conus, Wanda. 1962. *La topographie chrétienne de Cosmas Indicopleustès: Théologie et science au VIe Siècle*. Paris: Presses Universitaires de France.

Zeder, Melinda A. 1988. "Understanding Urban Process through the Study of Specialized Subsistence Economy in the Near East." *Journal of Anthropological Archaeology* 7: 1–55. https://doi.org/10.1016/0278-4165(88)90006-2.

Zeder, Melinda A. 1991. *Feeding Cities: Specialized Animal Economy in the Ancient Near East*. Washington, DC: Smithsonian Institution Press.

7

Faunal Remains and Subsistence at Monte Albán, Oaxaca

PATRICIA MARTÍNEZ-LIRA, MARCUS WINTER,
TERRY O'CONNOR, AND
JOAQUÍN ARROYO-CABRALES

In many parts of the world including Mesoamerica, faunal remains have been used to infer diet and subsistence strategies in both simple and complex societies (Foreman 2004; Martínez-Lira et al. 2011; Pohl 1985; Siracusano 2004). Wild and domesticated species contributed to the diet, and consumption in some cases varied over time and among different groups in a society (Sandefur 2001). Studies have determined whether species were obtained locally or from different areas or exchanged from farther away for different purposes among high-status members. This chapter focuses on the role of fauna in the economy at Monte Albán, one of the earliest complex societies in Mesoamerica.

At Monte Albán, manos and metates are common and show that households relied on maize as a staple food. Although animal bones have been found frequently at the site, discarded in household refuse, or used to produce implements and ornaments, our study provides the first detailed analysis of faunal remains that show that meat and, by inference, animal protein played an important role in the diet of the urban center's inhabitants. In order to characterize the use of fauna for subsistence at Monte Albán we focus on four topics: (1)

https://doi.org/10.5876/9781646422562.c007

identification of the animals used for food by the population, (2) detection of variation in subsistence patterns during different periods of time and in different areas of the site, (3) determination of what environmental zones provided the animals' food, and (4) comparison of the Monte Albán faunal assemblage with material from other contemporary sites in the Valley of Oaxaca and other regions of Mesoamerica.

BACKGROUND: MONTE ALBÁN

The archaeological site of Monte Albán, in the state of Oaxaca in Mexico's southern highlands, is situated 8 km southwest of Oaxaca City in the center of the Valley of Oaxaca. The valley floor is 1,550 m above sea level, and the surrounding mountains reach 2,000 m in height. The valley is divided into three branches or subvalleys: Etla, Tlacolula, and the Valle Grande (figure 7.1). The Etla Valley is drained by the Río Atoyac and the Tlacolula Valley by the Río Salado. These rivers merge in the center of the valley, east of Monte Albán, and continue as the Atoyac south through Oaxaca's southern highlands to the Pacific Coast.

Monte Albán was Oaxaca's first urban center. The site covers more than 20 km^2, and the intensively inhabited area measures 6.5 km^2 (650 ha) (Blanton 1978). Monte Albán was the center of a complex hierarchical society, and Classic period Zapotec culture was present in the Valley of Oaxaca and the mountainous immediately to the north and south. The Main Plaza and its surrounding buildings, including the North and South Platforms (400 m above the valley floor), comprise Monte Albán's civic ceremonial center (figure 7.2). Natural and artificial terraces with residential structures occur around the plaza. High-status residences tend to be near the city center and low-status ones farther away, though site subdivisions exist with their own high-status residences and public buildings. Monte Albán's population reached an estimated maximum of 25,000 to 30,000 people during the Late Classic (Blanton 1978).

Monte Albán was founded at approximately 500 BC and by the end of the Danibaan phase (300 BC) was the largest community in the Valley of Oaxaca, with an estimated 5,000 inhabitants. During the Pe (300–100 BC) and Nisa phases (100 BC–AD 200), Monte Albán grew in area and population and had widespread influence in the Valley of Oaxaca and beyond. During the Tani phase (AD 200–350), Monte Albán's political relationship with the central Mexican city of Teotihuacan was formalized with the establishment of the Barrio Oaxaqueño at Teotihuacan and then during the Pitao phase (AD 350–500) Teotihuacan took over Monte Albán (Winter 1998) as part of its general expansion in Mesoamerica. Following Teotihuacan's demise at approximately AD 550, Monte Albán underwent a second reorganization and florescence during the Peche (AD 500–650) and Xoo phases (AD 650–850). The city's poorly understood collapse at approximately AD 850 was part of a widespread Mesoamerican decline of Classic period urban centers.

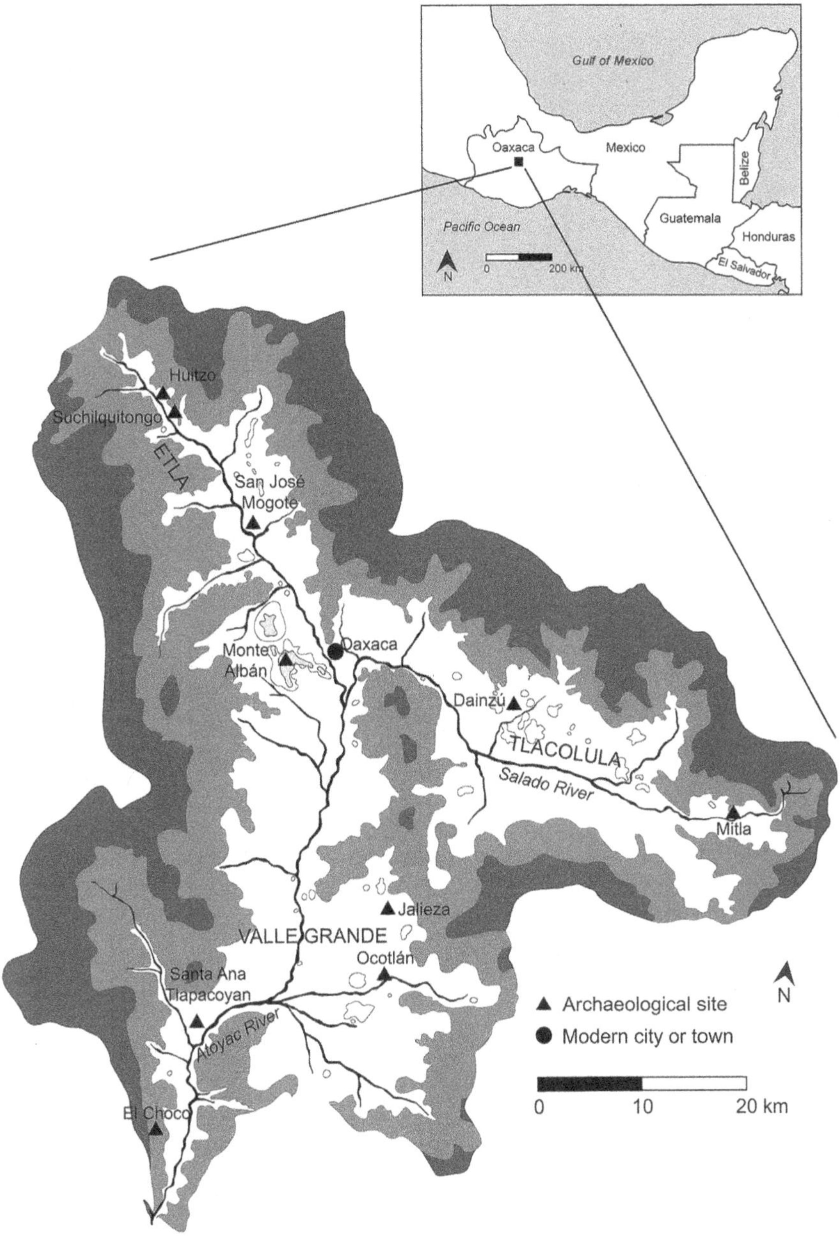

Figure 7.1. *Map of Mexico with location of Monte Albán (after Hutson 2002:54) and the Valley of Oaxaca with three subvalleys: Etla, Tlacolula, and Valle Grande (after Marcus and Flannery 1996:11).*

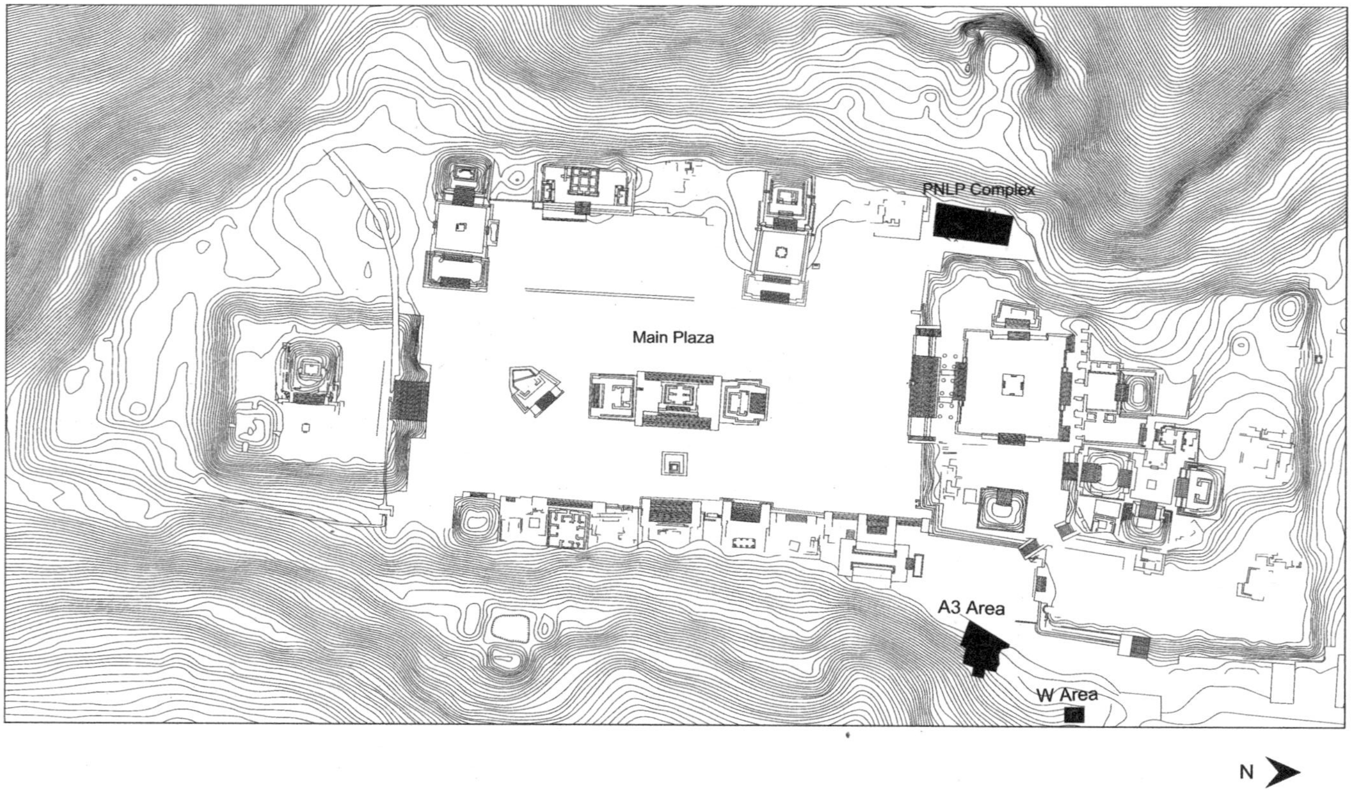

Figure 7.2. *Plan of the Main Plaza of Monte Albán (after Winter 1994:4).*

METHODS AND MATERIALS

The zooarchaeological material analyzed in this study was collected during the Monte Albán Special Project (1992–1994) directed by Marcus Winter. Each bag with animal bones was dated based on associated pottery, which allowed grouping by phases of material from different areas of the site. Study of the faunal remains included (1) identification of taxa and anatomic parts, (2) age determination, (3) quantification of the animal specimens based on minimum number of individuals (MNI) and number of identifiable specimens (NISP), (4) assessment of taphonomic processes, (5) data on procurement and transportation of skeletal parts to the archaeological site, and (6) identification of anatomical patterns present in the archaeofaunal assemblages. The faunal material was separated into the following groups: fish, reptiles, birds, and mammals. Categories of large, medium, and small mammals were established for the mammal bone fragments when identification to the species level was not possible. "Large" is represented by deer, "medium" by dog or peccary, and "small" by hare, rabbit, or rodent. Nonidentifiable specimens were counted, and evidence for taphonomic agents was registered. Identification was in part based on the reference collection of the Archaeozoology Laboratory in the National Institute of Anthropology and History (INAH) in Mexico City, as well as manuals and other literature (e.g., Gilbert 1993; Gilbert et al. 2006; Lawrence and Bossert 1967).

To facilitate identification, cranial and postcranial measurements were taken with a Fowler ultra-cal digital II caliper, following criteria proposed by A. von den Driesch (1999). To aid identification of closely related species—such as wolf, dog, and coyote; different deer taxa such as white-tailed and brocket deer; or hare and rabbit—measurements of modern skeletons were taken from the osteological reference collections of the Archaeozoology Laboratory "M. in C. Ticul Álvarez Solórzano," the National Collection of Mammals of the National Autonomous University of Mexico (UNAM), and the reference collection of the Archaeozoology Laboratory of the Arizona State Museum in Tucson.

Taphonomic agents were considered by examining each bone fragment carefully with a stereoscopic microscope and noting physicochemical, biological, and anthropogenic evidence such as weathering, root action, trampling, rodent and carnivore gnawing, burning, cut marks, percussion marks, and type of fractures (Behrensmeyer 1978; Binford 1981; Johnson 1989; Outram 2002).

To obtain data on procurement and transportation of mammalian skeletal parts to the archaeological site, H. Jackson and S. Scott's (2003) classification for deer was used. Low-utility deer parts include the skull, atlas, axis, cervical vertebrae, carpals, tarsals, metacarpals, metatarsals, and phalanges. Medium-utility elements include the thoracic vertebrae, ribs, and sternum, whereas high-meat content bones are represented by the scapula, forelimbs (humerus, radius, and ulna), pelvis, and hindlimbs (femur and tibia) (Jackson and Scott

2003). Bird anatomy varies from that of mammals, so different elements were considered as high utility, including the scapula, coracoid, sternum, humerus, and femur—particularly in the case of turkey. The radius, ulna, pelvis, and tibiotarsus were related to the medium-meat content range, and the low-meat utility category was formed by cranium, mandible, vertebrae, ribs, carpometacarpus, tarsometatarsus, and phalanges. Identification of high-, medium-, and low-utility elements is used to identify which parts of the animal were transported to and consumed at Monte Albán. These identifications are also used to determine whether patterns can be observed showing that cuts with higher meat content occur in high-status areas.

It is important to link bone transportation to skeletal element survival and taphonomic processes, in order to be certain that the anatomical patterns represented at Monte Albán are a consequence of human selection rather than natural processes (Faith and Gordon 2007). Dense elements with thick cortical walls and medullary cavities, such as long bones and mandibles, are classified as high-survival elements, as is the cranium, due to the presence of teeth (Cleghorn and Marean 2004; Faith and Gordon 2007). Low-survival bones include elements with thin cortical walls, low-density, and grease-rich cancellous portions, such as vertebrae, ribs, pelvises, scapulae and long-bone ends (Cleghorn and Marean 2004; Faith and Gordon 2007). Phalanges and small compact bones are considered part of the low-density group since they are frequently consumed or swallowed by carnivores (Cleghorn and Marean 2004; Faith and Gordon 2007).

The faunal remains considered in this study come from three areas of Monte Albán: Area A3, the PNLP Complex, and structures W1 and W2 of Area W (figure 7.2). Area A3 is located on the slope immediately east of the North Platform, and consisted of platforms and portions of residential structures, principally from the Danibaan, Pe, and Nisa phases. The PNLP Complex, located west of the south end of the North Platform, consisted of a patio surrounded by low platforms, designated structures PNLP-1 to PNLP-5 (structures 1 to 5), mostly of the Nisa phase. The complex has been interpreted as a garrison for guards controlling access in and out of the Main Plaza; a temple (Structure PNLP-1) indicates ritual activity in the complex (Martínez and Markens 2004; Winter et al. 2001).

Area W is located east of the North Platform and includes structures W1 and W2 (figure 7.2), which correspond to the Nisa, Pitao, Peche, and Xoo phases. Structure W1 consisted of three superimposed houses designated W1-A, W1-B, and W1-C. A typical closed residential format was present: a central patio surrounded by rooms with tombs under the west room, burials, midden deposits, and hearths. The W2 structures showed a distribution different from the closed pattern of the residences, though a hearth found in room W2-1 indicated that domestic activities took place. The northern part of the W2 terrace might have been used for growing corn or other plants, and the southern part could have been used to prepare or store foods. Terrace W2-B had a rectangular structure from the Xoo phase (Morales et al. 1999). Most of the analyzed samples correspond to three different time periods: the Pe, Nisa, and Pitao phases.

RESULTS

A total of 1,564 NISP and 784 MNI bone remains were identified to order, family, genus, and species level (table 7.1). An additional 1,040 fragments were identified to class level, and 1,184 unidentified (small splinters) completed the sample. Each species was considered in terms of four functions: diet, raw material, symbolism, and ritual. Evidence of this kind was observed in the faunal remains from all four areas.

In order to distinguish subsistence preferences, taxa related to human consumption were separated, taking into account the following criteria: species used for diet in other archaeological sites in Mesoamerica; faunal remains associated with contexts related to food preparation, such as hearths or midden deposits at Monte Albán; and other cultural taphonomic evidence on bones such as cut marks. In general, almost all of the species persisted throughout this sequence. Even though the political situation of Monte Albán changed, there was no evidence of a greater diversity of taxa being used or a considerable exploitation of different ecosystems. Identification of some species that were not part of the diet was based on the taxon represented in the sample, the type of context where they have been found at Monte Albán or elsewhere in Mesoamerica, their representation in codices and stelae, and sixteenth-century ethnohistoric sources (Carr 1985; Seler 2008; Tozzer 1941; Urcid 2005).

In this study, turkey was classified as a domestic species together with dog. All other taxa are considered wild. Dogs could have been used for many purposes besides subsistence, but cut marks observed on some bones and presence of burned bone fragments showed that dogs were part of the diet. Also, dog bones were found in domestic midden deposits, mixed with other elements of subsistence species such as turkey, deer, rabbits, and hares. Mammals comprised the majority of the zooarchaeological sample (70.6% NISP), birds a considerable portion (28.6% NISP), and only marginal numbers of reptiles (0.38% NISP) or fish (0.38% NISP). Therefore, we assume that subsistence was based more on wild and domestic terrestrial mammals and fowl than on riverine or marine resources.

The most frequent subsistence taxa in the total sample were common turkey (NISP=429), cervids (NISP=319, including fragments identified as white-tailed deer and brocket deer), canids (NISP=266, fragments identified as "dog" and "probable dog" constituted this category), collared peccary (NISP=189), and lagomorphs (NISP=122, fragments identified as lagomorphs, hare, white-sided jackrabbit, rabbit, Mexican cottontail, and eastern cottontail) (table 7.1). These

Table 7.1. Total of identified taxa from Monte Albán.

	Taxon	*Common Name*	*NISP*	*MNI*
Actinopterygii	*Centropomus* sp.	Snook	3	3
	Family Serranidae	Sea bass	1	1
	Ictiobus sp.	Buffalo fish	1	1
	Joturus pichardoi	Bobo mullet	1	1
Reptilia	Order Testudines/ Chelonia	Turtle	1	1
	Kinosternon	Mud turtle	2	2
	Trachemys scripta	Pond slider	1	1
	Chelonia mydas	Green turtle	1	1
	Family cf. Crocodylidae	Crocodylus	1	1
Aves	*Cassiculus melanicterus*	Yellow-winged cacique	1	1
	Corvus corax	Common raven	1	1
	Bubo virginianus	Great horned owl	1	1
	Family cf. Anatidae		1	1
	Family Anatidae	Duck	3	1
	cf. *Buteo* sp.		1	1
	Buteo sp.	Hawk	1	1
	Buteo jamaicencis	Red-tailed hawk	1	1
	Larus pipixcan	Franklin's gull	1	1
	Cyrtonix montezumae	Montezuma or harlequin quail	6	6
	cf. *Meleagris*		1	1
	Meleagris gallopavo	Common turkey	429	148
	cf. Crax	Curassow	1	1
Mammalia	cf. *Canis* sp.		2	2
	Canis sp.	Wolf, dog, coyotes	235	115
	cf. *Canis lupus familiaris*		4	3
	Canis lupus familiaris	Dog	25	22
	Canis cf. *latrans*	Coyote	1	1
	Canis cf. *lupus*	Wolf	4	2
	Urocyon cinereoargenteus	Gray fox, tree fox	2	2
	Procyon lotor	Northern raccoon	1	1
	Nasua narica	Coatimundi, white-nosed coati	1	1
	Puma concolor	Mountain lion	4	3
	Order Artiodactyla	Artiodactyl	183	96

continued on next page

Table 7.1.—*continued*

Taxon	Common Name	NISP	MNI
Dycotyles crassus	Collared peccary	189	89
Tayassu cf. *peccari*	White-lipped peccary	3	3
cf. *Odocoileus* sp.		4	3
Odocoileus sp.	Deer	22	19
Odocoileus virginianus	White-tailed deer	288	136
cf. *Mazama temama*		4	4
Mazama temama	Brocket deer	1	1
Order Lagomorpha	Lagomorph	13	12
Lepus sp.	Hare	33	25
Lepus callotis	White-sided jackrabbit	15	12
Sylvilagus sp.	Rabbit	28	18
Sylvilagus cf. *cunicularius*		1	1
Sylvilagus cunicularius	Mexican cottontail	9	8
Sylvilagus cf. *floridanus*		1	1
Sylvilagus floridanus	Eastern cottontail	22	18
Order Rodentia		1	1
Orthogeomys grandis	Giant pocket gopher	5	5
Peromyscus cf. *maniculatus*	White-footed or deer mouse	1	1
Peromyscus melanophrys	Plateau deer mouse	1	1
Liomys irroratus	Mexican spiny pocket mouse	1	1
Total		1,564	784

taxa were selected for analysis and for comparison by period and by excavation areas.

Taxa frequencies varied among Area A3, PNLP Complex, and the W1 and W2 structures. For instance, the highest percentage of deer (48.88% NISP) was observed in the PNLP Complex. The people (guards) who lived in this area may have had relatively more access to meat than other people if the meat were provided as tribute or tax by people entering the market, or if they obtained meat in exchange for ceramics and shell objects produced here (Martínez and Markens 2014). This complex could have also been used for rituals or public ceremonies, where higher numbers of people congregated and larger taxa were required. In this area, wild species were also more abundant than domestic animals. In Area W2, the number of cervids was also high compared to the rest of the subsistence taxa in this area (43.47% NISP). Area A3 presented a higher percentage of

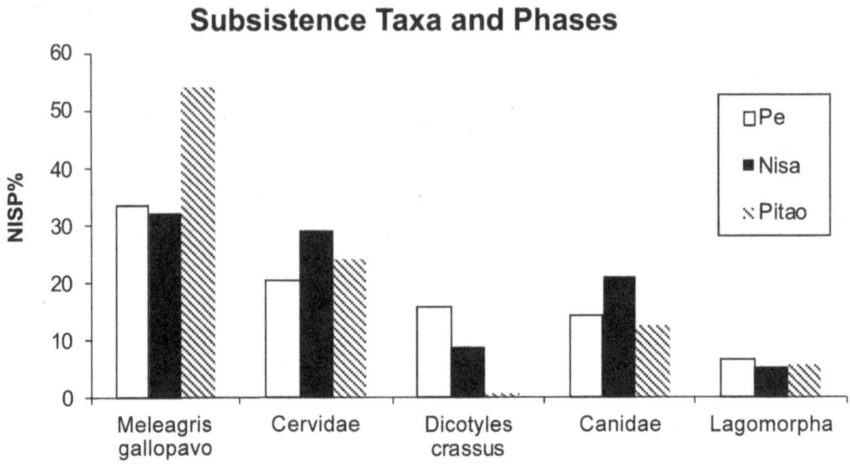

Figure 7.3. *Taxa used for subsistence in the Pe, Nisa, and Pitao phases.*

common turkey (36.69% NISP) than the other areas, and canids had a greater presence in Area W1 (29.91% NISP). The highest percentage of peccary was found in Area W2 (19.81% NISP), so it seems that in this place wild species were more frequent than domestic ones, as in the PNLP Complex.

Percentages of some but not all taxa changed by time period. Taxa used for subsistence varied during the Pe, Nisa, and Pitao phases (figure 7.3). For instance, a noticeable increase of common turkey can be seen from the Pe and Nisa phases to the Pitao phase, while collared peccary showed an opposite trend. The Lagomorph group (i.e., hares and rabbits) remained stable throughout the three phases. In the Pe phase the most prevalent species was the common turkey, followed by the group of cervids, collared peccary, canids, and lagomorphs. It is not certain if the relative drop in collared peccary percentage was due to overhunting this species, or to dietary preferences. Peccary may have been brought to the site less frequently or substituted by domestic species. Deer percentages reached their highest point in the Nisa and then dropped in the Pitao phase.

In general, deer, one of the most favored taxa, did not diminish drastically (suggesting that it may not have been overexploited), nor was it totally replaced by less-favored ones (smaller mammals or species with less meat content). Nor was there an increase in overall species diversity or a sharp drop of previously highly favored species. It seems that there was no need to incorporate new animals such as freshwater turtles, fish, wild birds, and small mammals, because common taxa did not diminish or become extinct through hunting (Broughton and Grayson 1993). The same taxa remained present, except for the significant drop of peccary, which might have been due to different causes. The presence of peccary at other sites and in other periods needs to be evaluated to confirm

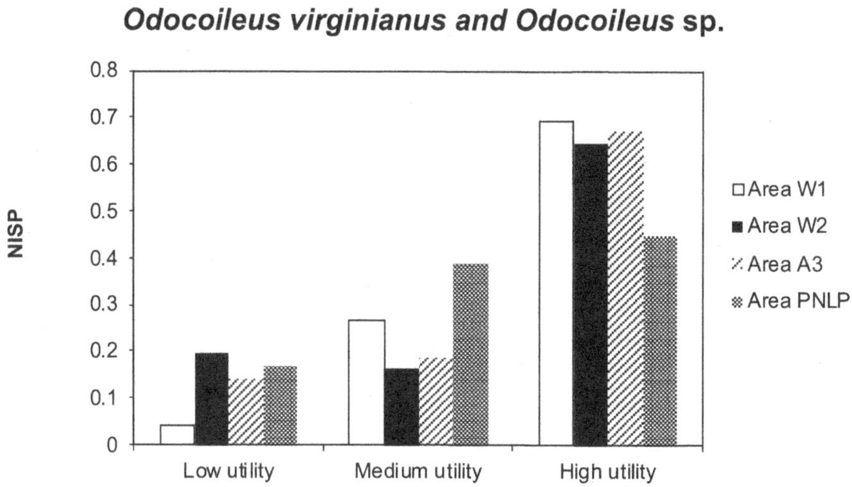

Figure 7.4. *Percentages of low-, medium-, and high-utility anatomical parts of* Odocoileus virginianus *and* Odocoileus *sp. in W1, W2, A3, and PNLP areas.*

that this trend persisted, and in order to infer with more clarity the reason for this decline.

Different parts of the skeleton (high-, medium-, and low-utility elements) of dog, turkey, peccary, hare, and rabbit were identified in all the areas, suggesting that these animals were butchered, prepared, eaten, and discarded at the site (Martínez-Lira 2014). In contrast, most of the anatomical parts of cervids represented in all the areas correspond to high- and medium-meat content (figure 7.4).

High-survival elements such as mandibles (1.27% NISP), teeth, or metapodials (1.27% NISP) are scarce in the sample, whereas low-survival bones are more abundant (97.46% NISP). The anatomical pattern of deer seems to be related to bone transportation decisions rather than to the preservation of bones. Since Monte Albán is located 400 m above the valley floor, it is possible that only high- and medium-utility portions were brought to the site or that deer were butchered in other areas of the site. If this were the case, large portions of the heavier or nonmeat sections would be found in the areas where deer were butchered, while the most desirable portions would occur in the elite residential and/or ceremonial contexts (Jackson and Scott 2003).

Another possibility is that low-meat content parts were used to manufacture tools. A case in point would be a deer metapodial used as a punch found in a tomb as part of the offering (Winter et al. 1995). There were more thoracic and lumbar than cervical vertebrae, which might indicate that the head was removed close to the shoulder during the initial butchering (Kelly 2000). In the Maya area, deer elements most used in ritual contexts such as caves were crania, antlers, and teeth (Pohl 1983). So it is quite possible that the missing anatomical parts of deer also might have been used in other contexts or transported to other sites. In the case of turkey, peccary, or rabbits, high-, medium-, and low-meat content bones were present in a more equal distribution, showing that complete skeletons were present or brought to the site.

DISCUSSION

In general, the Area A3, the PNLP Complex, and structures W1 and W2 of Area W showed a similar pattern of high-, medium-, and low-utility parts. There is not a marked difference of high-utility parts between these areas related to a higher status.

Dogs may have been used for consumption as well as for ritual purposes. Compared to the anatomical pattern of deer, it is not so obvious that all dog skeletal remains represent human consumption, since there was a similar proportion of high-, medium-, and low-meat-content bones. In general, in Mesoamerica, dogs were valued for both consumption and their symbolic meaning (Blank 2006; Garza 1997; Merino and Garcia Cook 1997).

According to S. Kansa and S. Campbell (2004), ritual or symbolic animals can sometimes be identified archaeologically by the degree of completeness of the skeleton. Dogs at Monte Albán are represented by different parts of the skeleton. Therefore, it is possible that some of these remains were also the result of symbolic or ritual acts, such as offerings or sacrifices. In Mesoamerica, dogs had important symbolic significance, since they were considered to be guides in the underworld, or Mictlán (Garza 1997). Dogs were sometimes sacrificed and buried with humans as part of the funerary offerings. Bones of *Canis familiaris* have been found in tombs and burials in Monte Albán and at other sites in the Valley of Oaxaca (Pérez and Winter 2014).

Dogs may well have been living with humans as companions or pets, and the whole carcass could have been discarded or buried when they died. Dogs were also used for food, since some bones found in domestic refuse showed burning and disarticulation cut marks. In Oaxaca, consumption of dogs is documented as early as the Guadalupe phase (900–700 BC); J. Marcus and K. V. Flannery (1996:116) reported a bell-shaped pit that contained the remains of five dogs that had been butchered systematically, possibly by the same individual. In the Tehuacán Valley, Puebla, dogs were consumed, and they generally constituted an important food resource in different regions of Mesoamerica, especially in times of a growing population (Flannery 1967; MacNeish 1967).

In Mesoamerica, common turkey was used for consumption and ritual, and bones were used as raw material (Corona-Martínez 2013a, 2013b; Seler 2008). During the Xoo phase in the Valley of Oaxaca, small birds were sometimes placed in tombs of high-status individuals (Urcid 2008:542), but at Monte Albán there is no evidence of turkey found in funerary contexts. Based on this evidence, it seems more likely that turkey remains were used as a food resource at Monte Albán than for ritual purposes.

The collared peccary and the white-lipped peccary were part of the subsistence inventory and have not been reported from ritual contexts at Monte Albán or other sites in Oaxaca. Lagomorphs could have had both ritual and dietary uses. According to ethnohistoric descriptions, rabbit was a high-status food in the Valley of Oaxaca (Horcasitas and George 1955). At the archaeological site of El Palmillo in the Valley of Oaxaca, rabbits were part of the diet among high-status members, and many animal offerings discovered in the terraces included rabbits (Haller et al. 2006). In Tomb 196 in Area W at Monte Albán, bones of two complete rabbit skeletons were placed in a ceramic vessel as part of the offering (Martínez et al. 2014:3). Bones of lagomorphs were discovered in refuse deposits at Monte Albán together with other taxa related to consumption, showing that this group of animals was also part of the diet.

Natural Environment of the Species Represented in the Sample

Faunal remains in archaeological assemblages may provide information about the kinds of environments exploited to obtain food or other types of resources. Species from diverse environments were present in the Monte Albán sample (table 7.2). All the species represented in the archaeological sample are still found today in the State of Oaxaca (Briones-Salas and Sánchez-Cordero 2004; Casas-Andreu et al. 2004; Martínez et al. 2004; Navarro et al. 2004), so some of the environments and habitats occupied by the species in the past may be inferred. Marine taxa and riverine species were rare. Monte Albán is located at the confluence of the Río Atoyac and Río Salado, and the fish identified in the assemblages from the four areas may have been obtained from those rivers.

Terrestrial taxa were the most abundant group, including the mammals. Domesticated species, such as dogs and turkeys, and other animals living near human settlements, cornfields, or other cultivated areas, constituted a large part of the assemblage. Deer and peccary would have inhabited the pine-oak zones in the mountains surrounding the valley. In the Monte Albán sample, white-tailed deer (NISP=288) are more abundant than brocket deer (NISP=5) (table 7.2). It is possible that the brocket deer species was found in habitats farther away from Monte Albán than white-tailed deer. Lagomorphs and other small mammals would have lived in the piedmont and also alluvial areas near the rivers. The Maya preferred to exploit the white-tailed, but brocket deer was also occasionally hunted, a trend corroborated by the lower frequency of brocket deer compared to white-tailed deer from all coastal and almost all the Maya inland sites (Foreman 2004). Some of these animals may have been attracted by the altered environment immediately around the settlements. Only a few taxa, such

Table 7.2. Habitats of animals identified by bone fragments from Monte Albán.

Taxon	*Common Name*	*Habitat*	*%*	*NISP*
Chelonia mydas	Green turtle	Marine	0.10	1
Testudines	Turtle	Riverine	0.10	1
Trachemys scripta	Pond slider	Riverine / lacustrine / pond	0.10	1
Kinostenon	Mud turtle	Riverine	0.20	2
Family Serranidae	Sea basses	Riverine	0.10	1
Ictiobus sp.	Buffalo fish	Riverine	0.10	1
Centropomus sp.	Snook	Riverine	0.31	3
Joturus pichardoi	Bobo mullet	Riverine	0.10	1
Family cf. Crocodylidae	Crocodile	Fresh water	0.10	1
Cyrtonix montezumae	Montezuma quail	Pine-oak / open woodland	0.41	4
Corvus corax	Common raven	Open field / dense vegetation	0.10	1
Puma concolor	Cougar, panther	Forest / grassland / desert	0.20	2
cf. *Mazama temama*	Brocket deer	Forest / woodland	0.10	1
Mazama temama	Brocket deer	Forest / woodland	0.41	4
Tayassu cf. *pecari*	White-lipped peccary	Forest	0.31	3
Canis cf. *lupus*	Wolf	Mountain forest / woodland	0.41	4
Sylvilagus floridanus	Eastern cottontail	Forest / marsh / prairie	1.84	18
Sylvilagus cunicularius	Mexican cottontail	Arid lowland / temperate highlands	0.71	7
Cassiculus melanicterus	Yellow-winged cacique	Cultivated area / wooded	0.10	1
cf. *Buteo* sp.	Hawk	Cultivated area / forest	0.10	1
Buteo sp.	Hawk	Cultivated area / forest	0.10	1
Buteo jamaicencis	Red-tailed hawk	Cultivated area / forest	0.10	1
Family Anatidae	Ducks	Cultivated area / rivers / lakes	0.41	4
cf. Crax	Curassow	Cultivated area / forest	0.10	1
Meleagris gallopavo	Common turkey	Cultivated area / open woodland / domestic	43.78	429
Odocoileus virginianus	White-tailed deer	Cultivated area / forest / thicket / desert	29.39	288
Dicotyles crassus	Collared peccary	Cultivated area / arid woodland / rainforest	15.51	152
Urocyon cinereoargenteus	Gray fox, tree fox	Cultivated area / forest–high brush / woodland	0.10	1
Canis cf. *latrans*	Coyote	Cultivated area / forest / grassland / desert	0.10	1
Nasua narica	White-nosed coati	Cultivated area / tropical / forest	0.10	1

continued on next page

Table 7.2.—*continued*

Taxon	*Common Name*	*Habitat*	*%*	*NISP*
Lepus callotis	White-sided jackrabbit	Cornfields/thicket/desert	1.43	14
Canis lupus familiaris	Dog	Domestic	2.96	29
Total			100	980

as the green turtle, were brought to the site from far away. This species was probably brought to the site from the Pacific Coast, since shells from that region have been found at Monte Albán (Melgar et al. 2010:18) and are more common than shells from the Atlantic or Caribbean areas.

Comparison of the Monte Albán Faunal Assemblage with Contemporary Sites

Food in relation to status is a topic of research in Mesoamerica. The elite of Monte Albán not only had greater access to prestigious materials such as jade, but also had differential access to specific food items, especially meat. According to isotope studies reported by J Blitz (1995), a statistical difference exists between the diet of people buried in tombs and those buried in other contexts, when all time periods are analyzed together, indicating that elite had more access to meat. However, when different periods are separated, only during the Classic period (AD 200–800) is a statistically significant dietary difference by burial type observed. High-status meat consumption is supported by ethnohistoric sources and archaeological evidence before and after the Classic period occupation of Monte Albán. Isotopic studies demonstrate that in the Classic period, meat consumption varied among members of different status groups (Blitz 1995). The faunal remains considered in the present study come from areas around the Main Plaza of Monte Albán, places that thus may have been of high meat consumption.

Faunal analysis from the Classic period at the El Palmillo archaeological site in the Valley of Oaxaca shows dietary variation between social classes. Remains of white-tailed deer, domestic dog, cottontail rabbit, and jackrabbit were more abundant in the upper terraces occupied by the elite, whereas reptile and turtle were more common in the lower terraces occupied by commoners. Species found in the upper terraces were present but less frequent in the lower ones. At Monte Albán the use of white-tailed deer, domestic dog, turkey, collared peccary, cottontail rabbit, and jackrabbit is documented for the Preclassic and Classic periods. Turtles were scarce in all four areas studied at Monte Albán, and no other reptiles were documented (table 7.1). This pattern coincides with that observed in the uppermost terraces of El Palmillo. Another similarity was that during the Classic period at Monte Albán, the percentage of collared peccary was very low, compared to the Preclassic. At El Palmillo the presence of this taxon was also very rare in the Classic period (Haller et al. 2006).

At the site of Ejutla, located on the alluvial floor at the southern end of the Valley of Oaxaca, during the Classic period, the diet was based more on small mammals than at the hilltop sites of El Palmillo and Monte Albán, where domesticated animals were more abundant than lagomorphs (Haller et al. 2006). El Palmillo was located in a dry area of the valley, where domestic species may have been crucial to survival. In contrast, Ejutla was situated in a fertile area, where small mammals, specially Lagomorpha, could have been found in or next to agricultural fields (Haller et al. 2006; Middleton et al. 2002). It will be interesting if future studies show this trend to be consistent between hilltop and valley sites.

The Maya were organized in city-states ruled by nobles linked by diverse and complex bonds of kinship, exchange, and political alliances (McKillop 2004). During the Late Preclassic (200 BC–AD 600), Classic (AD 200–800), and Postclassic periods (AD 800–1200), the Maya elite ate more meat and the best cuts; had a greater diversity and variety of animal resources and a larger number of domesticated animals and deer; showed management of wild animals, imported fish, and marine resources; and made greater use of wild birds than commoners (Emery 2003; Masson 1999; Pohl 1994). Results from Monte Albán showed that the diet consisted of domestic species during the Preclassic and Classic periods, similar to the taxa found in Maya high-status contexts (Carr 1985; Emery 2003, 2004; Masson 2004).

The Zapotecs at Monte Albán consumed similar faunal resources to those used by the Maya. In the Maya area, it seems that there was a continuum in the use of fauna with local and temporal variations (Masson 2004). Monte Albán results show that there was a continuum in the use of animal species with variations in frequencies of some species through time and among areas of the site. The most common subsistence resources among the Maya were the domesticated dog and turkey, both of them raised in households (Emery 2004; Wing 2004). At Monte Albán the two domestic species were also dog and turkey. In the Maya area, some research has focused on isotopic studies of dog, deer, and peccary to find out whether these animals were fed directly by humans (White and Schwarcz 1989; White et al. 2001). Analysis of Sr, Mg, and Zn demonstrated that deer and peccary from the Lamanai site were fed with maize (White and Schwarcz 1989). Isotopic studies of dogs from the Cuello site indicated 70% maize consumption (similar to that of humans), suggesting that people were feeding some dogs (Pohl 1994). Wild animals such as deer and peccary constituted a significant part of meat consumption, except for sites along the coast, where seafood represented an important part of the diet (McKillop 2004). At Monte Albán, deer was frequently used as a food resource and peccary to a lesser degree. Among the Maya, smaller wild mammals (lagomorphs), freshwater turtles and fish, shellfish, wild birds, and marine fish were also part of the diet (Pohl 1994; Wing 2004). Prestige and subsistence goods were exchanged from both near and more distant locations (McKillop 2004). These kinds of animals were not very abundant at Monte Albán and in some cases (marine fish) were absent.

During the Classic period in the Valley of Mexico, Teotihuacan became a city-state and a pan-Mesoamerican commercial and military power. This city and its allies had contact with societies in the Valley of Oaxaca, the Gulf Coast region of Mexico, West Mexico, and the Maya highlands and coast. At Teotihuacan, domesticated animals were not an important part of the diet and were not used to increase meat supply (Starbuck 1975). Only dogs and turkeys were available to Teotihuacanos, and they constituted no more than 10% of the meat consumed. In the Valley of Mexico, domestication did not become a significant dietary alternative until later, in the Postclassic period. By this time, continuous overhunting had seriously reduced the available supply of game animals in the Valley of Mexico (Starbuck 1987). However, it will be important to corroborate this trend with future and more recent studies.

CONCLUSIONS

Our study of faunal remains from Monte Albán has shown that inhabitants relied on species common in Mesoamerica, the most frequent in order of importance were deer, turkey, dog, peccary, and lagomorphs. Diet was based mainly on land mammals and domestic birds. Fish and turtles were obtained occasionally, the former probably from rivers near Monte Albán. Many mammals could have been found in local habitats near Monte Albán or in areas under cultivation, while other species were brought from further afield, possibly for ornamental or ritual purposes, such as cougar, common raven, and green turtle.

Variations were detected among species related to subsistence patterns in the different areas. For example, the PNLP Complex showed the highest percentage of cervids among the identified samples, and domestic animals were less prevalent than wild species, particularly deer. According to C. Martínez and R. Markens (2004), the PNLP Complex was used as a public space, where ceremonies or feasts took place, so animals with high meat content may have been consumed here more frequently than in common household contexts. The anatomical pattern observed of species used for subsistence did not vary significantly between the areas under study: high- and medium-meat-content bones were distributed similarly. The evidence does not indicate any differences among the areas regarding access to the most desirable anatomical parts with more meat content. However, it does indicate that a complex deer-provisioning system was practiced at Monte Albán, in which selected anatomical parts were supplied to the site.

The taxa used for subsistence varied between the Pe, Nisa, and Pitao phases, but there is no evidence of a greater diversity of taxa being used or a significant exploitation of different ecosystems. The presence of domesticated species such as common turkey at Monte Albán increased from the Preclassic to the Classic period, probably as a result of a subsistence strategy of increased reliance on domesticated species to deal with population growth.

The species consumed by the Zapotecs were similar to those used by Maya and Teotihuacanos (Emery 2004; McKillop 2004; Starbuck 1975, 1987). At Monte Albán, as at El Palmillo and in Maya area, differences in meat and species consumption existed between the elite and nonelite members of the community (Emery 2003, 2007; Haller et al. 2006; Masson 1999; Pohl 1994).

The zooarchaeological analysis reported here provides information about people at Monte Albán, their diet, and their relationship with their environment. It has also offered the possibility of comparing Zapotec subsistence patterns at Monte Albán with those in other sites in the Valley of Oaxaca and in other parts of Mesoamerica, and raises questions about the role of government and social mechanisms of obtaining and distributing resources that may be answered with future studies.

Acknowledgments. Special thanks are due to archaeologist Cira Martínez López for providing chronological data on the samples and for her general advice during the time of the first author's research. Martínez-Lira would also like to acknowledge the support of the Mexican National Council of Science and Technology (Conacyt) for awarding her a scholarship to carry out the study. We would also like to express our gratitude to Mr. Aurelio Ocaña for identifying the bird remains and the fragments of mammals that were uncommon in the sample; to biologist Norma Valentín, who helped identify the turtle remains; and to Dra. Fabiola Guzmán, who identified the fish remains presented in this study. We are also grateful to biologist Teresa Olivares for her support during the time the first author carried out the identification of Monte Albán bone remains in the Archaeozoology Laboratory of the INAH in Mexico City. Finally, we would like to thank archaeologist Elba Domínguez for preparing Figures 7.1 and 7.2 and to Maria Jessen for proofreading an earlier draft of this chapter.

WORKS CITED

Behrensmeyer, A. K. 1978. "Taphonomic and Ecologic Information from Bone Weathering." *Paleobiology* 4 (2): 150–162.

Binford, L. R. 1981. *Bones: Ancient Man and Modern Myth*. New York: Academic Press.

Blank, J. I. 2006. *Los perros del México antiguo*. Mexico City: Facultad de Medicina y Zootecnia, Universidad Nacional Autónoma de México.

Blanton, R. E. 1978. *Monte Alban: Settlement Patterns at the Ancient Zapotec Capital*. New York: Academic Press.

Blitz, J. B. 1995. "Dietary Variability and Social Inequality at Monte Albán, Oaxaca, Mexico." PhD diss., Department of Anthropology, University of Wisconsin, Madison.

Briones-Salas, M., and V. Sánchez-Cordero. 2004. "Mamíferos." In *Biodiversidad de Oaxaca*, edited by A. J. García-Mendoza, M. de J. Ordoñez, and M. Briones-Salas, 421–447. Mexico City: UNAM, Fondo Oaxaqueño para la Conservación de la Naturaleza, World Wildlife Fund.

Broughton, J. M., and D. K. Grayson. 1993. "Diet Breadth, Adaptive Change, and the White Mountains Faunas." *Journal of Archaeological Science* 20 (3): 331–336.

Carr, H. S. 1985. "Subsistence and Ceremony: Faunal Utilization in a Late Preclassic Community at Cerros, Belize." In *Prehistoric Lowland Maya Environment and Subsistence Economy*, edited by M. Pohl, 115–132. Cambridge, MA: Harvard University Press.

Casas-Andreu, G., F. R. Méndez-de la Cruz, and X. Aguilar-Miguel. 2004. "Anfibios y reptiles." In *Biodiversidad de Oaxaca*, edited by A. J. García-Mendoza, M. de J. Ordoñez, and M. Briones-Salas, 375–390. Mexico City: UNAM, Fondo Oaxaqueño para la Conservación de la Naturaleza, World Wildlife Fund.

Cleghorn, N., and C. W. Marean. 2004. "Distinguishing Selective Transport and *In Situ* Attrition: A Critical Review of Analytical Approaches." *Journal of Taphonomy* 2 (2): 43–67.

Corona-Martínez, E. 2013a. "El guajolote se pavonea fuera de América." *Tlacuache* 598: 1–4.

Corona-Martínez, E. 2013b. "Birds of the Pre-Hispanic Domestic Spheres of Central Mexico." In *The Archaeology of Mesoamerican Animals, Archaeobiology*, edited by C. Götz and K. F. Emery, 81–94. Atlanta: Lockwood Press.

Emery, K. F. 2003. "The Noble and the Beast: Status and Differential Access to Animals in the Maya World." *World Archaeology* 34 (3): 498–515.

Emery, K. F. 2004. "In Search of the Maya Diet: Is Regional Comparison Possible in the Maya Tropics?" *Archaeofauna* 13: 37–56.

Emery, K. F. 2007. "Assessing the Impact of Ancient Maya Animal Use." *Journal of Nature Conservation* 15 (3): 184–195.

Faith, T. J., and A. D. Gordon. 2007. "Skeletal Element Abundances in Archaeofaunal Assemblages: Economic Utility, Sample Size, and Assessment of Carcass Transport Strategies." *Journal of Archaeological Science* 34 (6): 872–882.

Flannery, K. V. 1967. "Vertebrate Fauna and Hunting Patterns." In *The Prehistory of the Tehuacan Valley: Environment and Subsistence*, edited by D. S. Byers, 132–177. Austin: University of Texas Press.

Foreman, L. 2004. "The Truth about Deer, Turtles, and Dogs: An Examination of the Ancient Maya Human-Faunal Interactions." *University of Western Ontario Journal of Anthropology* 12: 32–48.

Garza, M. de la. 1997. "El perro como símbolo religioso entre los mayas y los nahuas." *Estudios de Cultura Náhuatl* 27: 111–133.

Gilbert, B. M. 1993. *Mammalian Osteology*. Columbia: Missouri Archaeological Society.

Gilbert, B. M., L. D. Martin, and H. G. Savage. 2006. *Avian Osteology*. Columbia: Missouri Archaeological Society.

Haller, M. J., G. M. Feinman, and L. M. Nicholas. 2006. "Socioeconomic Inequality and Differential Access to Faunal Resources at El Palmillo, Oaxaca, Mexico." *Ancient Mesoamerica* 17 (1): 39–55.

Horcasitas, F., and R. George. 1955. "The Relación de Tlacolula y Mitla." *Notas Mesoamericanas* 3: 13–24.

Hutson, S. R. 2002. "Built in Space and Bad Subjects." *Journal of Social Archaeology* 2 (1): 53–80.

Jackson, H. E., and S. L. Scott. 2003. "Patterns of Elite Faunal Utilization at Moundville, Alabama." *American Antiquity* 68 (3): 552–572.

Johnson, E. 1989. "Human Modified Bones from Early Southern Plains Sites." In *Bone Modification*, edited by R. Bonnichsen and M. H. Sorg, 431–447. Orono: University of Maine Center for the Study of the First Americans.

Kansa, S. W., and S. Campbell. 2004. "Feasting with the Dead? A Ritual Bone Deposit at Domuztepe, South Eastern Turkey (c. 5550 ca. B.C.)." In *Behavior behind Bones: The Zooarchaeology of Ritual, Religion, Status and Identity*, edited by S. J. O'Day, W. van Neer, and A. Ervynck, 2–13. Oxford: Oxbow Books.

Kelly, L. S. 2000. "Spatial Implications of Faunal Provisioning for the Cahokia Site: Initial Mississippian, Lohmann Phase." PhD diss., Washington University, St. Louis.

Lawrence, B., and W. H. Bossert. 1967. "Multiple Character Analysis of *Canis lupus*, *latrans*, and *familiaris*, with a Discussion of the Relationship of *Canis niger*." *Zoologist* 7 (2): 223–232.

MacNeish, R. S. 1967. "A Summary of the Subsistence." In *The Prehistory of the Tehuacan Valley: Environment and Subsistence*, edited by D. S. Byers, 290–309. Austin: University of Texas Press.

Marcus, J., and K. V. Flannery. 1996. *Zapotec Civilization: How Urban Society Evolved in Mexico's Oaxaca Valley*. London: Thames and Hudson.

Martínez, C., M. Winter, and R. Markens. 2014. *Muerte y vida entre los Zapotecos de Monte Albán*. Arqueología Oaxaqueña 5. Oaxaca: Centro INAH.

Martínez, C., and R. Markens. 2004. "Análisis de la función político-económica del Conjunto Plataforma Norte Lado Poniente de la Plaza Principal de Monte Albán." In *Estructuras políticas en el Oaxaca antiguo: Memorias de la Tercera Mesa Redonda de Monte Albán*, edited by N. Robles, 75–99. Mexico City: Instituto Nacional de Antropología e Historia.

Martínez, E., I. Doadrio, and A. de Sostoa. 2004. "Peces continentales." In *Biodiversidad de Oaxaca*, edited by A. J. Garcia-Mendoza, M. de J. Ordoñez, and M. Briones-Salas, 357–373. Mexico City: UNAM, Fondo Oaxaqueño para la Conservación de la Naturaleza, World Wildlife Fund.

Martínez-Lira, P. 2014. "Faunal Remains and Zapotec Elite at Monte Albán during the Preclassic and Classic Periods." PhD diss., University of York, York, England.

Martínez-Lira, P., J. Arroyo-Cabrales, and J. Carpenter. 2011. "Faunal Remains and Subsistence Practices at the Archaeological Site *La Playa*, in Sonora, Mexico." *Kiva* 1 (77): 33–58.

Masson, M. A. 1999. "Animal Resource Manipulation in Ritual and Domestic Contexts at Postclassic Maya Communities." *World Archaeology* 31 (1): 93–120.

Masson, M. A. 2004. "Fauna Exploitation from the Preclassic to the Postclassic Periods at Four Maya Settlements in Northern Belize." In *Maya Zooarchaeology: New Directions in Methods and Theory*, edited by K. F. Emery, 97–122. UCLA: Cotsen Institute of Archaeology.

McKillop, H. 2004. *Salt: White Gold of the Ancient Maya*. Gainesville: University Press of Florida.

Melgar, E., R. Solís, and E. G. Licón. 2010. "Producción y prestigio en concha y lapidaria de Monte Albán." In *Producción de bienes de prestigio ornamentales y votivos de la América antigua: Arqueología mesoamericana*, edited by E. Melgar, R. Solís, and E. González, 6–21. Miami: Syllaba Press.

Merino, L., and A. García Cook. 1997. "Entrenamientos de perros durante el Formativo Temprano en el Noroeste de México." In *Homenaje al doctor Ignacio Bernal*, edited by L. Manrique and N. Castillo, 411–432. Mexico City: Instituto Nacional de Antropología e Historia.

Middleton, W. D., G. M. Feinman, and L. M. Nicholas. 2002. "Domestic Faunal Assemblages from the Classic Period Valley of Oaxaca, Mexico: A Perspective on the Subsistence and Craft Economies." *Journal of Archaeological Science* 29 (3): 233–249.

Morales, C., C. Martínez, and M. Winter. 1999. *Parte 2. Área W residencias*. Proyecto Especial Monte Albán 1992–1994, Informe Final. Vol. 9, Exploraciones en el Área W al Este de la Plataforma Norte. Archivo Técnico. Oaxaca: Centro INAH.

Navarro, A. G., E. A. García-Trejo, T. Peterson, and V. Rodríguez-Contreras. 2004. "Mamíferos." In *Biodiversidad de Oaxaca*, edited by A. J. García-Mendoza, M. de J. Ordoñez, and M. Briones-Salas, 391–421. Mexico City: UNAM, Fondo Oaxaqueño para la Conservación de la Naturaleza, World Wildlife Fund.

Outram, A. K. 2002. "Bone Fracture and Within-Bone Nutrients: An Experimentally Based Method for Investigating Levels of Marrow Extraction." In *Consuming Passions and Patterns of Consumption*, edited by P. Miracle and N. Milner, 51–63. Cambridge: McDonald Institute Monograph.

Pérez, S., and M. Winter. 2014. Restos de fauna de un área residencial de Monte Albán. Ponencia presentada en el X Simposio Internacional de Estudios Oaxaqueños. Oaxaca,Oaxaca, México 4–6 de Julio de 2014.

Pohl, M. D. 1983. "Maya Ritual Faunas: Vertebrate Remains from Burials, Caches, Caves, and Cenotes in the Maya Lowlands." In *Civilization in the Ancient Americas*, edited by R. Leventhal and A. Kolata, 55–103. Albuquerque: University of New Mexico Press.

Pohl, M. D. 1985. "The Privileges of Maya Elites: Prehistoric Vertebrate Fauna from Seibal." In *Prehistoric Lowland Mayas Environment and Subsistence Economy*, edited by M. D. Pohl, 133–143. Cambridge, MA: Harvard University Press.

Pohl, M. D. 1994. "The Economics and Politics of Maya Meat Eating." In *The Economic Anthropology of the State*, edited by E. M. Brumfiel, 121–149. New York: University Press of America.

Sandefur, E. C. 2001. "Animal Husbandry and Meat Consumption." In *Interdisciplinary Contributions to Archaeology*, edited by D. Altroy, N. Terence, and C. A. Hastorf, 179–198. New York: Kluwer Academic Press.

Seler, E. 2008. *Las Representaciones de los animales en manuscritos mexicanos y mayas*. Mexico City: Casa Juan Pablos.

Siracusano, G. 2004. "Animal Husbandry and Centralized Cultures: How Social and Political Factors Can Influence Rural Life." In *Behavior behind Bones: The Zooarchaeology of Ritual, Religion, Status and Identity*, edited by S. J. O'Day, W. Van Neer, and A. Ervynck, 190–197. Oxford: Oxbow Books.

Starbuck, D. 1975. "Man-Animal Relationships in Pre-Columbian Central Mexico." Unpublished PhD diss., Department of Anthropology, Yale University, New Haven, CT.

Starbuck, D. R. 1987. "Faunal Evidence for the Teotihuacan Subsistence Base." In *Teotihuacán: Nuevos datos, nuevas síntesis, nuevos problemas*, edited by E. McClung and E. C. Rattray, 75–90. Mexico City: UNAM.

Tozzer, A. M., ed. and trans. 1941. *Landa's relaciones de las cosas de Yucatán*. Papers No. 18. Cambridge: Peabody Museum of American Archaeology and Ethnology, Harvard University.

Urcid, J. 2005. "El simbolismo del jaguar en el suroeste de Mesoamérica." *Arqueología Mexicana* 12 (72): 40–45.

Urcid, J. 2008. "El Arte de pintar las tumbas: Sociedad e ideología zapotecas (400–800 d. C.)." In *La pintura mural prehispánica en México III: Oaxaca, tomo IV (Estudios)*, edited by B. de la Fuente and M. T. Uriarte, 513–627. Mexico City: Instituto de Investigaciones Estéticas, UNAM.

von den Driesch, A. 1999. *A Guide to Measurement of Animal Bones from Archaeological Sites*. Cambridge: Peabody Museum Bulletin 1.

White, C., and H. P. Schwarcz. 1989. "Ancient Maya Diet as Inferred from Isotopic and Elemental Analysis of Human Bone." *Journal of Archaeological Science* 16 (5): 451–474.

White, C. D., M. E. Pohl, H. P. Schwarcz, F. J. Longstaffe, and K. R. Law. 2001. "Social Complexity and Food Systems at Altun Ha, Belize: The Isotopic Evidence." *Latin American Antiquity* 12: 371–393.

Wing, E. 2004. "Maya Zooarchaeology from a Zooarchaeological Perspective." In *Maya Zooarchaeology: New Directions in Method and Theory*, edited by K. F. Emery, 249–254. Los Angeles: Cotsen Institute of Archaeology Press, University of California.

Winter, M. 1994. "El Proyecto Especial Monte Albán 1992–1994: Antecedentes, intervenciones y perspectivas." In *Monte Albán: Estudios recientes*, edited by M. Winter, 1–24. Contribución del Proyecto Especial Monte Albán, 1992–1994. Oaxaca: Centro INAH.

Winter, M. 1998. "Monte Alban and Teotihuacan." In *Rutas de intercambio en Mesoamerica: III Coloquio Bosch-Gimpera*, edited by E. Childs Rattray, 153–184. Mexico City: UNAM.

Winter, M., A. Rivero López, and C. Martínez. 2001. *Parte 2. Área Conjunto PNLP (Plataforma Norte Lado Poniente)*. Proyecto Especial Monte Albán 1992–1994, Informe Final. Vol. 13. Exploraciones en el Lado Oeste de la Plaza Principal. Parte 2. Área Conjunto PNLP (Plataforma Norte Lado Poniente). Unpublished report. Archivo Técnico. Oaxaca: Centro INAH.

Winter, M., C. Martínez, W. O. Autry, R. G. Wilkinson, and P. A. Juárez. 1995. *Enterros humanos de Monte Albán: Dos estudios*. Contribución No. 7 del Proyecto Especial Monte Albán 1992–1994. Oaxaca: Centro INAH.

8

For Love of the Game

Ancient Maya Deer Hunting as Sport, Symbolism, and Sustenance

SARAH E. NEWMAN

Across the Maya area, zooarchaeological studies suggest that white-tailed deer (*Odocoileus virginianus*) played a primary role in ancient subsistence. Although there are site-by-site variations (e.g., Emery 2012; Teeter and Chase 2004), skeletal remains of white-tailed deer often dominate faunal assemblages at coastal and inland sites; across social strata; in architectural fills, ritual contexts, and middens; and over time (e.g., Carr 1996; Götz 2008, 2014; Emery 2007:189; Montero-López 2009; Pohl 1983; Sharpe and Emery 2015; Sharpe et al. 2020). Given the comparative scarcity of big game and domesticated species in the ancient Americas, white-tailed deer provided a large, abundant, and easily acquired source of meat.

A consistent reliance on white-tailed deer, however, does not necessarily preclude differences or changes in the specific ways that the animal was procured; the symbolic, social, or political implications of the kill; or the products (edible and otherwise) and purposes (practical and otherwise) for which it was used. Faunal remains provide one valuable source of information on ancient consumption, but relative counts and contributions of particular species can also

https://doi.org/10.5876/9781646422562.c008

mask subtle distinctions in the meanings associated with meat. How else might we examine the particularities of subsistence economies in the past?

My aim in this chapter is to examine the close connections between deer hunting and the social and political ideologies of the royal courts that dominated much of Maya history. I begin by examining changing techniques, motivations, and meanings of deer hunting in the Maya lowlands, focusing on differences that can be observed over time and drawing primarily on ancient art and texts, historic sources, and modern ethnographic studies, as well as zooarchaeological data. Although they represent broad strokes, I employ the traditional periodizations of Maya archaeology: the Preclassic period (2000 BC–AD 250), during which village farming became firmly entrenched in the Maya area and the construction of cities, pyramid building, and mural painting began; the Classic period (AD 250–800), characterized by dated and inscribed stone monuments chronicling the events and individuals of dynastic rule; the Terminal Classic period (AD 800–900), in which varied cataclysms shook the lowlands and many Maya polities collapsed; and the Postclassic period (AD 900–1521), a time when Maya society reorganized and endured until the arrival of Europeans.

I then turn to a case study from the ancient Maya city of El Zotz, in present-day Guatemala, to ground the general observations gleaned from epigraphy, art history, and ethnography in the artifacts and analyses undertaken at a single archaeological site. The distinct areas and phases of occupation at El Zotz offer an ideal opportunity to track local changes in food production across the rise and fall of the local dynasty, further underscoring how patterns of procurement may have varied in ways and for reasons that are not always revealed by zooarchaeological assemblages alone.

A LONG HISTORY OF HUNTING

Hunting is featured prominently throughout Maya myth and history, often with remarkable continuity. For example, a series of first-century BC painted murals from San Bartolo, Guatemala, depict three young Maya men as hunters. Each individual carries and sacrifices an iconic food animal corresponding to one of the basic levels of the cosmos: a fish (the watery underworld), a deer (the surface of the earth), and birds (the celestial realm). Nearly 1,500 years later, a scribe in Yucatán sketched out a remarkably similar scene in the Dresden Codex, a bark-paper screenfold book. Before three trees, the very same animals are offered in bowls: a turkey, a fish, and a deer's haunch (Taube et al. 2010:26–27). Similar long-term continuities can be observed in the rituals performed by Maya hunters today, who make offerings to appease a supernatural protector of the animals, the contemporary version of a guardian who can be traced back to the hunting god of the ancient Maya (Brown 2005:131; Taube 1997:39, 2003:472).

Figure 8.1. *Hunting imagery from the height of Classic Maya courtly society shows large parties on parade. The figure at far right carries a deer head in his right hand, separated from the animal's body by the spear in his left. Justin Kerr, [K-1116], Justin Kerr Maya Vase Archive, Dumbarton Oaks, Trustees for Harvard University, Washington, DC.*

Figure 8.2. *A hunting party, accompanied by a dog, shows deer being butchered, trussed up, and carried in baskets and slings. The figure at far right blows a conch shell trumpet, coordinating the group. Justin Kerr, [K-1373], Justin Kerr Maya Vase Archive, Dumbarton Oaks, Trustees for Harvard University, Washington, DC.*

There are changes too, of course. Images from the height of Classic Maya courtly society illustrate not only hunters, tools, and trophies, but also the pomp and circumstance associated with elite hunting. One painted pottery scene portrays a lively representation of an elite hunt. A line of young men, their bodies covered in patches of black paint or ointment to camouflage their sight or smell in the tropical forest, writhe and dance on parade (Houston et al. 2006:220). Some smoke tobacco; some hoist their weapons and trophies in the air; others seem to be smiling or singing. A deer is depicted as well: its head is separated from its body by a spear (figure 8.1). Another Late Classic vessel provides a glimpse that may portray the hunt itself (figure 8.2). A dog accompanies the party, expectantly awaiting the reward for its assistance. Progressing from right to left, the deer is shown before and after being butchered; first as its haunches are removed and later neatly trussed up and carried in a tumpline basket, the traditional Mesoamerican means of carrying heavy loads by transferring weight across the forehead with a sling. The spotted men wear headdresses in the shape of deer—symbols frequently used to mark real and performative hunters and hunting gods (see

Figure 8.3. *Deer caught in a snare or trap in the Madrid Codex (Madrid 45B, after Villacorta C. and Villacorta 1976:314).*

below)—and carry conch shells, perhaps to signal to one another, coordinate the group, or as a means of attracting deer (Olivier 2014:147; Thompson 1963:95–96; Tozzer [1907] 1982:72, 96). The shell trumpets may also serve to herald the triumphant return of successful parties or as vehicles for the voices of hunting deities or instruments for invoking those gods (see Looper 2019:66).

Later Postclassic depictions or historical and modern accounts, however, emphasize opportunistic hunting over the ceremonial, communal events shown on Classic-period painted pottery. In the Madrid Codex, a fifteenth-century bark-paper book, a series of illustrations depicts deer caught in spring snares or traps (figure 8.3). Deer are also shown being captured in a pit or hunted with projectiles (Carr 1996:252). Based on associated texts and imagery, Gabrielle Vail (1997:97) proposed that the pages of the Madrid Codex provide seasonal information on hunting, indicating the appropriate times of year when deer might be culled by illustrating young bucks with prominent testicles but without antlers (although cf. Pohl [1981:516], who suggests that the deer in the Madrid Codex have had their antlers removed as a part of ritual sacrifice). Pierre Colas

(2006), on the other hand, argued that the Madrid Codex illustrates particular hunting rituals, rather than actual hunts, which may explain some of the more fantastic imagery, including deer with scorpion tails or human limbs. The hunting *methods* depicted, however, are probably realistic. In the twentieth century, Thomas Gann (1918:24) observed deer caught by Maya hunters making use of a "springy young sapling" and a noose to entrap both large and small game along paths to watering holes. Similar spring snares were a common way of trapping deer throughout the pre-Columbian Americas (e.g., Custred 1979; Osborne and Riddell 1978).

This is not to suggest that group hunting ceased after the fall of Classic-period dynasties. Agustín Cano (1984:10), a Dominican friar who entered the Petén in the late seventeenth century, writes of finding a group of thirty Itzá Maya deer hunters, armed with shields, spears, and bows and arrows and accompanied by hunting dogs, in the savannas to the south of Lake Petén Itzá. Anthropologist Charles Wisdom (1941:70–71) observed group deer hunting in the early 1930s, in which one man in the group (the "professional hunter") carried a gun and hid himself in the underbrush near a trail. The others spread out from his camouflaged position, formed a line spaced several hundred yards apart, and drove the game before them. Although smaller animals usually escaped with this method, deer were successfully forced along the trail and shot by the man with the gun. Even today, traditional Maya hunters in Yucatán engage in group hunting (*p'uuj*), which focuses exclusively on white-tailed deer and peccary and can involve as many as fifteen to twenty participants (Rodríguez et al. 2012:215).

As with many activities of courtly life, however, deer hunting became less performative and took place less frequently or at smaller scales in Postclassic and colonial Maya society. At the Postclassic capital of Mayapán, Marilyn Masson and Carlos Peraza Lope (2008:179–180; 2014:401–402) have marshalled evidence to argue that deer were heavily managed, if not bred and raised in captivity. Unusually high proportions of full-size, subadult white-tailed deer were recovered at Mayapán—not only from elite residences in the city center, but also from outlying households. Those zooarchaeological patterns mimic those of the only domestic mammal among the Maya (the dog) and are unlike those observed for wild species, such as brocket deer and peccaries. There is also no comparative evidence (zooarchaeological or ethnographic) to suggest such patterns might be produced by selective hunting. Moreover, possible animal pens and corrals were found adjacent to domestic house lots at Mayapán, echoing descriptions of Maya deer management in documentary accounts (e.g., Pohl and Feldman 1982:295; Ximénez [1722] 1967:57). A specific term for deer raised in a dwelling (*ah may*) can even be found in the colonial-period Motul dictionary of Yucatec Mayan (Pohl 1985:140).

Figure 8.4. *A ritual deer hunting scene. Blood flows from the neck of a wounded buck while the elaborately dressed figure second from left raises his atlatl and dart. The young attendant at far left holds the deer by one of its hind legs while the central figure takes aim. Justin Kerr, [K-5857], Justin Kerr Maya Vase Archive, Dumbarton Oaks, Trustees for Harvard University, Washington, DC.*

A NOBLE SPORT

It is no surprise that the royal courts of the Classic Maya incorporated hunting as an exaggerated, performative display. Across ancient societies, from Neo-Assyrian Mesopotamia (Thomason 2014) to Shang China (Campbell 2014) to the Aztec of Central Mexico (Díaz del Castillo 2008), the organization of successful elite hunts displayed a leader's special abilities to marshal labor and individuals (both human and animal), often demonstrated with pomp and circumstance well beyond the confines of city centers and to subjects far removed from courtly society. One Late Classic (ca. AD 650) Maya polychrome vase recalls the *venationes* of the Roman Republic, in which animals were killed in staged hunts (Latin's *venatus*, "hunted," is the source of the Spanish term *venado* for "deer" [Corominas and Pascual 1983:765]). The vase shows a lord or ruler, elaborately adorned with a deer headdress and jade jewelry, readying an atlatl (a spear/dart thrower) to finish off a wounded buck. As he prepares to throw his dart, his young attendant holds the creature by a leg, ensuring a successful kill (figure 8.4; Looper 2019:94–95). As Thomas Allsen (2006:8) argues for Eurasian history, "the royal hunt thus served as an effective reaffirmation of a ruler's capacity to manage large-scale enterprises, that is, to govern." For the Classic Maya, the hunt—as an act, experience, and symbol—encompassed the foundational mythologies, very real responsibilities, and successful perpetuation of rulership.

A primordial figure known as 1-Ajaw, whose name is based on a particular day sign, but also carries the connotation of "First Lord," served as a model for certain features of Maya kingship. Royal accession, often referred to in Maya texts as "fastening the headband," references his most distinctive marker: the bark-paper headband "crown" of Classic Maya kings. 1-Ajaw, along with his brother, are Classic-period versions of characters better known as the Hero Twins from colonial-period texts. They are cunning, skilled, and fearless youths, besting the lords of death in an underworld ballgame and vanquishing avian monsters with their blowguns. As Karl Taube (2003) has argued, they encompass the necessary abilities and power of the king: 1-Ajaw serves as the personified office of lordship over humans, while his twin brother, with jaguar pelt markings covering his face and body, embodies dominion over the forest and the wild. Dominion over humans and animals comprise two sides of the same coin—each realm controlled and protected by the Classic Maya king when he "fastened the headband." Hunters' spotted bodies on polychrome vases (see figures 8.1 and 8.2) mimic 1-Ajaw's twin brother, with his jaguar pelt markings. Stephen Houston (2010) has noted other images in which 1-Ajaw is shown with a deer headdress accompanied by a swirling curl, which is often shown on the ears and faces of deer or peccaries, conveying the strong, earthy musk of animals. These scenes of 1-Ajaw, garbed as a hunter and smelling like a deer, suggest the spots represent the application of scent maskers or scent attractors, a practice common among modern hunters.

Images of hunters also recall Huk Xib (later Huk Sip), the Maya hunting god. This deity, known in Classic-period and colonial texts, as well as among contemporary Maya communities (Redfield and Villa Rojas 1934:117–118; Thompson 1970:308; Zender 2017), is often understood as a kind of caretaker and protector of animals, deer in particular. He is easily identified by his distinctive deer attributes—a large deer ear and antler protruding from his brow—as well as his conch shell trumpet (figure 8.5). That conch trumpets were emblematic of hunting is underscored not only in painted scenes, but also in an actual carved shell from a private collection, which proclaims that its owner "spears deer [*u juluw chij*]" on a certain date (Houston et al. 2006:264; Zender 2010:84), commemorating a successful hunt (Looper 2019:33).

Hunting was not only carried out in fields and forests, but also symbolically enacted in city centers, within the context of a better-known Maya sport: the ballgame. Ballgame players are often shown as hunters—wearing animal headdresses, particularly deer, or characteristic broad-brimmed hats and dark body paint (Whittington 2001). Nicholas Hellmuth (1991:146) argues that one ballgame scene shows a theatric recreation of the hunt: the central figure wears a headdress in the likeness of the old hunting god's dark face, while the remaining players are all portrayed as deer. The final figure even blows a conch shell, signaling and coordinating the game in every sense (figure 8.6). In the late 1920s, J. Eric Thompson documented deer headdresses worn during traditional Q'eqchi' Maya hunting dances in the town of San Antonio, in what is

Figure 8.5. *A carved Late Classic vase shows the Maya hunting god, Huk Sip, burning* milpa *fields with a deer at his feet. He carries a torch in his left hand, setting fire to a personified tree. With his right hand, he blows a conch shell trumpet. Justin Kerr, [K4336], courtesy of Justin Kerr and Kerr Associates.*

Figure 8.6. *Ballgame players in varied deer headdresses surround a kneeling central figure, whose black-faced headdress may represent the Maya hunting god. The figure at far right blows a conch shell trumpet, coordinating the game/staged hunt, much like in figure* 8.2. *Justin Kerr, [K-1871], Justin Kerr Maya Vase Archive, Dumbarton Oaks, Trustees for Harvard University, Washington, DC.*

now Belize. Although the deer headdresses are made of solid wood, they are "quite realistic" and bear a remarkable similarity to those depicted in Classic-period imagery (Thompson 1930:103). In addition to ancient painted vessels and twentieth-century ethnographic accounts, the remains of an actual deer headdress were recovered during archaeological investigations at the well-preserved site of Cerén, El Salvador. Formed from the cranium of an adult white-tailed deer stag, the headdress was recovered with bits of twine (presumably to secure it on the wearer) still wrapped around the antler bases (Brown 2001:374).

Whether real pursuits or symbolic ballgames, hunting provided a stage to enact and affirm various roles within the Classic Maya court. Individuals' skills and physical fitness are celebrated, but success ultimately rests on a collaborative hierarchy and the groups' coordinated efforts. Elite hunting thus may have served as an outlet for social tensions and competition within the royal court, as Thomas Allsen (2006:26) has argued for fifth-century Armenian ring hunts. Hunting also represents an unusual example of elite action demonstrated beyond city centers and to subjects removed from courtly society, a rare activity replicated by and relatable to those beyond the confines of palaces.

Finally, the skills required to organize and participate in the hunt translated directly to another political arena as well. Warriors are shown carrying the same spears and conch shell trumpets used by hunters, suggesting that coordinated movements practiced in the hunt were also used on the battlefield (Houston et al. 2006:220, see also Looper 2019:95–113). Captives are often equated to hunted animals not only among the Classic Maya but throughout Mesoamerica, to deer in particular (Olivier 2014). Warriors spear, butcher, and bundle their prizes in identical fashion to hunters with their catches, even showing human "haunches" bent over and tied up, just as a deer's. The *Chilam Balam of Chumayel*—an eighteenth-century Maya book of prophecies, chronicles, rituals, and other miscellany—describes a graphic scene of human slaughter using the term *ah-cehob* ("he of deer" or "deer-hunter" in Yucatec), identifying the executioners as deer slayers and the prisoners as their prey (Carr 1996:252; Taube 1988:334).

Some painted scenes and figurines even show captives being made to look and act as deer. Tightly bound to scaffolds on all fours, sending a clear message that the human has been reduced to an animal, the unfortunate victims are shown with deer heads placed atop their own or their hair styled into antlers. Karl Taube (1988:333–334) interprets these scenes of human sacrifice as metaphorical hunts, with the victim speared as a deer and the leaf-covered scaffolding serving as a symbolic portrayal of the forest. Perhaps the ultimate debasement is shown on another painted vessel, where a naked human on all fours, wearing a deer headdress and even a small tail, defecates onto a disgraced and presumably defeated combatant in a scene of ritual fighting and drinking (Taube and Zender 2009:177–178). Like captives sacrificed as deer, deer could be sacrificed as humans. In fact, in Central Mexico, sacrificing a deer was considered equivalent to that of a war captive (Olivier 2015:435–457). Deer offerings were an important part of many traditional Maya ceremonies (e.g., Bricker 1991; Pohl 1981). Colonial accounts mention hunters discovering "the blood of sacrificed deer" in a cave or throwing animal hearts into fires (Tozzer 1941:76, 163), perhaps echoed in scenes from the Madrid Codex that Colas (2006:83) argued depict ritual bloodletting and heart extraction being practiced on deer.

Figure 8.7. *In a complex Classic-period scene, a buck carries off the wife of the elderly Maya hunting god. Justin Kerr, [K-1182], Justin Kerr Maya Vase Archive, Dumbarton Oaks, Trustees for Harvard University, Washington, DC.*

GAME, PLAYER, AND PRIZE: WHY WHITE-TAILED DEER?

Why the emphasis on deer in particular? Even the term the Classic Maya used generally for "hunter," *ajchij*, like that in Yucatec, literally translates as "He of the Deer" (Boot 2009:16). Deer feature prominently in Maya mythology, but in ways that remain poorly understood. They interacted with and substituted for human beings; hunting them could emulate warfare, symbolize sex, and recall myth. Even seemingly realistic depictions of deer often include confounding or supernatural elements, many of them overtly sexual. For example, a series of codex-style vessels show the old hunting god in sickness or death, attended by anthropomorphic and realistic deer congregating around his bed. The associated text on one of the vessels tells of the deer "carrying off the wife of Huk Xib," matched by the image of a voluptuous woman riding naked on the back of a larger-than-life buck (figure 8.7; Stone and Zender 2011:185). The deer wears the characteristic conch shell trumpet of the cuckolded old god around his neck, emphasizing that the "game" has changed—the hunted has become the hunter (see Looper 2019:81–93 and Zender 2017 for detailed discussions of the complex mythology behind the "Dying God" vessels).

An even more overtly sexual and later scene, in the Madrid Codex, shows a deer in rare frontal view, its four legs splayed to reveal its erect penis (figure 8.8). The sexual connotations of deer hinted at in ancient art are recounted in contemporary Maya folklore. Across Mesoamerica, a variety of myths and stories portray deer as lustful beings or equate capturing a doe with getting a woman and vice versa (e.g., Braakhuis 2001; Olivier 2014). Incantations to lure deer or to ensure success in deer hunting have erotic connotations among both the Nahua (Ruiz de Alarcón 1987:161–166) and the Maya. In the *Ritual of the Bacabs*, a manuscript

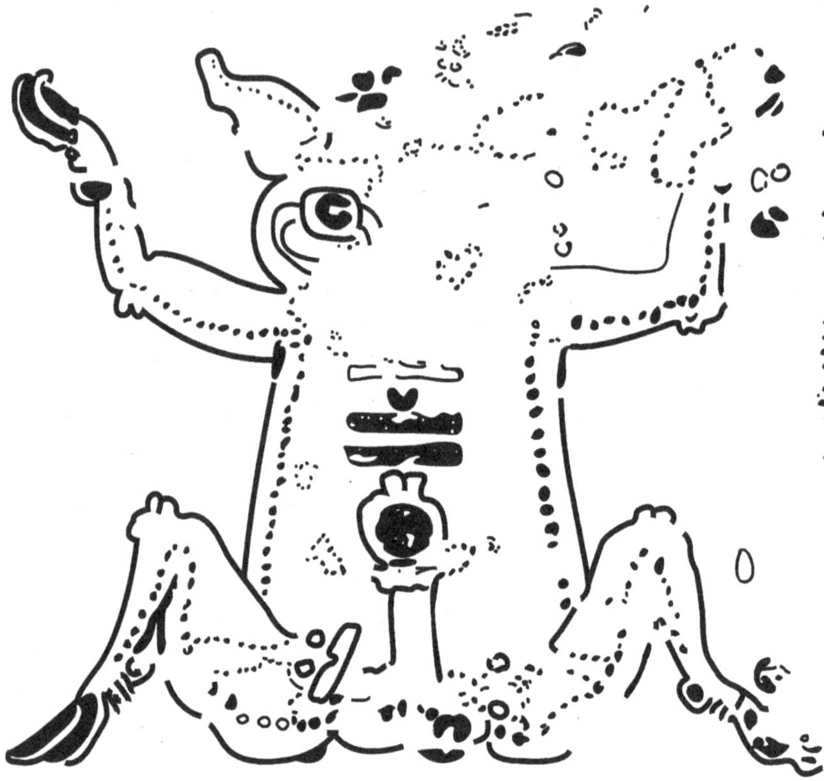

Figure 8.8. *An explicitly sexual Postclassic depiction from the Madrid Codex shows a deer with its legs splayed and an erect penis (Madrid 42B, after Villacorta C. and Villacorta 1976:308).*

of Maya incantations in colonial Yucatán, the "words to call deer" anticipates the animal's capture in explicitly sexual terms (Arzápalo 1987:419–420):

> I remember the fornication chant; that was sung ten times
>
> His masculinity is inciting and with the liquid of his member he lubricates the entrance.
>
> They transcend my song, extend my songs by the great winds.
>
> Here they go, passing subtly right by the deer.
>
> Go to meet her, to take from her the virginity, the beauty, of your little deer.
>
> Come to place yourself above the pleasure of your little deer until the tenth level of the underworld, where the wind fades away . . .
>
> Well numbed is the tail, he has the deer captured . . .

In the seventeenth century, Indigenous people from Zacatecas and Tamaulipas offered deer in exchange for the bride in marital rites (Olivier 2015:67).

Traci Ardren (2002:80) has suggested that the close association of deer with female sexuality may be connected to the raising of deer in and around household compounds, with the reproductive power of women extended to the deer they nurtured. Although game management or dedicated stands of forest for hunting are not definitively known among the Classic Maya, they are alluded to by colonial-period sources (see also Masson and Peraza Lope 2008:172–173 and discussion of deer raised in captivity at Mayapán, above). Recording the travels of Hernán Cortés and his men through the Peten in 1525, the Spanish conquistador Bernal Díaz del Castillo details their arrival in an area known as the Mazatecas, which he translates as "the pueblos or lands of deer" (2010:30–31). There, treeless savannas and flat plains were filled with abundant deer surprisingly unafraid of horses and humans. When asked, their guides explained that their gods had ordered them not to kill or frighten the animals (30–31). Diego de Landa, the Second Bishop of Yucatán, wrote that Maya women "let the deer suck their breasts, by which means they raise them and make them so tame that they will never go into the woods, although they take them and carry them through the woods and raise them there" (Tozzer 1941:127). This idea is bolstered by figurines found at Altar de Sacrificios and Lubantan and a painted vessel showing women suckling small animals (Ardren 2002:80), as well as ethnographic observations from the 1930s, which note three families in the Yucatec Maya village of Pisté as having pet deer (Steggerda 1941:145). A particular hieroglyphic phrase, *sak chij we'*, has been translated by Marc Zender as "white or 'artificial' venison food," based on the meaning of *sak* as "a thing made with human artifice" in Yucatec (Zender 2000:1044, cited in Houston et al. 2006:108). The use of the phrase on ceramic serving vessels may indicate that the meat they once offered came from tame or controlled deer populations.

Much remains to be understood, particularly the complex substitution of deer for humans: as sacrifices and trophies, but also as sexual creatures, as beings cared for and desired by women, but killed by men. This brief review, however, suggests that ancient Maya deer hunting revolved around politics and performance as much as it did around protein.

A TASTE FOR DEER: CHANGING ACQUISITION PATTERNS AT EL ZOTZ

In what follows, I highlight zooarchaeological evidence for shifts in hunting derived from a single site: the ancient Maya polity of El Zotz, located in northern Guatemala's Department of Petén. Archaeological faunal remains reveal that smaller and more diverse prey played a greater role in subsistence before and after the establishment of the royal dynasty at El Zotz, which was founded in the fourth century AD and collapsed toward the end of the tenth century AD (Houston, Newman, Román, and Carter 2015; Newman et al. 2018). During the Classic-period height of the kingdom, however, preferences shifted to a few species, particularly white-tailed deer. I consider the faunal data from El Zotz in comparison to complementary indices of local hunting practices and prey availability at the site itself—changes in social and political organization, lithic technologies, and the immediate environment. The specific evidence from El Zotz complements the iconographic, historic, and ethnographic sources presented above. That is, the marked political, ideological, and mythic importance of white-tailed deer resulted in an increased emphasis on hunting that particular species during the Classic period.

The archaeological site of El Zotz occupies an elevated position within a corridor known as the Buenavista Valley (Garrison and Houston 2018:5–7; Houston, Newman, Román, and Carter 2015). The valley connects the northeast and northwest department of Petén, providing a key route from Chetumal Bay to the bay of Campeche, in the shadow of its defining feature: the Buenavista Escarpment, the largest in the Petén, which rises nearly 400 m above sea level in some places along the valley's northern edge, before transitioning to the uplands of the Petén Karst Plateau.

Beginning in 2006, the El Zotz Archaeological Project conducted an extensive program of survey and mapping; test units; and vertical, horizontal, and tunneling excavations at El Zotz and surrounding sites and satellite groups in the region. This work revealed an occupational history across nearly two millennia, from the Preclassic through the Postclassic periods (ca. 800 BC–AD 1250), as well as architecture, burials, and artifacts varying widely in date, function, scale, or elaboration (see Garrison and Houston 2018).

The physical landscape at El Zotz often reflects changes in the political one, characterized by waxing and waning relationships with more powerful polities in the region. Over time, primary areas of occupation at the site transition from the edges of the local El Palmar *cival*, or wetland, to the high edges of the escarpment, to the valley at its base. Construction at the site often occurs in fits and starts, with monumental constructions built in single episodes (Carter et al. 2018) or erected, modified multiple times, and abandoned within a short time frame (Houston, Newman, Román, and Garrison 2015; Román et al. 2018). When the local dynasty collapsed around the turn of the tenth century AD (at the end of the Terminal Classic period), a resilient population remained for several centuries after the fall of the royal court, reorienting itself spatially, socially, and economically in an area just to the south of the city center (Kingsley and Gámez 2018). This finding means that occupational horizons at El Zotz are often distinct, both temporally and spatially, and that faunal remains from different areas of the site provide clear indications of general changes over time. In this chapter, I present the zooarchaeological data from El Zotz according to the chronological periods defined by the El Zotz Archaeological Project, each of which is marked by significant changes in terms of populations, architecture, and/or artifacts

Table 8.1. Skeletal elements included in modified number of individual specimens (NISP) quantification

Limb Bones	*Vertebrae*	*Skull Elements/ Parts*	*Isolated Teeth*
Distal scapula	Axis	Basioccipital	M3
All proximal and distal end fragments of long bones (including epiphyses)	Atlas	Occipital	dP4
All carpals	Sacrum	Petrous	
Patella		Temporal	
All tarsals		Zygomatic	
All phalanges		Premaxilla with teeth	
All pelvis fragments with portion of the acetabulum		Maxilla with teeth	
		Mandible with teeth	

(see Czapiewska-Halliday 2018:table 8.1). These are the Preclassic (800 BC–AD 250), the Early Classic (AD 250–550), the Late Classic (AD 550–850), the Terminal Classic (AD 850–980), and the Early Postclassic (AD 980–1250).

In order to examine changes in the types and quantities of species procured at El Zotz over time, the relative proportions of different taxa exploited and estimates for species diversity and equitability were calculated for each chronological period. A modified version of the number of identifiable specimens (NISP) method of quantification was used, to prevent overcounting repetitive elements from single individuals—such as vertebrae, teeth, and the scutes of armadillo or turtle shells. Only specimens identifiable as the elements listed in table 8.1 were included in calculations. Table 8.2 records the number of individual specimens and relative abundance of the species identified for each chronological period at El Zotz.

Species diversity refers to the variety of animals used (the relative importance of species present), while equitability refers to the evenness with which those animals are represented. To assess both diversity and equitability, the Shannon-Weaver formula was used (Reitz and Wing 208:245–247). The formula calculates the Shannon-Weaver diversity index value (*H'*), based on the relative abundance of individuals for each taxon in the assemblage (p_i) and the equitability value (*V'*) based on the number of taxonomic categories included in the assemblage (*S*):

$$H' = -\Sigma(p_i)(\log_e p_i)$$
$$V' = H' / \log_e S$$

Table 8.2. Number of individual specimens (NISP) and relative abundance (% of total NISP) for each taxon represented in the faunal assemblage from El Zotz (separated according to chronological period)

Taxon	*Common Name*	*Preclassic NISP*	*Early Classic NISP*	*Late Classic NISP*	*Terminal Classic NISP*	*Postclassic NISP*
Actinopterygii	Bony fish		4			
Amphibia	Unidentified amphibians					2
Anura	Frogs/toads	9		2		3
Bufo/Rhinella sp.	Toads			1		1
Reptilia	Unidentified reptiles	1			3	
Crocodylus sp.	Crocodiles	1	2	1	1	6
Iguanidae	Iguanas			3	2	
Testudines, large–intermediate	Turtles, large–intermediate		1			8
Testudines, intermediate	Turtles, intermediate	4	1			
Testudines, small	Turtles, small		1		1	
Kinosternidae	Mud/musk turtles	1				1
Staurotypus triporcatus	Giant mud turtle	1				3
Dermatemys mawii	Central American river turtle			1		3
Trachemys venusta	Common slider		1	1		1
Aves	Unidentified birds		5			
Aves, large	Birds (turkey sized)	1	2	1	10	
Aves, intermediate	Birds (duck or owl sized)		1	6	8	20
Aves, small	Birds (pigeon or smaller)	2	5		2	17
Colinus sp.	Quail		3	1	3	1
Meleagris sp.	Turkey	1	1	8	10	95
Penelope purpurascens	Crested guan				1	
Mammalia, large–intermediate	Mammals (deer sized)	15	22	4	5	
Mammalia, intermediate	Mammals (peccary-sized)	8	2	2	7	6
Mammalia, intermediate–small	Mammals (raccoon sized)	6	1	3	2	18
Mammalia, small	Mammals (rat sized)	1	8	1	4	20
Didelphidae	Opossums	2		2	2	28

continued on next page

Table 8.2.—*continued*

Taxon	*Common Name*	*Preclassic NISP*	*Early Classic NISP*	*Late Classic NISP*	*Terminal Classic NISP*	*Postclassic NISP*
Philander opossum	Gray four-eyed possum	3			1	1
Primates	Primates					1
Alouatta pigra	Howler monkey	1				
Dasypus novemcinctus	Nine-banded armadillo	6	4	1	7	52
Sylvilagus sp.	Rabbit		7	1	1	4
Rodentia	Rodents		2		1	
Sciurus sp.	Squirrel				2	10
Orthogeomys sp.	Pocket gopher		1		2	3
Cuniculus paca	Lowland paca	3	1	1	8	96
Dasyprocta punctata	Agouti	3	4	5	11	122
Carnivora	Carnivores		2			9
Canidae	Dogs, wolves, and foxes	4	2	3	2	23
Canis lupus familiaris	Domestic dog		5			
Urocyon cinereoargenteus	Gray fox			2	1	7
Procyonidae	Raccoon/coati	1		1		3
Procyon lotor	Raccoon					1
Nasua narica	White-nosed coati	3				
Felidae	Felids	10	2		1	19
Puma concolor	Puma		1		1	
Leopardis pardalis	Ocelot		4		4	1
Panthera onca	Jaguar		1	3	1	1
Tapirella bairdii	Baird's tapir		4		1	1
Tayassuidae	Peccaries	17	10	5	10	73
Cervidae	Deer		2			
Mazama sp.	Brocket deer	7	19	9	24	62
Odocoileus virginianus	White-tailed deer	21	123	71	118	89
Totals		132	254	139	257	811

Using the Shannon-Weaver measure of diversity, samples with an even distribution of abundance among taxa have a greater index than samples with the same number of taxa but with disproportionately high abundance of a few

Table 8.3. Diversity (H') and equitability (V') values for each chronological period at El Zotz

Time Period	*H' (Diversity)*	*V' (Equitability)*
Preclassic (800 BC–250 AD)	2.805	0.861
Early Classic (AD 250–550)	2.248	0.637
Late Classic (AD 550–850)	2.127	0.653
Terminal Classic (AD 850–980)	2.317	0.663
Postclassic (AD 980–1250)	2.765	0.768

species. Samples with higher H' values are thus considered to be "more diverse" than those with lower H' values. This measure of diversity combines species richness (the number of species) with equitability (the degree to which species are equally abundant). Equitability independent of richness is represented by V', with values ranging from 0 to 1.0. Higher values are more equitable than lower values. That is, equitability values close to 1.0 indicate even distribution of taxa, while lower values suggest dominance of one taxon or a few taxa (Reitz and Wing 2008:111–114). The diversity and equitability values for each chronological period at El Zotz are presented in table 8.3.

Looking at the relative abundance of species across the occupational periods at El Zotz (table 8.2), a spike in white-tailed deer during the Classic period is clear. During the Early, Late, and Terminal Classic periods (those in which the El Zotz dynasty rose to power, controlled the Buenavista Valley, and eventually collapsed), white-tailed deer consistently represent almost half of the faunal remains recovered (48.43%, 51.08%, and 45.91%, respectively). Before and after the existence of the royal court at El Zotz, white-tailed deer represent only 15.91% and 10.97% of the faunal assemblage, respectively. The diversity and equitability indices are comparatively lower for the Early, Late, and Terminal Classic periods as well, reflecting heavy reliance on a single species. The relative abundances of other wild and domestic fauna are distinct from those of white-tailed deer, either remaining fairly steady (dogs, brocket deer) or increasing during the Postclassic period (agoutis, pacas, turkeys, peccaries). This general trend—an increased use of artiodactyls to the exclusion of other animal species from the Preclassic to Late Classic periods—has been noted at over thirty Maya sites (e.g., Emery 2007; Götz 2008; Sharpe et al. 2014).

But how do the variations in these patterns relate to changing practices of procurement at El Zotz? What, if anything, was changing in the way people hunted animals, large and small? Like many traditional societies of the New World, the foundations of ancient Maya subsistence lay in the practice known as "garden hunting" (Linares 1976), in which people hunt and trap animals inhabiting their agricultural fields and home gardens—often opportunistically, but also selectively. Archaeological faunal data suggest that garden hunting has a long history in Mesoamerica, beginning in earnest as early as the first millennium BC (Vanderwarker 2006), while ethnographic observations of traditional subsistence and resource-management techniques of the Lacandon Maya in Chiapas, Mexico, point to continuity. The faunal data from El Zotz—particularly the Postclassic period sample—echo the patterns originally described by Olga Linares (1976) in her proposal of the neotropical garden-hunting model and accord with trends observed in follow-up studies (e.g., Greenberg 1992; Nations and Nigh 1980; Smith 2005), not only in terms of general diversity and equitability but also in the high proportions of caviomorph rodents (agoutis and pacas) being procured. These findings suggest a consistent underlying pattern of garden hunting, with an additional emphasis on elite white-tailed deer hunting during the Classic period.

As a complement to faunal remains, paleoenvironmental data indicate that the El Zotz region was ideally suited to white-tailed deer throughout its ancient occupation. Sheryl Luzzadder-Beach and colleagues (2016:10) explicitly describe the borderland between Tikal and El Zotz during the Late Classic period as a "forest garden," with both agriculture and reforestation (see also Beach et al. 2018; Ford and Nigh 2009). Slash-and-burn milpa agriculture, in particular, provides habitats that are attractive to a variety of animals—deer, especially—and generally encourages a greater diversity and density of small animals than those found in forested environments (e.g., Linares 1976; Neusius 2008).

White-tailed deer are opportunistic browsers, preferring vegetation mosaics and transitional zones between biomes, particularly the edges of agricultural fields (Harlow and Guynn 1994). Paleoecological research at the El Palmar *cival* (a perennial wetland swamp) and the local *aguada* (reservoir) at El Zotz revealed that even when humans impacted the local environment by planting maize, squash, and other economic species, at least half of the pollen evidence recovered came from tropical forest species (see also Emery and Thornton 2008). This picture of El Zotz aligns with other studies of ancient Maya forest composition (e.g., Emery and Thornton 2008; Ford and Emery 2008), as well as ethnohistoric accounts such as Agustín Cano's (1984:20), in which he describes an area of the Petén close to El Zotz (from Mopán to Lake Petén Itza) as a landscape of woods that "are not so thick . . . they alternate with pine groves and very beautiful fields which abound exceedingly with deer, wild boar [peccaries], tapir, turkeys—which they call hens of the earth, and with other animals."

Fire, used to clear the land and prepare the ground for planting, was also commonly used in the pre-Columbian Americas to hem in animals and direct them toward killing zones (Mancall 2018:34). One carved Maya vase likely shows the burning of milpa fields, with the hunting god Huk Xib carrying a torch and setting fire to a personified tree and beckoning deer from the forest (see figure 8.5;

Finamore and Houston 2010:116–117). This image also recalls ethnographic descriptions of night hunts. Wisdom (1940:71) states that among the Ch'orti', "deer are nearly always hunted at night," while Gann (1918:24) describes night hunting as a "favorite method of hunting the larger game animals." In those ethnographic settings, a pine torch attached to the hat of the hunter not only attracts animals of all kinds, but also reflects the eyes of inquisitive prey, offering an easy mark.

Among the contemporary Lacandon Maya, fallow fields are also manipulated to facilitate hunting. Known as *pak che kol*, or "planted tree milpa," fallow agricultural plots are often sown with extra seeds to attract animals, then used for hunting game (Greenberg 1992:25; Nations and Nigh 1980:15). Isotopic studies of white-tailed deer bone in the Maya area indicate that although deer diets were primarily wild, animals also clearly grazed in agricultural fields. Notably, a specimen from Lagartero (White et al. 2004:154) had an isotopic signature suggesting an almost exclusively maize-based diet, adding some weight to the notion that the Maya raised or managed deer. Tame deer may have also been used to attract their wild counterparts for hunts, as in other parts of the ancient world (Olivier 2015:176).

Finally, as reviewed above, hunting imagery from painted polychrome vases and bark-paper books suggests that hand spears and atlatls were the primary means of acquiring deer during the Classic period, with a shift toward snares and traps during the Postclassic, colonial, and modern periods. Stone tools from El Zotz also seem to reflect this change, with the kinds of thin bifaces used for spear and atlatl points best represented at the height of the Classic period, when they peak in comparison to stone bifaces with agricultural functions (Hruby 2018:fig. 9.3). These patterns of stone tool production could also indicate increased warfare during the Late and Terminal Classic periods at El Zotz, but that interpretation would contradict the dispersion of El Zotz's settlement away from defensible hilltop locations after the Early Classic period (e.g., Carter et al. 2018) and broadening gifting and trade networks in which El Zotz participated during the Late and Terminal Classic periods (Eppich et al. 2015; Newman et al. 2018).

CONCLUSION

The patterns observed in faunal remains from El Zotz are not unique. The shift from a marked preference for white-tailed deer toward smaller-bodied prey and an overall increase in the variety of taxa consumed also describe assemblages recovered from many ancient Maya cities (e.g., Emery 2007, 2008). One way of understanding those trends has been through the application of optimal foraging theories and prey choice models from behavioral ecology. Those theories, which assume that predators (including human hunters) selectively seek out the prey that provides the greatest nutritional return for their efforts, suggest that such diversification in the size and species of hunted animals is an indicator of resource depression, a reduction in the availability of the most desirable resource, because of factors such as overhunting, behavioral changes, or decreasing habitat availability (e.g., Codding and Bird 2015; Emery 2007, 2008; Grayson 2001; Lupo 2007). That is, fewer deer remains are found in later Maya faunal assemblages simply because there were fewer deer to hunt (Emery and Brown 2012:110).

In an oft-cited treatise on hunting, José Ortega y Gassett (1995:105) wrote, "One does not hunt in order to kill; on the contrary, one kills in order to have hunted." Meat is food, of course, and deer hunters throughout Maya history certainly enjoyed the nutritional benefits of their catch. Artistic representations of meals and feasts highlight deer haunches served in bowls and stacks of tamales accompanied by hieroglyphs describing them as filled with venison (Taube 1988). But meat is also power and pleasure.

In the context of the royal courts of the Classic Maya, hunting was about sport, symbolism, and sociality as much as it was about sustenance. Most archaeological faunal remains recovered at Maya sites come from city centers and the upper ranks of Maya society (e.g., Emery 2012; Pohl 1990; Sharpe and Emery 2015), including those studied here from El Zotz. It seems rash, or at least imprudent, to ignore the impact of courtly taste and elite competition on those samples, to assume strictly rational behaviors on behalf of those enmeshed in what Houston and Takeshi Inomata (2009:150) call "an elaborate tournament of competition, largesse, and consumption." Much like other practices perhaps more readily identified with the culture of courtly life, such as artistry reflected in stone sculptures or painted polychrome pottery, deer hunting shifted in both form and meaning when royal court systems collapsed toward the end of the first millennium AD.

WORKS CITED

Allsen, Thomas T. 2006. *The Royal Hunt in Eurasian History*. Philadelphia: University of Pennsylvania Press.

Ardren, Traci. 2002. "Death Became Her: Images of Female Power from Yaxuna Burials." In *Ancient Maya Women*, edited by Traci Ardren, 68–88. Walnut Creek, CA: Altamira Press.

Arzápalo, Ramón, ed. and trans. 1987. *Ritual de los Bacabes*. Mexico City: Universidad Nacional Autónoma de México.

Beach, Timothy, Sheryl Luzzadder-Beach, Colin Doyle, and William Delgado. 2018. "Environments of El Zotz: Water and Soil Chemistry, the El Zotz Dam, and Long-Term Environmental Change." In *An Inconstant Landscape: The Maya Kingdom of El Zotz, Guatemala*, edited by Thomas G. Garrison and Stephen Houston, 163–188. Boulder: University Press of Colorado.

Boot, Erik. *The Updated Preliminary Classic Maya-English, English-Classic Maya Vocabulary of Hieroglyphic Readings*. Last modified April 2009. http://www.mesoweb.com/resources/vocabulary/Vocabulary-2009.01.pdf.

Braakhuis, H.E.M. 2001. "The Way of All Flesh: Sexual Implications of the Mayan Hunt." *Anthropos* 96 (2): 391–409.

Bricker, Victoria R. 1991. "Faunal Offerings in the Dresden Codex." In *Sixth Palenque Round Table, 1986*, edited by Merle Green Robertson, 285–292. Norman: University of Oklahoma Press.

Brown, Linda A. 2001. "Feasting on the Periphery: The Production of Ritual Feasting and Village Festivals at the Cerén Site, El Salvador." In *Feasts: Archaeological and Ethnographic Perspectives on Food, Politics, and Power*, edited by Michael Dietler and Brian Hayden, 368–390. Washington, DC: Smithsonian Institution Press.

Brown, Linda A. 2005. "Planting the Bones: Hunting Ceremonialism at Contemporary and Nineteenth-Century Shrines in the Guatemalan Highlands." *Latin American Antiquity* 16 (2): 131–146.

Campbell, Roderick. 2014. "The Wild and the Sacred: The Shang Royal Hunt." Paper presented at the 79th Society for American Archaeology Annual Meeting, Austin, TX.

Cano, Agustín. 1984. *Manche and Peten: The Hazards of Itza Deceit and Barbarity*. Ed. Frank E. Comparato, trans. Charles P. Bowditch and Guillermo Rivera. Culver City, CA: Labyrinthos.

Carr, H. Sorayya. 1996. "Precolumbian Maya Exploitation and Management of Deer Populations." In *The Managed Mosaic: Ancient Maya Agriculture and Resource Use*, edited by Scott L. Fedick, 251–261. Salt Lake City: University of Utah Press.

Carter, Nicholas P., Yeny M. Gutiérrez-Castillo, and Sarah Newman. 2018. "Border Lords and Client Kings: El Zotz and Bejucal in the Late Classic Period." In *An Inconstant Landscape: The Maya Kingdom of El Zotz, Guatemala*, edited by Thomas G. Garrison and Stephen Houston, 93–115. Boulder: University Press of Colorado.

Codding, Brian F., and Douglas W. Bird. 2015. "Behavioral Ecology and the Future of Archaeological Science." *Journal of Archaeological Science* 56: 9–20.

Colas, Pierre R. 2006. "The Hunting Scenes in the Madrid Codex: A Planner for Hunting Rituals." *Sacred Books, Sacred Languages: Two Thousand Years of Ritual and Religious Maya Literature. Proceedings of the 8th European Maya Conference, Madrid, November 25–30, 2003*, edited by Rogelio Valencia Rivera and Geneviève Le Fort, 81–92. Markt Schwaben, Germany: Verlag Anton Saurwein.

Corominas, Joan, and José A. Pascual. 1983. *Diccionario crítico etimológico castellano e hispánico*. Vol. 5. Madrid: Editorial Griegos.

Custred, Glynn. 1979. "Hunting Technologies in Andean Culture." *Journal de la Société des Américanistes* 66: 7–19.

Czapiewska-Halliday, Ewa. 2018. "The Study of Value: Social, Economic and Political Dimensions of Palace Complexes at El Zotz." PhD diss., University College London.

Díaz del Castillo, Bernal. 2008. *The History of the Conquest of New Spain*, edited by Davíd Carrasco. Albuquerque: University of New Mexico Press.

Díaz del Castillo, Bernal. 2010. *The True History of the Conquest of New Spain*. Vol. 4, edited by G. García. Cambridge: Cambridge University Press.

Emery, Kitty F. 2007. "Assessing the Impact of Ancient Maya Animal Use." *Journal for Nature Conservation* 15 (3): 184–195.

Emery, Kitty F. 2008. "A Zooarchaeological Test for Dietary Resource Depression at the End of the Classic Period in the Petexbatun, Guatemala." *Human Ecology* 36 (5): 617–634.

Emery, Kitty F. 2012. "The Motul de San José Animals in an Economic Perspective." In *Motul de San José: Politics, History, and Economy in a Classic Maya Polity*, edited by Antonia E. Foias and Kitty F. Emery, 291–325. Gainesville: University Press of Florida.

Emery, Kitty F., and Linda A. Brown. 2012. "Maya Hunting Sustainability: Perspectives from Past and Present." In *The Ethics of Anthropology and Amerindian Research: Reporting on Environmental Degradation and Warfare*, edited by Richard J. Chacon and Rubén G. Mendoza, 79–116. New York: Springer Science and Business Media.

Emery, Kitty F., and Erin Kennedy Thornton. 2008. "Zooarchaeological Habitat Analysis of Ancient Maya Landscape Changes." *Journal of Ethnobiology* 28 (2): 154–178.

Eppich, Keith, Griselda Pérez Robles, Caroline Parris, Sarah Newman, James Fitzsimmons, Matthew Moriarty, Mélanie Forné, and Juan Carlos Pérez. 2015. "Cerámica de Petén Occidental: Una perspectiva regional." Paper presented at the XXIX Simposio de Investigaciones Arqueológicas en Guatemala. National Museum of Archaeology and Ethnology, Guatemala City, July 20–24, 2015.

Finamore, Daniel and Stephen Houston, eds. 2010. *The Fiery Pool: The Maya and the Mythic Sea*. New Haven, CT, and Peabody Essex Museum, Salem: Yale University Press.

Ford, Anabel, and Kitty F. Emery. 2008. "Exploring the Legacy of the Maya Forest." *Journal of Ethnobiology* 28 (2): 147–153.

Ford, Anabel, and Ronald B. Nigh. 2009. "Origins of the Maya Forest Garden: A Resource Management System." *Journal of Ethnobiology* 29 (2): 213–236.

Gann, Thomas W.F. 1918. *The Maya Indians of Southern Yucatan and Northern British Honduras*. Bureau of American Ethnology, Bulletin 64. Washington, DC: Smithsonian Institution.

Garrison, Thomas G., and Stephen Houston, eds. 2018. *An Inconstant Landscape: The Maya Kingdom of El Zotz, Guatemala*. Boulder: University Press of Colorado.

Götz, Christopher M. 2008. "Coastal and Inland Patterns of Faunal Exploitation in the Prehispanic Northern Maya Lowlands." *Quaternary International* 191 (1): 154–169.

Götz, Christopher M. 2014. "La alimentación de los mayas prehispánicos: Vista desde la zooarqueología." *Anales de Antropología* 4 (1): 167–199.

Grayson, Donald K. 2001. "The Archaeological Record of Human Impacts on Animal Populations." *Journal of World Prehistory* 15 (1): 1–68.

Greenberg, Laurie S.Z. 1992. "Garden Hunting among the Yucatec Maya: A Coevolutionary History of Wildlife and Culture." *Etnoecología* 1 (1): 23–33.

Harlow, Richard F., and David C. Guynn Jr. 1994. "Whitetail Habitats and Ranges." In *Deer*, edited by Duane Gerlach, Sally Atwater, and Judith Schnell, 169–173. Mechanicsburg, PA: Stackpole Books.

Hellmuth, Nicholas M. 1991. "A Hunting God and the Maya Ballgame of Guatemala: An Iconography of Maya Ceremonial Headdresses." In *The Mesoamerican Ballgame: Papers Presented at the International Colloquium "The Mesoamerican Ballgame 2000 BC–AD 2000,"* edited by Gerard W. Van Bussel, Paul L.F. Van Dongen, and Ted J.J. Leyenaar, 135–159. Leiden, Netherlands: Riijksmuseum voor Volkenkunde.

Houston, Stephen. 2010. "Maya Creatures I: Maya Musk." Last modified June 17, 2010. https://decipherment.wordpress.com/2010/06/17/maya-musk/.

Houston, Stephen D., and Takeshi Inomata. 2009. *The Classic Maya*. Cambridge: Cambridge University Press.

Houston, Stephen, Sarah Newman, Edwin Román, and Nicholas Carter. 2015. "A Temple over Time." In *Temple of the Night Sun: A Royal Tomb at El Diablo, Guatemala*, edited by Stephen Houston, Sarah Newman, Edwin Román, and Thomas Garrison, 30–83. San Francisco: PreColumbia Mesoweb Press.

Houston, Stephen, Sarah Newman, Edwin Román, and Thomas Garrison. 2015. *Temple of the Night Sun: A Royal Tomb at El Diablo, Guatemala*. San Francisco: PreColumbia Mesoweb Press.

Houston, Stephen D., David Stuart, and Karl A. Taube. 2006. *The Memory of Bones: Body, Being, and Experience among the Classic Maya*. Austin: University of Texas Press.

Hruby, Zachary. 2018. "Lithic Technologies and Economies at El Zotz." In *An Inconstant Landscape: The Maya Kingdom of El Zotz, Guatemala*, edited by Thomas G. Garrison and Stephen Houston, 228–254. Boulder: University Press of Colorado.

Kingsley, Melanie J., and Laura Gámez. 2018. "In the Wake of 'Collapse': The Postdynastic or Early Postclassic Period at El Zotz." In *An Inconstant Landscape: The Maya Kingdom of El Zotz, Guatemala*, edited by Thomas G. Garrison and Stephen Houston, 140–160. Boulder: University Press of Colorado.

Linares, Olga F. 1976. "Garden Hunting in the American Tropics." *Human Ecology* 4 (4): 331–349.

Looper, Matthew. 2019. *The Beast Between: Deer in Maya Art and Culture*. Austin: University of Texas Press.

Lupo, Karen D. 2007. "Evolutionary Foraging Models in Zooarchaeological Analysis: Recent Applications and Future Challenges." *Journal of Archaeological Research* 15 (2): 43–189.

Luzzadder-Beach, Sheryl, Timothy Beach, Thomas Garrison, Stephen Houston, James Doyle, Edwin Román, Steven Bozarth, Richard Terry, Samantha Krause, and Jonathan

Flood. 2016. "Paleoecology and Geoarchaeology at El Palmar and the El Zotz Region, Guatemala." *Geoarchaeology* 32: 90–106. https://doi.org/10.1002/gea.21587.

Mancall, Peter C. 2018. *Nature and Culture in the Early Modern Atlantic*. Philadelphia: University of Pennsylvania Press.

Masson, Marilyn A., and Carlos Peraza Lope. 2008. "Animal Use at the Postclassic Maya Center of Mayapán." *Quaternary International* 191 (1): 170–183.

Masson, Marilyn A., and Carlos Peraza Lope. 2014. *Kukulcan's Realm: Urban Life at Ancient Mayapán*. Boulder: University Press of Colorado.

Montero-López, Coral. 2009. "Sacrifice and Feasting among the Classic Maya Elite and the Importance of the White-Tailed Deer: Is there a Regional Pattern?" *Journal of Historical and European Studies* 2: 53–68.

Nations, James D., and Ronald B. Nigh. 1980. "The Evolutionary Potential of Lacandon Maya Sustained-Yield Tropical Forest Agriculture." *Journal of Anthropological Research* 36 (1): 1–30.

Neusius, Sarah W. 2008. "Game Procurement among Temperate Horticulturalists: The Case for Garden Hunting by the Dolores Anasazi." In *Case Studies in Environmental Archaeology*, edited by Elizabeth Reitz, Margaret C. Scarry, and Sylvia J. Scudder, 297–314. New York: Springer-Verlag.

Newman, Sarah, José Luis Garrido, and Nicholas P. Carter. 2018. "Collapse, Continuity, Change: El Zotz in the Terminal Classic Period." In *An Inconstant Landscape: The Maya Kingdom of El Zotz, Guatemala*, edited by Thomas G. Garrison and Stephen Houston, 116–139. Boulder: University Press of Colorado.

Olivier, Guilhem. 2014. "Venados melómanos y cazadores lúbricos: Cacería, música y erotismo en Mesoamérica." *Estudios de Cultura Náhuatl* 47: 121–168.

Olivier, Guilhem. 2015. *Cacería, sacrificio y poder en Mesoamérica: Tras las huellas de Mixcóatl, "Serpiente de Nube."* México City: Universidad Nacional Autónoma de México, Instituto de Investigaciones Históricas, Fondo de Cultura Económica, Centro de Estudios Mexicanos y Centroamericanos.

Ortega y Gasset, José. 1995. *Meditations on Hunting*. New York: Charles Scribner's Sons.

Osborne, Carolyn M., and Harry S. Riddell. 1978. "A Cache of Deer Snares from Owens Valley, California." *Journal of California Anthropology* 5: 101–109.

Pohl, Mary D. 1981. "Ritual Continuity and Transformation in Mesoamerica: Reconstructing the Ancient Maya Cuch Ritual." *American Antiquity* 46 (3): 513–529.

Pohl, Mary D. 1983. "Maya Ritual Faunas: Vertebrate Remains from Burials, Caches, Caves, and Cenotes in the Maya Lowlands." In *Civilization in the Ancient Americas: Essays in Honor of Gordon R. Willey*, edited by Richard M. Leventhal and Alan M. Kolata, 55–103. Albuquerque: University of New Mexico Press.

Pohl, Mary D. 1985. "The Privileges of Maya Elites: Prehistoric Vertebrate Fauna from Seibal." In *Prehistoric Lowland Maya Environment and Subsistence Economy*, edited by Mary D. Pohl, 133–145. Cambridge, MA: Harvard University.

Pohl, Mary D. 1990. "The Ethnozoology of the Maya: Faunal Remains from Five Sites in the Peten, Guatemala." In *Excavations at Seibal, Department of Peten, Guatemala, No. 3*, edited by Gordon R. Willey, 144–174. Cambridge, MA: Peabody Museum of Archaeology and Ethnology, Harvard University.

Pohl, Mary D., and Lawrence H. Feldman. 1982. "The Traditional Role of Women and Animals in Lowland Maya Economy." In *Maya Subsistence: Studies in Memory of Dennis E. Puleston*, edited by Kent V. Flannery, 295–311. New York: Academic Press.

Redfield, Robert, and Alfonso Villa Rojas. 1934. *Chan Kom: A Maya Village*. Carnegies Publication No. 448. Washington, DC: Carnegie Institute of Washington.

Reitz, Elizabeth J., and Elizabeth S. Wing. 2008. *Zooarchaeology*. 2nd ed. Cambridge Manuals in Archaeology. Cambridge: Cambridge University Press.

Rodríguez, Mariana, Salvador Montiel, María D. Cervera, María T. Castillo, and Eduardo J. Naranjo. 2012. "The Practice and Perception of *Batida* (Group Hunting) in a Maya Community of Yucatan, Mexico." *Journal of Ethnobiology* 32 (2): 212–227.

Román, Edwin, Thomas G. Garrison, and Stephen Houston. 2018. "Ruling through Defense: The Rise of an Early Classic Dynasty at El Zotz." In *An Inconstant Landscape: The Maya Kingdom of El Zotz, Guatemala*, edited by Thomas G. Garrison and Stephen Houston, 70–92. Boulder: University Press of Colorado.

Ruiz de Alarcón, Hernando. 1987. "Tratado de las supersticiones y costumbres gentilicas que oy viuen entre los indios naturales desta Nueua España." In *El alma encantada*, edited by Francisco Benítez, 125–223. Mexico City: Fondo de Cultura Económica.

Sharpe, Ashley E., and Kitty F. Emery. 2015. "Differential Animal Use within Three Late Classic Maya States: Implications for Politics and Trade." *Journal of Anthropological Archaeology* 40: 280–301.

Sharpe, Ashley E., Takeshi Inomata, Daniela Triadan, Melissa Burham, Jessica MacLellan, Jessica Munson, and Flory Pinzón. 2020. "The Maya Preclassic to Classic Transition Observed through Faunal Trends from Ceibal, Guatemala." *PLoS ONE* 15 (4): e0230892. https://doi.org/10.1371/journal.pone.0230892.

Sharpe, Ashley E., William A. Saturno, and Kitty F. Emery. 2014. "Shifting Patterns of Maya Social Complexity through Time: Preliminary Zooarchaeological Results from San Bartolo, Guatemala." In *Animals and Inequality in the Ancient World*, edited by Benjamin S. Arbuckle and Sue Ann McCarty, 85–105. Boulder: University Press of Colorado.

Smith, Derek A. 2005. "Garden Game: Shifting Cultivation, Indigenous Hunting, and Wildlife Ecology in Western Panama." *Human Ecology* 33(4): 505–537.

Steggerda, Morris. 1941. *Maya Indians of Yucatan*. Publication 531. Washington, DC: Carnegie Institute of Washington.

Stone, Andrea, and Marc Zender. 2011. *Reading Maya Art: A Hieroglyphic Guide to Ancient Maya Painting and Sculpture*. New York: Thames and Hudson.

Taube, Karl A. 1988. "A Study of Classic Maya Scaffold Sacrifice." In *Maya Iconography*, edited by Elizabeth P. Benson and Gillett G. Griffin, 331–351. Princeton, NJ: Princeton University Press.

Taube, Karl A. 1997. "A God Named Zip." *Archaeology* 50: 39.

Taube, Karl A. 2003. "Ancient and Contemporary Maya Conceptions about Field and Forest." In *The Lowland Maya Area: Three Millennia at the Human-Wildland Interface*, edited by Arturo Gómez-Pampa, Michael F. Allen, Scott L. Fedick, and Juan J. Jiménez-Osornio, 461–492. New York: Food Products Press.

Taube, Karl A., William A. Saturno, David Stuart, and Heather Hurst. 2010. *The Murals of San Bartolo, El Petén, Guatemala, Part 2: The West Wall*. Barnardsville, NC: Boundary End Archaeology Research Center.

Taube, Karl A., and Marc Zender. 2009. "American Gladiators: Ritual Boxing in Ancient Mesoamerica." In *Blood and Beauty: Organized Violence in the Art and Archaeology of Mesoamerica and Central America*, edited by Heather Orr and Rex Koontz, 161–220. Los Angeles: Cotsen Institute of Archaeology Press.

Teeter, Wendy G., and Arlen F. Chase. 2004. "Adding Flesh to Bones: Using Zooarchaeology Research to Answer the Big-Picture Questions." *Archaeofauna* 13: 155–172.

Thomason, Allison. 2014. "The Royal Hunt in Neo-Assyrian Mesopotamia." Paper presented at the 79th Society for American Archaeology Annual Meeting, Austin, TX.

Thompson, J. Eric S. 1930. *Ethnology of the Mayas of Southern and Central British Honduras*. Chicago: Field Museum of Natural History.

Thompson, J. Eric S. 1963. *Maya Archaeologist*. Norman: University of Oklahoma Press.

Thompson, J. Eric S. 1970. *Maya History and Religion*. Norman: University of Oklahoma Press.

Tozzer, Alfred M. 1941. *Landa's Relación de las Cosas de Yucatán: A Translation*. Cambridge: Peabody Museum of Archaeology and Ethnology.

Tozzer, Alfred M. (1907) 1982. *Mayas y lacandones: Un estudio comparativo*. Mexico City: Instituto Nacional Indigenista.

Vail, Gabrielle. 1997. "The Deer-Trapping Almanacs in the Madrid Codex." *Papers on the Madrid Codex*, edited by Victoria R. Bricker and Gabrielle Vail, 73–110. New Orleans: Middle American Research Institute, Tulane University.

Vanderwarker, Amber M. 2006. *Farming, Hunting, and Fishing in the Olmec World*. Austin: University of Texas Press.

Villacorta C., J. Antonio, and Carlos A. Villacorta. 1976. *Códices mayas*. 2nd ed. Guatemala City: Tipografía Nacional.

White, Christine D., Mary D. Pohl, Henry P. Schwarcz, and Fred J. Longstaffe. 2004. "Feast, Field, and Forest: Deer and Dog Diets at Lagartero, Tikal, and Copán." In *Maya Zooarchaeology: New Directions in Method and Theory*, edited by Kitty F. Emery, 141–158. Los Angeles: Cotsen Institute of Archaeology Press.

Whittington, E. Michael, ed. 2001. *The Sport of Life and Death: The Mesoamerican Ballgame*. New York: Thames and Hudson.

Wisdom, Charles. 1940. *The Chorti Indians of Guatemala*. Chicago: University of Chicago Press.

Ximénez, Francisco. (1722) 1967. *Historia natural del Reino de Guatemala*, edited by José de Pineda Ibarra. Guatemala City: Sociedad de Geografía e Historia de Guatemala, Special Publication 14.

Zender, Marc. 2000. "A Study of Two Uaxactun-Style Tamale-Serving Vessels." In *The Maya Vase Book: A Corpus of Rollout Photographs of Maya Vases*, 6, edited by Justin Kerr, 1038–1055. New York: Kerr Associates.

Zender, Marc. 2010. "The Music of Shells." In *The Fiery Pool: The Maya and the Mythic Sea*, edited by Daniel Finamore and Stephen Houston, 83–85. New Haven, CT, and Peabody Essex Museum, Salem: Yale University Press.

Zender, Marc. 2017. "The Maize God and the Deer Lord's Wife." Paper presented at the 22nd Annual European Maya Conference, Malmö, Sweden.

9

Garden Hunting and Food Sharing during the Mississippian Period in the American South

TANYA M. PERES

Food is one of the basic necessities of life. It is so important to the survival of the human species that communities focus on a particular subsistence strategy to lessen subsistence risk and uncertainty. Traditional ecological knowledge was a beneficial means of avoiding subsistence uncertainty in the past, avoiding food shortfalls, and making decisions that were risk averse. One way to mitigate variance in food availability is to diversify the types of subsistence activities practiced (Winterhalder et al. 1999). During the late prehistoric Mississippian period (AD 1000–1475) of the American South, people practiced a system of agriculture centered on the growing of imported domesticated crops and native cultigens, hunting native wild animals, and harvesting native fruits and nuts (Steponaitis 1986). Previous studies have shown that in terms of Mississippian period animal exploitation, the range of taxa was reduced from previous periods. This reduction is attributed to scheduling conflicts that arose with an intensification of agricultural activities and the environmental changes that resulted (Jackson and Scott 2003; Muller 1997; Scott 1983). A subsistence strategy that included farming,

https://doi.org/10.5876/9781646422562.c009

gathering, and hunting enabled communities to lessen the potential for food shortfalls and uncertainty.

This chapter examines the animal portion of the diet from two Mississippian period sites located in Middle Tennessee. These two sites are part of the regional cultural tradition known as the Middle Cumberland Region (MCR) and include a farmstead and a village. My study examines how changes in settlement patterns and sociopolitical structure influenced decisions about subsistence risk and uncertainty. The faunal records from these sites are used to determine if increased attention to farming that coincided with population aggregation into villages and changes in sociopolitical structure resulted in a shift in other subsistence activities (hunting) and food sharing.

THE MISSISSIPPIAN PERIOD IN THE AMERICAN SOUTH

The archaeological cultures of the late Holocene (ca. AD 100–1450) in the American South are referred to as Mississippian (Steponaitis 1986). General hallmarks of the Mississippian period in the southeastern United States include the production of shell-tempered ceramics; intensive cultivation of maize and other domesticates; large, densely populated settlements often focused around earthen mound centers; increased social stratification; and elaboration of mortuary treatments and grave goods (Schroedl 1998). In Tennessee, localized differences can be seen between major river drainage basins located across the state (i.e., Mississippi, Tennessee, and Cumberland rivers). The Cumberland River valley is home to the Central Basin physiographic feature and the cultural tradition known as the Middle Cumberland Region.

The Middle Cumberland Region during the Mississippian Period

The Middle Cumberland Region is a cultural tradition situated in the Central Basin of Middle Tennessee. The Central Basin covers an area more than 7,500 mi.^{2}, with an average elevation of around 500 ft. The area is nearly surrounded by the Highland Rim, which averages 1,000 ft. in elevation (Gildrie 2018). The formation of the basin dates to the Ordovician period, about 430 million years ago. Periodic uplifting of bedrock created the Nashville Dome, which has since eroded into the Central Basin (Reesman and Stearns 1989). The resulting topography comprises karst landforms, such as sinkholes and caves (Kingsbury et al. 1999). One of the most prominent features in the Central Basin landscape is the Cumberland River, which has been the setting of human occupation for millennia.

The terrain in this area consists of soils characterized as deep, well-drained, clayey and silty, making it one of the best upland farming areas in Tennessee (Springer and Elder 1980). Middle Cumberland Region sites occur within the Western Mesophytic Forest Region, an area distinguished by upland climax communities of oak, hickory, tulip tree, beech, and chestnut (Braun 1950). Most of Middle Tennessee is within the Carolinian Biotic Province (Dice 1943). This province is marked by a rich and diverse fauna that includes such large game as white-tailed deer, elk, and black bear, as well as smaller game such as bobcat, otter, and cottontail rabbit. Other important resources include birds (owl, turkey, and ducks), snakes, frogs, turtles, fish, and mollusks.

In Tennessee, the MCR is recognized as the regional manifestation of the larger Mississippian period culture, defined in part by distinctive mortuary practices, artistic styles, and ceramic typologies (Moore and Smith 2009; Moore et al. 2006). Subsistence activities in the MCR follow those of the larger American South. People practiced an increasingly intensive system of agriculture centered on growing imported domesticated crops (maize, beans, and squash) as well as native cultigens (sunflower, chenopod, bottle gourd) (Steponaitis 1986). In the MCR, the early Mississippian period, designated Regional Periods I (Emergent Mississippian, AD 1000–1100) and II (West-to-East expansion and Mississippianization, AD 1100–1200), saw a population that was still somewhat dispersed, with single-family groups living in farmsteads scattered across the landscape (Moore and Smith 2009). Mississippian period farmsteads were typically composed of a single-family house, a kitchen or cooking shed, and associated yard features such as middens, drying racks, and a corn crib (Hinson 2018; Smith 1992; Smith et al. 1993). This site type was situated on arable land and lacked a ceremonial or communal structure.

A noticeable shift in settlement structure occurred ca. AD 1250 (Regional Period III, "Proliferation of Chiefdoms"), when populations appear to aggregate into larger communities consisting of a hierarchy of villages and mound sites (Moore and Smith 2009:208). The large and more densely populated villages included a number of structures such as platform mounds, conical burial mounds, domestic houses, special-use structures, formal cemeteries, and palisade walls with bastions (Hinson 2018; Smith 1992). There was a marked increase in interpersonal violence as evidenced by population aggregation into villages and the construction of fortifications (walls, earthen embankments, ditches) around these communities.

Farming and hunting were important to the subsistence economy at this time, yet not until recently has much attention been given to studying Middle Cumberland Mississippian foodways beyond species lists (Clinton and Peres 2011; Ledford 2018; Ledford and Peres 2018; Peres 2010a, 2018; Peres and Ledford 2016). Earlier zooarchaeological data were generated for technical reports that resulted from salvage projects in the 1980s and 1990s. The data were used to make generalizations based on species lists and relative abundances. For instance, Emanuel Breitburg (1998; Breitburg and Moore 2016) generalizes to argue that the hunting strategies of Middle Cumberland Mississippian communities were focused on large terrestrial game animals, specifically white-tailed deer (*Odocoileus virginianus*), elk (*Cervus canadensis*), black bear (*Ursus americanus*), and eastern wild turkey

(*Meleagris gallopavo silvestris*). Breitburg (Breitburg and Moore 2016:114) notes that even though freshwater fish and shellfish were abundant in the rivers and streams of Middle Tennessee, aquatic taxa constituted a "very small percentage" of the diet. However, I found that these conclusions were based on the culturally defined "edible meat weights" and not on more telling measures such as minimum number of individuals (MNI), biomass, or diversity and equitability values (Peres 2010a).

Studies conducted since 2010 show that managing food resources and subsistence risk was more complicated than site species lists indicate. Resource management strategies may have included hunting to maximize the capture of animals from in and around agricultural fields (i.e., garden hunting) (Clinton and Peres 2011), the management of turkey populations to ensure a stable supply of meat and eggs (Ledford 2018; Ledford and Peres 2018; Peres and Ledford 2016), and the butchering of white-tailed deer for meat and bone marrow (Peres 2018). The current study further examines the strategy of hunting animals attracted to agricultural fields at a time when population and community-based settlements grew and became more socially and politically stratified. This change created an elite class that did not produce its own food but relied on other members of the community for provision of necessary foodstuffs.

It is expected that agricultural fields larger and more productive than house gardens were necessary to successfully harvest sufficient crop yields to feed all segments of society in these larger Mississippian period communities. Creating these fields required landscape management and modification, such as clearing of forested areas and cleaning out of existing fields after the harvest. This increased focus on farming obligated people to stay near their agricultural fields and gardens, diverting time and energy away from hunting and fishing activities (VanDerwarker 2006; Zeder 2012). Garden hunting is one solution to alleviating the competing time and labor demands of hunting and agriculture (Linares 1976; Neusius 2008; VanDerwarker 2006).

The concept of garden hunting is based on the idea that as people focused more of their efforts on farming to help feed families and communities, they had less time to spend on long-distance hunts of large game animals (VanDerwarker 2006). In the American South, this may not have been the case when native cultigens were the main farming crops. C. Margaret Scarry (2008) suggests that the husbandry practices used for Indigenous crops in the American South (such as chenopod) were potentially less labor and time intensive than those needed for their imported domesticated counterparts (such as maize, beans, and squash). For instance, chenopods were planted by the broadcast sowing of seeds on lightly tilled soils. Based on ethnohistoric sources, women and children sowed the seeds in rows or in a random fashion in a prepared area in the fall or early spring. Seeds from domesticated Indigenous sunflowers, squashes, and sumpweed may have been planted in hills set around the edges of fields, to accommodate their sprawling vines (Scarry 2008; Wilson 1917). Scarry (2008:397) suggests that this more labor-intensive method of planting may have been the precedent for the method used to plant maize, beans, and squash. Thus, while farming Indigenous plants may not have limited hunting, the adoption and widespread farming of crops such as maize would have.

The chronicles of Spanish explorers note that the communities they encountered in the American South practiced communal farming of maize, beans and squash, with tasks often divided by gender (Scarry 2008). Men prepared fields by clearing out trees and underbrush from new areas and burning weeds and grasses from existing fields in the late winter and early spring. Some accounts describe men trenching the fields for planting. Women then created rows of hills spaced out at 1 m (3 ft.) intervals using digging sticks and hoes. Multiple maize seeds were placed in each hill, sometimes interspersed with squash and beans. Once the seedlings reached a certain size, the women thinned the plants and spent the growing season managing the care of the crops, including weeding (Díaz et al. 1936; Scarry 2008; Swanton 1946).

While this is a brief and general summary of Indigenous farming practices as they apply to both native and adopted plants, it is clear that the two groups of plants required different methods of planting (and also harvesting) and were maintained on a different seasonal schedule. Scarry (2008) suggests that because imported and native crops were planted and harvested at different times of the year, farmers were actively growing crops year-round. This practice would mean that Indigenous farmers' schedules were tuned to the seasonal rhythms of plants in ways they had not been prior to the adoption of maize. Ethnographic data from the Guyamí and Cuna peoples of Panama indicate that they spend an enormous amount of time protecting their crops from pest animals (Linares 1976:347). To achieve this, they practiced garden hunting as their main hunting strategy. This resulted in the dual benefit of having meat to eat and fewer pests feeding on their crops.[1]

In the next section I describe models of garden hunting and the expectations for this activity in the archaeological record of the MCR. I then describe expected patterns of food sharing (provisioning) at the household (farmstead) and community (village) levels in the Mississippian period. I then use previously published zooarchaeological data from two Mississippian period sites in Middle Tennessee to test the garden-hunting model of animal exploitation and the degree to which food was shared at the household and community levels.

GARDEN HUNTING TO MITIGATE SUBSISTENCE RISK AND UNCERTAINTY

Garden hunting is a subsistence strategy practiced in response to a reorganization or intensification of agricultural-related activities. Garden hunting is a form of risk avoidance. It minimizes time spent procuring meat resources, and it reduces competition for a farmer's resources by killing the larger pests that destroy crops. Hunting pest animals attracted to cleared fields, gardens, crops, and secondary growth around fields is a way to protect crops and acquire meat. Managing subsistence risk and uncertainty using this strategy can be seen through patterns in the zooarchaeological data.

There are three working models of garden hunting and their archaeological signatures. Olga Linares (1976) proposed the original "garden-hunting" model for sites in the American tropics, specifically Panama. This model suggests that farming communities utilized selective hunting that targeted populations of large mammals living in forest-edge environments (e.g., collared peccary and white-tailed deer) and smaller animals that live in the underbrush or in burrows (e.g., caviomorph rodents and armadillo) (Linares 1976:344). According to this strategy, the resulting faunal assemblage will consist of animal taxa that travel in small numbers over small ranges, tend to be passive, and are conducive to living in edge environments. These animals are easy to catch in traps and favor cultivated crops for their diets. In this model of garden hunting, "animal protein and carbohydrates are spatially concentrated" (Linares 1976:347).

Building on Linares's description of garden hunting in Panama, Sarah Neusius (2008) proposes a revised model of this hunting adaptation based on her work with the Dolores Anasazi in the American Southwest. The Neusius model suggests humans were more opportunistic and nonselective, hunting any taxon available in and around fields. If cultivated fields contain a high diversity of plants, then there would be a corresponding high diversity of animals. Archaeologically, the faunal assemblage will yield a high species diversity in comparison with the species diversity of natural spaces, and the represented species will be those most able to tolerate changes in vegetation (Neusius 2008). This model is supported by the fact that cultivation places further constraints on people's time. Local human groups would have had little time for hunting, so they merely gathered game when and where they could (Neusius 2008). A nonselective garden hunting strategy addresses the scheduling conflicts created by agricultural activities.

Amber VanDerwarker (2006) presents a garden-hunting model based on her work in Mesoamerica on Olmec sites. This model is similar to the others, except VanDerwarker argues that the adaptability of this strategy represents risk management. The "entire premise of the garden-hunting strategy is the economy of resources" and that local human groups chose a "selective or opportunistic approach depending on availability" (151). There is an organic continuum between selective and opportunistic strategies within this model. Farmers could be more selective in the animals hunted when crop harvests were good, resulting in restricted species diversity in the archaeological faunal assemblage. Conversely, when crops failed farmers may have used a "take what you can get" approach to hunting animals in and around their fields (151). This more opportunistic strategy would result in zooarchaeological assemblages with high species diversity.

In addition to archaeological samples, modern ethnographic research supports several aspects of the garden-hunting model. Lisa Naughton-Treves and colleagues (2003:1112) conducted research in the Peruvian Amazon that showed "shortly after maize was planted, wildlife visits to the disturbed areas peaked and was statistically higher than the amount of wildlife that visited fallow fields or forests." This research demonstrated that fewer animals were attracted to intensively managed areas (Naughton-Treves et al. 2001:1107). Ethnographic and ethnohistoric evidence indicate the application of both selective and nonselective strategies in the past and present (Linares 1976:347; Neusius 2008:300). The choice depends on the reliability of the agricultural yields (VanDerwarker 2006:150). In areas where agricultural yields are predictable and high, agriculturalists are more likely to hunt with increasing selectiveness, whereas in areas where yields are unpredictable, people exhibit less selectivity in hunting animals.

As people cleared land for agricultural fields, they provided the opportunity for an increase in the abundance of high-quality edible vegetation. This shift led to an increase in animals attracted to the cleared areas with edible cultivated crops (VanDerwarker 2006:148). Certain animals (e.g., white-tailed deer or wild turkey) are drawn to disturbed environments such as home gardens or forest edges because of the concentration of crops and weedy plants (Eaton 1992; Neusius 2008; Nowak and Paradiso 1983; VanDerwarker 2006). Linares (1976:347) refers to these animals as commensals, while VanDerwarker (2006:149) and others refer to them as crop pests. They usually travel in small groups and therefore need smaller home territories. Crop pests lack an overly aggressive nature and are able to recover quickly from overexploitation and other population pressures. I follow VanDerwarker's (2006:159–160) definition of crop pests as those animals that prefer secondary growth, forest edges, agricultural fields, and urban/suburban areas.

Through the adoption of a garden-hunting scheme, people are able to hunt in cultivated fields and home gardens with no special preparation as was required for lengthy and/or long-distance hunting parties. Garden hunting was less time consuming because it happened while performing other cultivation requirements. Garden hunting does not necessarily require a huge expenditure of energy and would have reduced the need for long-distance hunting trips during critical agricultural activities (VanDerwarker 2006). Additional benefits included killing pests that destroy crops, thus reducing the competition for farmer's resources, while providing easy access to readily exploitable sources of protein. In the following section I outline the zooarchaeological expectations for determining which type of garden-hunting strategy was used in the MCR.

Garden Hunting in the Middle Cumberland Region

The expected archaeological correlates of Mississippian period garden hunting in MCR combine elements of the models described by Linares (1976), Neusius (2008), and VanDerwarker (2006) but most heavily draw from VanDerwarker's work in Mesoamerica. I look at species diversity and equitability measures, relative abundance of pest animals, and ratios of terrestrial and aquatic taxa to determine if residents of two Mississippian period sites in the MCR were following a selective strategy of garden hunting or an opportunistic strategy.

If the site residents practiced a *selective strategy* for balancing protein needs with agricultural activities, we would expect to find a moderately diverse and inequitable assemblage with a relatively higher proportion of large game animals (e.g., deer, turkey) versus small terrestrial mammals (e.g., squirrel, raccoon, rabbit, etc.), and relatively few freshwater fishes and shellfish. If an *opportunistic strategy* was employed, we can expect to find a relatively high species diversity (many different types of animals) represented by a relatively high number of smaller prey animals.

Species diversity and equitability are calculated using the Shannon-Weaver function. The Shannon-Weaver function uses the following formula:

$$H' = -S\,(p_i)\,(\mathrm{Log10}\,p_i)$$

where:

H' = information content of the sample (can be biomass, NISP, MNI)

p_i = the relative abundance of the ith taxon within the sample

Log p_i = the logarithm of p_i. This can be to the base 2, e, or 10.

In this formula, assemblages with an even distribution of abundance between taxa have a higher diversity (H') than samples with the same number of taxa but with less even distribution of these taxa (where one or a few taxa have high abundance) (Reitz and Wing 2008:111). Samples that have a high number of taxonomic categories and a similar degree of equitability have greater diversity values. Equitability (V) values range from 0 to 1. Assemblages with a value nearing 1.0 have an even distribution among taxa (Reitz and Wing 2008:113). Samples with values closer to 0 have an uneven distribution of taxa, or dominance by one or a few taxa (Peres 2010b; Reitz and Wing 2008:113).

Knowing the type of garden hunting strategy employed at sites in the MCR allows me to look further into the redistribution of hunted food resources within communities. The next section first reviews a study on food redistribution (provisioning) during the Mississippian period in the Black Warrior River valley in Alabama. This review is followed by the expectations for faunal assemblages if animal meat was redistributed in a community. These expectations are then tested with the available data from two MCR sites: Brandywine Pointe and Rutherford-Kizer.

MISSISSIPPIAN PERIOD FOOD REDISTRIBUTION AT FARMSTEAD AND VILLAGE COMMUNITIES

Redistribution of food is an important aspect of communal life, especially in terms of reducing food uncertainties and the creation and maintenance of social and political structures. Food redistribution can take several forms or occur for different reasons. These include sharing, trade, gifting, obligatory exchange, taxation, and commandeering of resources. The extent to which the rules of redistribution in a given society are codified varies, and is not always clear from the archaeological record. In societies where food "producers" (farmers, hunters) provisioned the consumers / non–food producers (craftspeople, administrators, religious and/or political leaders), "the redistribution and/or marketing of meat and other animal products should produce some degree of patterning of faunal assemblages" (Crabtree 1990:158).

Recent research on provisioning in the Mississippian period in the American South comes from the Moundville community, located in Alabama (Jackson et al. 2016; Scarry et al. 2016) (figure 9.1). The results of the provisioning study suggest that meat, especially deer, was supplied to the elite and/or urban residents of Moundville from rural communities throughout the history of the community, but with noticeable shifts in hunting and butchering practices (Jackson and Scott 1995; Jackson et al. 2016). The changing demography of the Moundville community resulted in increased demands for food provisions for elites and the people involved in mound construction. An eventual decrease in food demands resulted from a decrease in the Moundville population, with the exception of the elites in the late occupational periods. Jackson and colleagues (Jackson et al. 2016:232) identify these as structural and social changes at Moundville and outlying communities.

In the earliest periods of the Moundville community, it is likely that kin from outlying communities shared food with their relatives living or working at the newly situated political center. During the height of Moundville's occupation, there is clear evidence of provisioning with deer meat in the form of high-utility or meatier portions, especially forequarters. Edwin Jackson et al. (2016:217) suggest this could be due to increased processing of deer carcasses in the field as a way to lessen transport costs. This evaluation may hold true for deer use but is not necessarily valid for smaller game animals (e.g., squirrels and rabbits), which for some parts of Moundville were brought in as whole carcasses. The faunal assemblage from elite contexts at Moundville further differed from rural or commoner deposits in the type and quantity of special/dangerous/exotic taxa

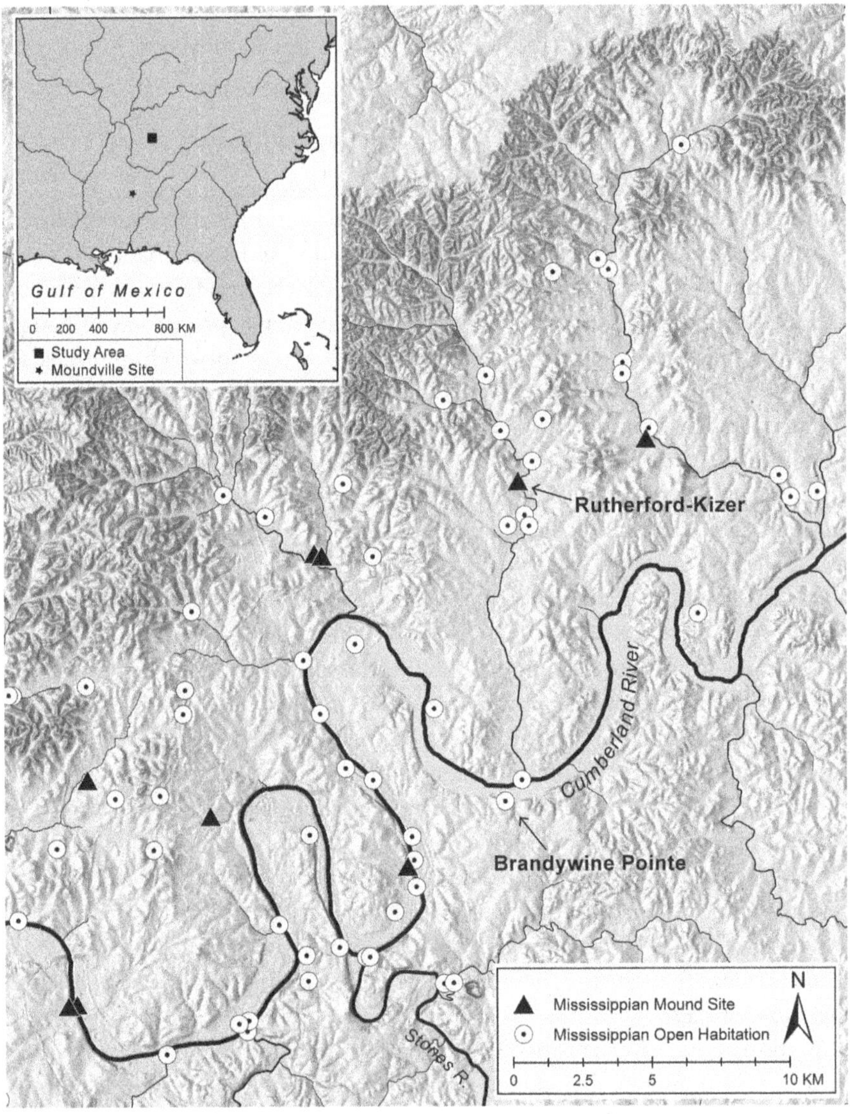

Figure 9.1. *Location of study area and sites discussed in the text.*

included. It is further noted that the variety of animals found in urban/elite food refuse is directly correlated to social and ceremonial factors. In sum, it appears that at Moundville, elites were provisioned with higher-utility and meatier parts of deer and with exotic/dangerous/special taxa (e.g., raptors, owls, woodpeckers, passerine birds, sandhill crane, bear, cougar, bobcat, snakes) (Jackson and Scott 1995, 2003). The findings from Moundville can be tested with data from the MCR to determine if and how villages and/or elites were provisioned.

Archaeological Expectations for Meat Redistribution

To determine if a faunal assemblage is the result of food redistribution within a community, I look at the data in terms of identified species, demographic patterns of killed animals, and the parts of the animal that were discarded. According to Pamela Crabtree (1990), the expectations for identifying redistribution at farmstead and village community sites from faunal data include data on the range of species present and relative importance of different animal species, kill patterns and sex ratios of main mammalian species, and body part distributions for the main vertebrate species. The faunal data from Moundville show that elites were provisioned with higher-utility and meatier parts of deer and with exotic or special taxa.

Based on the above expectations and the patterns seen at Moundville, I hypothesize that

- Family farmstead faunal assemblages will have *lower* diversity than those from village communities because of the hunting focus on pest taxa from garden plots and the scheduling of hunting and trapping around agricultural activities. The assemblages from village communities will have a *higher* diversity than rural sites.
- While smaller mammals and fish may be present in village community assemblages, the focus of meat procurement/provisioning efforts will be those animals that produce the largest amount of meat per individual; in the MCR, this is most likely deer and turkey.
- The parts of deer represented in a provisioned village community will be those that are meatier or of higher utility—such as hindquarters and forequarters.
- Exotic or "special" taxa will be present in village community faunal assemblages and nearly or completely absent from farmstead assemblages.

In the next section, I use the faunal data from Brandywine Pointe and Rutherford-Kizer to assess the type of garden hunting that was employed followed by an analysis of the data to determine the presence of provisioning in the village community.

ASSESSING GARDEN HUNTING IN THE MIDDLE CUMBERLAND REGION

In order to address these questions about changes in hunting strategies and provisioning systems, I use previously published faunal data from two Mississippian sites in the MCR of Tennessee. These data are used to derive the species diversity and equitability indices and to compare relative abundances of terrestrial to aquatic animals in each of the samples to determine the type of garden hunting employed at a Mississippian Regional Periods I and II farmstead (Brandywine Pointe) and a Mississippian Regional Periods III and IV mound and village site

(Rutherford-Kizer) (figure 9.1). I then compare the faunal assemblages (table 9.1) from Brandywine Pointe and Rutherford-Kizer to determine whether the data support the hypothesis that the residents of Rutherford-Kizer were provisioned with meat.

Middle Cumberland Mississippian Farmstead—Brandywine Pointe

The Brandywine Pointe site (40DV247) is a rural farmstead occupied during Regional Periods I and II based on radiocarbon dates and ceramic types (Moore and Smith 1993; Smith and Moore 1994). The site consists of a single square post-in-ground and wall trench house with interior features that include a hearth, an infant stone-box burial, and a limestone-lined cooking feature (Smith and Moore 1994). Exterior to the house were posts that likely belonged to a covered work area or storage facility, as well as a midden, pits, and remnants of a possible drying rack. Radiocarbon dates from intact deposits and ceramic chronologies at Brandywine Pointe suggest the site was occupied between AD 1000–1250, with "a high likelihood of actual occupation between AD 1210 and 1230" (Smith and Moore 1994:205). Moore and Smith (1993:21) note that houses of this style (post-in-ground) in the American South needed to be renovated every twenty years (or less). There was no evidence for renovation of the Brandywine Pointe house, suggesting that "the structure was occupied for substantially less than three decades" before it was abandoned (Moore and Smith 1993:21).

The zooarchaeological data available for Brandywine Pointe include taxonomic identifications, number of identified specimens (NISP), and MNI (weights and biomass estimates are not available). The NISP recovered from the Mississippian period occupation of Brandywine Pointe is fifty-three (analysis by E. Breitburg as reported in Moore and Smith 1993). Reasons for the small quantity of faunal remains include moderate to highly acidic soils that result in a lack of preservation of bone (as noted by the excavators); the structure and affiliated features were occupied for a relatively short time (potentially only twenty years), thus fewer opportunities for bones to be deposited; and the possibility that food waste was deposited further away from the structure (i.e., in cultivation fields or near the river) and, thus, outside the excavated area. While this number is small, the information gained from this sample should not be underestimated. The overall subsistence data at Brandywine Pointe show a reliance on terrestrial animals including white-tailed deer, wild turkey, and eastern box turtle (*Terrapene carolina*) (Smith and Moore 1994; see Peres 2010a) (table 9.1).

The Brandywine Pointe faunal assemblage is diverse ($s = 10$ taxa, $H' = 0.9818$), and highly equitable ($V' = 1.146$). This means that the faunal assemblage is diverse in terms of species represented in relation to the overall number of elements, and it is not dominated by any one taxon. This is what the opportunistic model predicts.

Table 9.1. Identified taxa and MNI: Rutherford-Kizer and Brandywine Pointe

Taxon	*Common Name*	*Rutherford-Kizer MNI**	*Brandywine Pointe MNI*†
Didelphis virginiana	Opossum	2	0
Scalopus aquaticus	Common mole	2	0
Canis familiaris	Domestic dog	2	0
Canis lupus	Gray wolf	1	0
Urocyon cinereoargenteus	Gray fox	1	0
Mephitis mephitis	Striped skunk	2	0
Procyon lotor	Raccoon	1	1
Ursus americanus	Black bear	2	0
Cervus canadensis	Elk	2	0
Odocoileus virginianus	White-tailed deer	24	1
Castor canadensis	Beaver	1	1
Marmota monax	Woodchuck	1	1
Ondatra zibethicus	Muskrat	1	0
Rodentia	Rodents	0	1
Oryzomys palustris	Marsh rice rat	7	0
Sciurus carolinensis	Eastern gray squirrel	5	1
Sciurus niger	Eastern fox squirrel	7	0
Tamias striatus	Chipmunk	1	0
Sylvilagus floridanus	Eastern cottontail rabbit	2	0
Aves	Birds	0	1
Branta canadensis	Canada goose	1	0
Colinus virginianus	Bobwhite	2	0
Meleagris gallopavo	Wild turkey	9	1
Corvus brachyrhynchos	Common crow	1	0
Strix varia	Barred owl	1	0
Grus canadensis	Sandhill crane	1	0
Ectopistes migratorius	Passenger pigeon	1	0
Anas sp.	Duck	1	1
Passerine	Perching birds	1	1
Testudines	Turtles	0	1
Terrapene carolina	Box turtle	10	1
Chelydra serpentina	Snapping turtle	1	0
Chrysemys/ Graptemys spp.	Sliders/cooters	1	0

continued on next page

Table 9.1.—*continued*

Taxon	*Common Name*	*Rutherford-Kizer MNI**	*Brandywine Pointe MNI†*
Trionyx ferox	Softshell turtle	2	0
Colubridae	Nonvenomous snakes	1	0
Viperidae	Venomous snakes	1	0
Bufo sp.	Toad	0	1
Rana/Bufo sp.	Frogs and toads	1	0
Osteichthyes	Bony fish	0	1
Amia calva	Bowfin	1	0
Catostomidae	Suckers	2	0
Moxostoma sp.	Redhorse	1	0
Ictalurus spp.	Catfish	1	0
Ictalurus punctatus	Channel catfish	5	0
Aplodinotus grunniens	Drumfish	5	0
Cyprinidae	Minnows	1	0
	Total MNI	115	14

* Rutherford-Kizer data are from Breitburg and Michael Moore (2001).

† Brandywine Pointe data are from Moore and Kevin Smith (1993).

I follow VanDerwarker's (2006:159–160) definition of "disturbance taxa" as those animals that prefer secondary growth, forest edges, agricultural fields, and urban/suburban areas. Disturbance taxa account for nearly 75% of the faunal remains identified at Brandywine Pointe and 50% of the MNI values. These data suggest that the residents of Brandywine Pointe relied most heavily on terrestrial animals, especially those that are attracted to agricultural fields and house gardens. Overall, the data suggest that the residents of Brandywine Pointe were opportunistic in their animal exploitation choices.

Middle Cumberland Mississippian Village—Rutherford-Kizer

While the Brandywine Pointe site gives us a look at subsistence on the family level, Rutherford-Kizer allows us to look at the subsistence of a larger community. The Rutherford-Kizer site was occupied during Regional Periods III and IV (Deter-Wolf 2016:xvii), with the majority of the occupation dating to circa AD 1280–1485 (Moore 2016:67). Rutherford-Kizer is a village that consists of a mound, numerous domestic structures and associated features, burials, and a palisade wall with bastions (Moore and Smith 2001:73). From 1993 to 1995, the Tennessee Division of Archaeology excavated the site, and Emanuel Breitburg analyzed the faunal assemblage (as he did for the Brandywine Pointe Site) (Breitburg and

Moore 2001; Deter-Wolf and Moore 2016). The available faunal data recovered from all proveniences at Rutherford-Kizer consist of taxonomic identifications and MNI (MNI = 115) (see table 9.1).

Results of the faunal analysis at Rutherford-Kizer also show a reliance on white-tailed deer, wild turkey, and box turtle. The Rutherford-Kizer faunal assemblage is diverse (s = 41 taxa, H' = 0.844377) but not equitable, based on MNI (V' = 0.53843647). This finding means that the faunal assemblage at Rutherford-Kizer is dominated by one or a few taxa, specifically white-tailed deer (MNI = 24, or 21% of the total MNI). Overall the diversity and equitability values suggest that the residents of Rutherford-Kizer, while eating animals that preferred disturbed and forest-edge environments, were doing so selectively.

Terrestrial animals comprise nearly 80% of the assemblage at Rutherford-Kizer, while aquatic animals just under 21%, based on MNI. These data suggest that the residents of Rutherford-Kizer relied most heavily on terrestrial animals, especially those that are attracted to agricultural fields and house gardens, with disturbance taxa accounting for nearly 55% of the animals identified. It appears that the residents of this site were clearing primary forests for agricultural and construction purposes and, in turn exploiting those animals that were attracted to the newly disturbed environments.

ASSESSING PROVISIONING IN THE MIDDLE CUMBERLAND REGION

To test for the presence of provisioning at Rutherford-Kizer, I compare faunal data from Rutherford-Kizer and Brandywine Pointe, addressing assemblage diversity, species represented, cuts of meat of the larger taxa, and the presence of exotic or "specially charged" taxa.

The Rutherford-Kizer faunal assemblage represents a village community, and Brandywine Pointe is the rural family farmstead. The faunal assemblage from Rutherford-Kizer is more diverse than Brandywine Pointe (RK: s = 41 taxa; BwPt: s = 10 taxa), but less equitable than Brandywine Pointe based on MNI (RK: V' = 0.53843647; BwPt: V'= 0.9818).

The Brandywine Pointe assemblage comprises disturbance taxa, but all are equally represented. Deer dominate the Rutherford-Kizer assemblage (MNI = 24) and are one of the three largest terrestrial land mammals in the southeastern United States. The other two identified large mammals are elk and black bear, both of which are represented by two individuals each at Rutherford-Kizer but are absent from the Brandywine Pointe assemblage. These two taxa would have been procured for reasons other than subsistence (see below).

I next look at body part distribution of white-tailed deer at Rutherford-Kizer. Of the 722 identified deer elements, 355 (49.17%) are either from the hindquarter or the forequarter. Both of these areas are associated with high-utility cuts of meat or meatier portions of the deer carcass. The hindquarter includes the femur, patella, and tibia. The forequarter includes the scapula, humerus, radius, and ulna. The forequarter elements are more frequent ($n = 231$) than hindquarter elements ($n = 124$). Axial elements (ribs, vertebrae, sacrum) comprise 23.55% ($n = 170$); feet (phalanges, calcaneus, astragalus) comprise 14.54% ($n = 105$); and cranial elements (skull, auditory bulla, mandible, teeth) comprise 12.74% ($n = 92$).

There are a number of identified taxa in the Rutherford-Kizer assemblage that are included in the category of exotic, or "special," taxa. These include bear, elk, wolf, fox, barred owl, sandhill crane, passenger pigeon, and colubrid and viperid snakes. Special or exotic taxa of any kind are completely absent from the Brandywine Pointe sample. As has been argued elsewhere (Jackson and Scott 1995, 2003; Peres 2010a), it is likely that these animals were not part of the everyday quotidian diet but, rather were either reserved for consumption during special food-centered events, were used during ceremonial or ritual events, or were not food at all and served other uses.

In terms of the four areas of data analysis, there are clear differences between the farmstead and village faunal assemblages. The Rutherford-Kizer faunal assemblage is more diverse and less equitable than that of Brandywine Pointe. Both assemblages include forest-edge and pest taxa, such as deer, turkey, and raccoons. Deer dominates the Rutherford-Kizer sample. Unfortunately the available data for Brandywine Pointe do not allow for an analysis of deer parts. At Rutherford-Kizer, the hindquarters and forequarters dominate the identified elements. The farmstead site did not yield any animals considered to be exotic or specially charged. The Rutherford-Kizer assemblage does contain taxa in this category, including bear, elk, and snakes.

DISCUSSION AND CONCLUSIONS

Although the current data sets are admittedly limited, this analysis shows marked differences between these assemblages. The data presented in this chapter suggest that Mississippian period farmers living in the MCR minimized subsistence uncertainty by hunting animals that were attracted to their agricultural fields and garden plots. Disturbance taxa, or crop pests—such as deer, turkey, raccoons, and squirrels—were part of the quotidian diet, especially in rural areas.

I suggest there is a correlation between political centralization and the organization of subsistence activities in the MCR. During the Mississippian period, there was increased social and political stratification in the MCR, resulting in people rearranging themselves on the landscape (Moore and Smith 2009). While some families certainly still lived in rural farmstead settings, many people abandoned this lifestyle and moved into village and town communities. Exactly why is unclear, though it may be in part due to increased violence across the region and the security that fortified village life brought (Moore and Smith 2009;

VanDerwarker and Wilson 2016). There is a correlation between this increased population aggregation and an increased focus on farming and maize agriculture specifically. The expansion of maize agriculture and the concomitant time and labor demands resulted in people restructuring their subsistence activities and schedules to minimize subsistence risk and uncertainty. Garden hunting, both opportunistic and selective, was practiced as a means to offset the loss of crops due to pest taxa and a way to ensure meat was available.

Supporting the political infrastructure likely meant acquiring meat to provision any number of people beyond one's immediate family. The rural farmers provided food for their own family members, while those who either lived in the town and farmed outside the village walls, or possibly extended kin living across the countryside, needed to provide food for the non–food producers in the village. The non–food producers at Moundville were the elites and their families. It is clear that others provisioned them with food—whether the others were kin from outlying villages, or religious and political followers, is less certain.

The four data markers I used to determine if provisioning was an aspect of the foodways in the MCR include assemblage diversity, equitability of species, cuts of meat, and presence and type of exotic or special taxa. The assemblage from Rutherford-Kizer was more diverse and less equitable than that from Brandywine Pointe. At the former, deer dominated the assemblage (21%), while at the latter the animals were represented more equitably. It is notable that at Moundville, Jackson and Susan Scott (2003:560) found that deer also dominated the faunal assemblage and comprised 13–15% of the site MNI.

One of the expected indicators that the residents of the village were provisioned is a preponderance of higher-utility or meatier parts of deer. These higher-utility parts are the forequarters and hindquarters, excluding any of the foot/ankle bones (Jackson and Scott 1995, 2003). Unfortunately, information about element representation is missing from the available primary data (Moore and Smith 1993). The element data for deer from the Rutherford-Kizer site shows that the highest percentage of deer parts is from the forequarters and hindquarters. This figure compares favorably to Moundville (Jackson and Scott 2003).

Some animals identified from faunal assemblages in the southeastern United States were likely charged with extra meaning beyond nutritional profiles (Jackson and Scott 1995, 2003). Jackson and Scott (1995, 2003) note that these animals are not usually abundant and are recovered from elite-associated areas. There are at least nine taxa identified from the Rutherford-Kizer faunal assemblage that fall into this category. This is similar to special taxa representation from Moundville (Jackson and Scott 2003). In contrast, there are no taxa that are included in this category identified from the Brandywine Pointe faunal assemblage.

In terms of meat provisioning of village residents, the data are highly suggestive that this was a common practice. I am confident that with additional data sets and analysis, we can tease out the redistributive relationships between farmsteads and villages that coexisted during the Mississippian period in the MCR. Recent data compilation from the Moundville polity and neighboring rural communities is a model for what these relationships may have looked like.

On the surface, the species lists for sites in Middle Tennessee tell a story of people hunting locally available wild animals to feed themselves and their families. By taking a closer look at the assemblage compositions in terms of diversity, equitability, ratio of terrestrial to aquatic, and the preference for some animals to take up residence in disturbed or edge environments, we are able to show a more nuanced picture of the lives of Mississippian peoples. Their ability to maximize resources through opportunistic and strategic garden hunting allowed them to minimize food shortage events and thrive in Middle Tennessee.

Acknowledgments. I appreciate the insightful and useful comments of Benjamin S. Arbuckle, Levent Atici, and an anonymous reviewer on the original version of this chapter. I am grateful for the continued and unwavering assistance, enthusiasm, and collaborative spirit of my colleagues at the Tennessee Division of Archaeology, especially Aaron Deter-Wolf and Mike Moore. Aaron Deter-Wolf created figure 9.1. Any omissions or errors are mine alone.

WORKS CITED

Braun, Lucy. 1950. *Deciduous Forests of Eastern North America*. Philadelphia: Blakiston Company.

Breitburg, Emanuel. 1998. "Chapter IX. Faunal Remains." In *Gordontown: Salvage Archaeology at a Mississippian Town in Davidson County, Tennessee*, edited by M. C. Moore and E. Breitburg, 147–168. Nashville: Tennessee Department of Environment and Conservation.

Breitburg, Emanuel, and Michael C. Moore. 2001. "Faunal Remains." In *Archaeological Excavations at the Rutherford Kizer Site: A Mississippian Mound Center in Sumner County, Tennessee*, edited by Michael C. Moore and Kevin E. Smith, 119–134. Nashville: Tennessee Department of Environment and Conservation.

Breitburg, E., and M. C. Moore. 2016. "Faunal Remains." In *Archaeological Excavations at the Rutherford-Kizer Site: A Mississippian Mound Center in Sumner County, Tennessee* (revised electronic edition), edited by A. Deter-Wolf, M. C. Moore, 105–114. Division of Archaeology Research Series No. 13 (Original edition 2001), revised electronic edition. Nashville: Tennessee Department of Environment and Conservation.

Clinton, Jennifer M., and Tanya M. Peres. 2011. "Pests in the Garden: Testing the Garden-Hunting Model at Rutherford-Kizer Site, Sumner County, Tennessee." *Tennessee Archaeology* 5 (2): 131–141.

Crabtree, Pamela J. 1990. "Zooarchaeology and Complex Societies: Some Uses of Faunal Analysis for the Study of Trade, Status, and Ethnicity." In *Archaeological Method and Theory*. Vol. 2, edited by M. B. Schiffer, 155–205. Tucson: University of Arizona Press.

Deter-Wolf, Aaron, and Michael C. Moore. 2016. *Archaeological Investigations at the Rutherford-Kizer Site: A Mississippian Mound Site in Sumner County, Tennessee*. Rev. electronic ed. Nashville: Tennessee Department of Environment and Conservation.

Díaz, Vara Calder, Wenhold, Lucy L., and Swanton, John Reed. 1936. "A 17th Century Letter of Gabriel Díaz Vara Calderón, Bishop of Cuba, Describing the Indians and Indian Missions of Florida." *Smithsonian Miscellaneous Collections* 95 (16): 1–14.

Dice, Lee R. 1943. *The Biotic Provinces of North America*. Ann Arbor: University of Michigan Press.

Eaton, S. 1992. "Wild Turkey (*Meleagris gallopavo*)." In *The Birds of North America*. Vol. 22, edited by P. Stettenheim and F. Gill, 1–28. Washington, DC: Academy of Natural Sciences.

Gildrie, Richard P. 2018. "Ecological Systems." *Tennessee Encyclopedia*. http://tennesseeencyclopedia.net/entries/ecological-systems/.

Hinson, Lindsey R. 2018. "Characteristics and Functions of Non-Mound Mississippian Sites: A Case Study of Fitzner North End (9SN256)." MA thesis, Department of Sociology and Anthropology, Georgia Southern University. https://digitalcommons.georgiasouthern.edu/etd/1763.

Jackson, H. Edwin, C. Margaret Scarry, and Susan Scott. 2016. "Domestic and Ritual Meals in the Moundville Chiefdom." In *Rethinking Moundville and Its Hinterland*, edited by Vincas P. Steponaitis and C. Margaret Scarry, 187–233. Gainesville: University Press of Florida.

Jackson, H. Edwin, and Susan Scott. 1995. "The Faunal Record of the Southeastern Elite: The Implications of Economy, Social Relations, and Ideology." *Southeastern Archaeology* 14 (2): 103–119.

Jackson, H. Edwin, and Susan Scott. 2003. "Patterns of Elite Faunal Utilization at Moundville, Alabama." *American Antiquity* 68 (3): 552–572.

Kingsbury, J. A., A. B. Hoos, and M. D. Woodside. 1999. Environmental Setting and Water-Quality Issues in the Lower Tennessee River Basin: US Geological Survey Water-Resources Investigations Report 99-4080, 44 pp.

Ledford, Kelly L. 2018. "Somewhere between Wild and Domestic: An Examination of the Human-Turkey Relationship during the Mississippian Period in Middle Tennessee." MS thesis, Department of Anthropology, Florida State University, Tallahassee.

Ledford, Kelly L., and Tanya M. Peres. 2018. "Turkey Foodways: The Intersection of Cultural, Social, and Economic Practices in the Mississippian Period Southeast." In *Baking, Bourbon, and the Black Drink: Foodways Archaeology in the American Southeast*, edited by Tanya M. Peres and Aaron Deter-Wolf, 51–62. Tuscaloosa: University of Alabama Press.

Linares, Olga F. 1976. "'Garden Hunting' in the American Tropics." *Human Ecology* 4 (4): 331–349.

Moore, Michael C. 2016. "Radiocarbon Dates." In *Archaeological Investigations at the Rutherford-Kizer Site: A Mississippian Mound Site in Sumner County, Tennessee*, edited by Aaron Deter-Wolf and Michael C. Moore, 67. Nashville: Tennessee Department of Environment and Conservation.

Moore, Michael C., Emanuel Breitburg, Kevin E. Smith, and Mary Beth Trubitt. 2006. "One Hundred Years of Archaeology at Gordontown: A Fortified Mississippian Town in Middle Tennessee." *Southeastern Archaeology* 25 (1): 89–109.

Moore, Michael C., and Kevin E. Smith. 1993. *A Report on the 1992 Archaeological Investigations at the Brandywine Pointe Site (40DV247), Davidson County, Tennessee*. Nashville: Tennessee Department of Environment and Conservation.

Moore, Michael C., and Kevin E. Smith. 2001. *Archaeological Excavations at the Rutherford-Kizer Site: A Mississippian Mound Center in Sumner County, Tennessee*. Nashville: Tennessee Department of Environment and Conservation.

Moore, Michael C., and Kevin E. Smith. 2009. *Archaeological Explorations of the Peabody Museum in Middle Tennessee, 1877–1884*. Nashville: Tennessee Department of Environment and Conservation.

Muller, Jon. 1997. *Mississippian Political Economy*. New York: Plenum Press.

Naughton-Treves, Lisa, Jose Luis Mena, Adrian Treves, Nora Alvarez, and Volker Christian Radeloff. 2003. "Wildlife Survival beyond Park Boundaries: The Impact of Slash-and-Burn Agriculture and Hunting on Mammals in Tambopata, Peru." *Conservation Biology* 4 (17): 1106–1117.

Neusius, Sarah W. 2008. "Game Procurement among Temperate Horticulturists: The Case for Garden Hunting by the Dolores Anasazi." In *Case Studies in Environmental Archaeology*. 2nd ed., edited by Elizabeth J. Reitz, C. Margaret Scarry, and Sylvia J. Scudder, 297–314. New York: Springer.

Nowak, R. M., and J. L. Paradiso. 1983. *Walker's Mammals of the World*. 4th ed. Baltimore: Johns Hopkins University Press.

Peres, Tanya M. 2010a. "Zooarchaeological Remains from the 1998 Fewkes Excavations, Williamson County, Tennessee." *Tennessee Archaeology* 5 (1): 100–125.

Peres, Tanya M. 2010b. "Methodological Issues in Zooarchaeology." In *Integrating Zooarchaeology and Paleoethnobotany: A Consideration of Issues, Methods, and Cases*, edited by Amber M. VanDerwarker and Tanya M. Peres, 15–36. New York: Springer Press.

Peres, Tanya M. 2018. "Splitting the Bones: Marrow Extraction and Mississippian Period Foodways." In *Baking, Bourbon, and the Black Drink: Foodways Archaeology in the Southeast*, edited by Tanya M. Peres and Aaron Deter-Wolf, 30–50. Tuscaloosa: University of Alabama Press.

Peres, Tanya M., and Kelly L. Ledford. 2016. "Archaeological Correlates of Population Management of the Eastern Wild Turkey (*Meleagris gallopavo silvestris*) with a Case

Study from the American South." *Journal of Archaeological Science: Reports* 10: 547–556. https://doi.org/10.1016/j.jasrep.2016.11.014.

Reesman, A. L., and R. G. Stearns. 1989. "The Nashville Dome, an Isostatically Induced Erosional Structure and the Cumberland Plateau Dome, an Isostatically Suppressed Late Paleozoic Extension of the Jessamine Dome." *Southeastern Geology* 30 (3): 147–174.

Reitz, E. J., and E. S. Wing. 2008. *Zooarchaeology*, 2nd ed. Cambridge: Cambridge University Press.

Scarry, C. Margaret. 2008. "Crop Husbandry Practices in North America's Eastern Woodlands." In *Case Studies in Environmental Archaeology*. 2nd ed., edited by Elizabeth Reitz, C. Margaret Scarry, and Sylvia J. Scudder, 391–404. New York: Springer Press.

Scarry, C. Margaret, H. Edwin Jackson, and Mintcy D. Maxham. 2016. "Late Prehistoric Social Practice in the Rural Black Warrior River Valley." In *Rethinking Moundville and Its Hinterland*, edited by Vincas P. Steponaitis and C. Margaret Scarry, 162–186. Gainesville: University Press of Florida.

Schroedl, Gerald F. 1998. "Mississippian Towns in the Eastern Tennessee Valley." In *Mississippian Towns and Sacred Spaces: Searching for an Architectural Grammar*, edited by R. B. Lewis and C. B. Stout, 64–92. Tuscaloosa: University of Alabama Press.

Scott, Susan L. 1983. "Analysis, Synthesis, and Interpretation of Faunal Remains from the Lubbub Creek Archaeological Locality." In *Prehistoric Agricultural Communities in West Central Alabama*, edited by Christopher S. Peebles, 272–290. Mobile: Report submitted to the US Army Corps of Engineers, Mobile District.

Smith, Kevin E. 1992. "The Middle Cumberland Region: Mississippian Archaeology in North Central Tennessee." PhD diss., Department of Anthropology, Vanderbilt University, Nashville.

Smith, Kevin E., and Michael C. Moore. 1994. "Excavation of a Mississippian Farmstead at the Brandywine Pointe Site (40DV247), Cumberland River Valley, Tennessee." *Midcontinental Journal of Archaeology* 19 (2): 198–222.

Smith, Kevin E., C. Parris Stripling, and Michael C. Moore. 1993. "The Brick Church Business Park Site (40DV301) Salvage Excavations at a Mississippian Hamlet." *Tennessee Anthropologist* 18 (2): 95–112.

Springer, M. E., and J. A. Elder. 1980. *Soils of Tennessee*. University of Tennessee Agricultural Experiment Station Bulletin 596. Knoxville: USDA-SCS.

Steponaitis, Vincas P. 1986. "Prehistoric Archaeology in the Southeastern United States, 1970–1985." *Annual Review of Anthropology* 15: 363–404.

Swanton, John R. 1946. *The Indians of the Southeastern United States*. Bureau of American Ethnology Bulletin 137. Washington, DC: Government Printing Office.

VanDerwarker, Amber M. 2006. *Farming, Hunting, and Fishing in the Olmec World*. Austin: University of Texas Press.

VanDerwarker, Amber M., and Greg Wilson. 2016. "War, Food, and Structural Violence in the Mississippian Central Illinois Valley." In *The Archaeology of Food and Warfare:*

Food Insecurity in Prehistory, edited by Amber M. VanDerwarker and Greg D. Wilson, 75–106. New York: Springer Press.

Wilson, Gilbert L. 1917. "Agriculture of the Hidatsa Indians: An Indian Interpretation." *Studies in the Social Sciences* 9: 1–115.

Winterhalder, Bruce, Flora Lu, and Bram Tucker. 1999. "Risk-Sensitive Adaptive Tactics: Models and Evidence from Subsistence Studies in Biology and Anthropology." *Journal of Archaeological Research* 7 (4): 301–348.

Zeder, M. A. 2012. "Pathways to Animal Domestication." In *Biodiversity in Agriculture: Domestication, Evolution, and Sustainability*, edited by P. Gepts, T. R. Famula, S. B. Betting, A. B. Brush, P. E. Damania, and C. O. McGuire, 227–259. Cambridge: Cambridge University Press.

Index

Page numbers followed by *f* indicate figures. Page numbers followed by *t* indicate tables.

Contributors

Benjamin S. Arbuckle is a professor in the Department of Anthropology at UNC–Chapel Hill. He is an anthropological archaeologist and zooarchaeologist whose research focuses on human-animal interactions in ancient Southwest Asia, especially Anatolia. He received his PhD from the Department of Anthropology at Harvard University with a thesis focusing on pastoralism in Anatolian prehistory.

Joaquín Arroyo-Cabrales is head at the Archaeozoology Lab, National Institute of Anthropology and History. His research focuses on Late Quaternary vertebrates and their contribution to understanding the paleoenvironments in which humans survived; in doing so, he has undertaken studies on taxonomy, biogeography, taphonomy, and paleoecology, mostly on Mexican Pleistocene mammals.

Levent Atici is a professor of anthropology and archaeology at the Department of Anthropology, University of Nevada, Las Vegas. With his technical expertise in zooarchaeology, his research covers the full spectrum of human-animal interactions with a special emphasis on prehistoric foraging, origins and spread of domesticated animals, and specialized pastoral economies of early complex societies in Southwest Asia in general and Turkey in particular. Atici received his PhD from the Department of Anthropology at Harvard University.

Fiona Beglane is a faculty member and member of the Centre for Environmental Research, Innovation and Sustainability at Atlantic Technological University, Sligo, Ireland. Her research focuses mainly on medieval landscapes, zooarchaeology, hunting, community archaeology, and scientific techniques in archaeology. She has a particular interest in integrating scientific and social/cultural interpretations of archaeology and in examining the interaction between humans and animals.

Roderick Campbell is an associate professor of East Asian archaeology and history at the Institute for the Study of the Ancient World, NYU. His focus is on the Chinese Bronze Age, and he is involved in assemblage analysis at several Shang production sites. His works include *Archaeology of Bronze Age China: From Erlitou to Anyang*, and *Violence, Kinship and the Early Chinese State: The Shang and their World*.

Patricia Martínez-Lira is an independent scholar. Her research focuses on the study of zooarchaeological remains to understand the subsistence strategies of pre-Hispanic cultures and their relation with their environment. Her interests also include ritual practices and symbolic meaning of animals in Mesoamerica. She has undertaken morphometric and taphonomic studies.

Jacqueline S. Meier is an assistant professor of anthropology in the Department of Sociology, Anthropology and Social Work at the University of North Florida. Her zooarchaeological research investigates human adaptations to the challenges of resource provisioning, focusing on the development of agricultural lifeways. Her research spans from the Paleolithic to the Iron Age in Greece, Israel, and France. She has authored several recent publications on the application of contextual taphonomic methods to detect the remains of past daily meals, rites (i.e., feasting), and norms of refuse management.

Sarah E. Newman is an assistant professor at the University of Chicago. She is an anthropological archaeologist specializing in Mesoamerica, with a focus on the ancient Maya. Her research examines human interactions with ancient environments, including human-animal relationships, cultural and historical changes in the concept of "waste," and anthropogenic landscapes.

Terry O'Connor is Professor Emeritus of Archaeological Science at York University. He explores the relations between past peoples and the animals around them. Within that, he is particularly interested in how archaeological bone assemblages form, beginning with the disposal decisions that people make and continuing on through the action of scavengers, sediment chemistry, and the sampling decisions taken on sites.

Tanya M. Peres, PhD, RPA, is an associate professor of anthropology Department of Anthropology, Florida State University. She examines the various ways that humans incorporate animals into both their cuisine and cultural worldview in the Americas. Her research is two-pronged: foodways in ancient America and the nonfood roles of animals in Indigenous societies.

Dr. Gypsy C. Price is a biological anthropologist at SEARCH, Inc., specializing in biogeochemistry in the archaeological record and how it can inform sociopolitical processes in the past. While Dr. Price's field interests largely focus on Late Bronze Age Greece, she is also active on projects throughout eastern North America and the Caribbean.

Kim S. Shelton is an associate professor of classics and the Graduate Group in Ancient History and Mediterranean Archaeology and the director of the Nemea Center for Classical Archaeology at the University of California, Berkeley. The author of several publications on Mycenaean pottery, figurines, cemeteries, the Tsountas House Area of the Cult Center, and her ongoing excavation at Petsas House in the settlement of Mycenae, she also has ongoing excavations at the Panhellenic Sanctuary of Zeus in Nemea, where her research is centered on questions of the prehistory and protohistory of the sanctuary area and the development of cult, and in collaboration with the Korinthian Ephorate of Antiquities at the Mycenaean cemetery of Aidonia; there the TAPHOS project is preserving cultural heritage through the excavation of partly looted and unlooted chamber tombs together with public outreach and education.

Marcus Winter is Profesor de Investigación Científica Emérito in the Oaxaca office of Mexico's Instituto Nacional de Antropología e Historia (INAH). His interests include the pre-Hispanic archaeology of Oaxaca, particularly the origins and development of village and urban life and the relation of archaeological evidence to present-day linguistic and ethnic groups in Oaxaca.

Helina S. Woldekiros is an assistant professor in the Department of Anthropology, Washington University in St. Louis, whose work focuses on human adaptations in the Horn of Africa during the beginnings of food production, agricultural diets, pastoralism, and mobile responses to climatic change in extreme ecological/environmental settings. She also has a particular interest in the organization of early states in the Horn of Africa from 800 BCE to modern times.